Microsoft Press

Instrument Flight Techniques

with Microsoft®
Flight Simulator 98

Michele Chambre
Ben Chiu

PUBLISHED BY
Microsoft Press
A Division of Microsoft Corporation
One Microsoft Way
Redmond, Washington 98052-6399

Library of Congress Cataloging-in-Publication Data
Chambre, Michele, 1969-
    Instrument Flight Techniques with Microsoft Flight Simulator 98 /
Michele Chambre, Ben Chiu.
        p.   cm.
    Includes index.
    ISBN 1-57231-628-4
    1. Microsoft flight simulator (Computer file)   2. Instrument
flying--Computer simulation.   I. Chiu, Ben, 1963-   . II. Title.
TL712.8.C49   1997
629.132'5214'02855369--dc21

97-29193
                                                            CIP

Printed and bound in the United States of America.

1 2 3 4 5 6 7 8 9   MLML   3 2 1 0 9 8

Distributed to the book trade in Canada by Macmillan of Canada, a division of Canada Publishing Corporation.

A CIP catalogue record for this book is available from the British Library.

Microsoft Press books are available through booksellers and distributors worldwide. For further information about international editions, contact your local Microsoft Corporation office. Or contact Microsoft Press International directly at fax (425) 936-7329. Visit our Web site at mspress.microsoft.com.

Direct3D, DirectDraw, DirectPlay, DirectX, Microsoft, Microsoft Press, SideWinder, Windows, and Windows NT are registered trademarks and MSN, ZoneMatch, and ZoneMessage are trademarks of Microsoft Corporation.

The Personal Computing Press is an imprint of The PC Press, Inc.

Other product and company names mentioned herein may be the trademarks of their respective owners.

"The Art of the Instrument Scan," copyright 1997 and 1991, by Rod Machado, is reprinted from *Rod Machado's Instrument Pilot's Survival Manual,* courtesy Rod Machado.

This product contains aeronautical information reproduced from NOAA and FAA charts, forms, and maps. This reproduction is not for use in navigation. Other maps and charts are also used for illustrative and educational purposes only, and no presentation of information, maps, or charts herein is intended to be used or relied on for actual flight planning or navigation.

Acquisitions Editor: Kim Fryer
Project Editor: Stuart J. Stuple

Dedication

To Mom and Dad, thanks.

Michele Chambre

To two real life heroes, Chuck Yeager and Neil Armstrong,
for inspiring a young boy to reach for the skies and
follow his dreams.

Ben Chiu

Acknowledgments

I would like to thank Michele Chambre, Ben Chiu, and Dave Gwinn
for the many weeks and months they collectively invested in creating this book,
and the many others who labored behind the scenes to bring it to completion.
At The PC Press, Inc., especially Phill Powell, Kathleen Ingram, and Kim Davis;
at Microsoft Press, Kim Fryer and Stuart Stuple, and at
Microsoft Games the entire Flight Simulator group.
Finally, our thanks go to Robert Burns for his kind assistance to Michele
during this process, and to Rod Machado for his contribution
of his years of experience.

Robert C. Lock
President and Editor-in-Chief
The PC Press, Inc.

Contents

Foreword

SIMULATED FLIGHT

Welcome to the world of aviation and the education you'll find within Microsoft Flight Simulator 98!

The challenge of simulated flight—whether accomplished on a sophisticated multi-million dollar airline simulator or on your PC with your Flight Simulator 98 program—has many similarities. On the big sims, we too are lacking wind velocities that give aural clues; and as pilots, we always bemoan the absence of kinetics, the "seat-of-the-pants" inputs that bespeak an airplane's attitude and changes to it.

Absent that broad sensory assistance, Flight Simulator 98 can certainly help you achieve important goals: a critical one is to perfect an instrument "scan" pattern. A skilled simulator pilot will always be a talented instrument aviator, if only by mastery of the instruments used to control the airplane.

The accomplished instrument aviator must scan faster, see and absorb information quickly, move to other parameters before they change, and accept the liabilities inherent within those challenges. Perhaps the airline pilot does not have the peripheral distractions that you might have with the domestic ambience surrounding your computer screen. Therefore, focus intently, be part of the scene.

I have flown computer simulators and was impressed with Flight Simulator 98. I performed magnificently (please accept my word for that, although I do not give demonstrations!)

I am convinced my own road into instrument ratings and flying would have been facilitated by a program like this one you have purchased. With this book, and Flight Simulator 98, you will learn how instruments react to control inputs, as I did in an expensive airplane and accompanied by a costly flight instructor.

Experienced PC-simulator pilots will enjoy the variety, sophistication, and challenges of Simulator 98. Novice computer pilots will learn the many challenges facing pleasure and professional pilots in handling aircraft in various weather conditions. Professional pilots have learned to do a difficult job and make it look easy. I think you'll find that many of those skills were honed through study and hard work to fine edges before "easy" was possible.

Enjoy this splendid experience. When you're frustrated and performing badly, find a plane and scenario to enjoy. After 30 years in aviation, I have to say "It's been FUN!" I trust you will have fun in sharing some sky of your choosing, in planes that please you, and in challenges that reward your sense of accomplishment.

TWA Captain David Gwinn
Contributing Editor: *Plane & Pilot Magazine* and Technical Editor: *Instrument Flight Training with Microsoft Flight Simulator 98*

Introduction

Instrument flight training gives you the ability to fly and land when there is little, or even no, visibility. Although learning IFR (Instrument Flight Rules) skills and procedures is challenging, these rules will allow you to take advantage of advanced Microsoft Flight Simulator 98 features. For example, you will be able to fly in all the weather conditions available in Flight Simulator and make better use of your cockpit instruments. Although Flight Simulator models real-life dangers during IFR flight operations—including some that IFR skills may not conquer, such as thunderstorm clouds and icing conditions—with the information in this book you will be able to tackle most of the weather conditions the Flight Simulator programmers have in store for you.

You will also better understand how to use navigational aids and compensate for their limitations—variables now modeled in Flight Simulator. In fact, you will learn how to use these aids to land in low visibility. Many pilots compare these instrument-aided landings to playing a video game. Therefore, you can be sure the instrument landings you practice in Flight Simulator are "as real as it gets."

This book will also help you understand how control inputs effect aircraft performance. Therefore, you will be able to get the aircraft to perform exactly the way you want it to. This will make you much more proficient and professional in your style of flying.

One final note: this book is not intended to teach real-world aviation and under no circumstances is this book intended to be a substitute for flight training by a certified flight instructor. In short, this book is not meant to be a manual for private pilots training for an instrument flight rating. It has been designed to teach instrument flight training as it relates specifically to Microsoft Flight Simulator 98. Actual aviation knowledge not relevant to Flight Simulator has not been included. To effectively use this book, you should have some basic flying skills in Flight Simulator. For example, you should be able to take off, fly level, and land. To become more skilled in these areas, you may want to read the *Microsoft Flight Simulator 98: Inside Moves* book, also from Microsoft Press.

Michele Chambre

A Few Words About The Instrument Flight Training Book Team:

Michele Chambre *has an FAA Commercial Pilots License for single- and multi-engine aircraft and an Instrument Flight Rating. She has logged over 400 hours in the air including 100 hours of instrument flight time. Michele received an MBA with a specialization in aviation management from Embry Riddle Aeronautical University in 1995. She regularly uses Microsoft Flight Simulator to practice IFR skills.*

Ben Chiu *is a multi-engine and instrument-rated pilot experienced in over a dozen low- and high-performance fixed-wing and rotor aircraft and a nationally-known air combat simulation writer. Chiu is the author of the monthly column, "The Air Combat Advisor," for* Computer Games Strategy Plus Magazine. *He has published numerous articles about flying and flight simulation, as well as regular features appearing in the magazines* Radio Control Model Cars *and* Model Builder. *He is the author of three previous books:* Flight Simulator 98: Inside Moves *(Microsoft Press/The PC Press, 1997),* Official Air Warrior II Strategy Guide *(Sybex, 1997), and* The Best Simulation Games: Strategies and Secrets *(Sybex,1996).*

TWA Captain **David Gwinn** *is well known in the aviation industry as a columnist for* Plane & Pilot Magazine, *with a multitude of articles in many publications:* IFR, Flight Training, Trend, Navy's Approach, *the Army's* Aviation Safety Journal *and ALPA periodicals. He is the recognized authority and educator in the use of Airborne Weather Radar in professional aviation. Gwinn returned to St. Louis-based line-flight after a decade as an Instructor in TWA's pilot training center. An Airline Transport Rated Pilot with over 13,000 hours experience, he is rated as an Advanced and Instrument Ground Instructor, and has held Certified Flight Instructor ratings in Airplanes, Helicopters, Gyroplanes, Seaplanes and Gliders.*

Chapter One

CHECK BEFORE FLIGHT—
PREFLIGHTING YOUR COMPUTER

The world of aviation is chock full of expressions like propwash and center of pressure. To the uninitiated, these phrases seem to suggest something totally different from what they mean to aviators. For example, the former term is the rearward airflow from propeller operation—not a type of propeller soap. (And just to keep the record straight, the latter does not refer to the location where you take FAA written exams!) Conversely, the phrase "flying solely by reference to instruments" (the essence of instrument flying) doesn't usually suffer from these creative fictional double-entendres; it is generally considered to be synonymous with precision flight.

The ability to fly precisely is typically tied to the level of a pilot's flying skills and knowledge (we'll address both in this book). However, what many people overlook is the aircraft's role in this equation. For example, if your aircraft is stable, one that does what you tell it (by reacting adequately and promptly to your control inputs), naturally you'll fly better. On the other hand, if you're flying an aircraft that demands all of your attention to keep it in the air, your abilities to track a course or maintain altitude will be proportionally hampered. This relationship remains the same whether you're flying a real aircraft or a simulated one.

In this chapter we'll look at the factors that will tend to help or hurt your interaction with Microsoft Flight Simulator 98's computer-generated aircraft. Specifically, we'll discuss Flight Simulator 98's configuration options and controller setup. Both of these areas will affect how your computer returns feedback feel and reacts to your control inputs. As you advance in this book you'll see that success with instrument flight (and, ultimately, your ability to enjoy Flight Simulator 98) hinges on your computer setup. A few minutes spent reading this chapter can really increase your enjoyment and prevent frustration as well.

Graphics and Hardware Issues

One of the oldest quandaries about computer games and simulations is what many call the look and feel dilemma. Unless you're riding the absolute cutting edge of computer hardware technology or are in the "hardware-of-the-week upgrade club," you (like the rest of us) will be forced to make the decision to fly sims that either look good and feel bad, or feel good and look bad.

Fortunately there are two characteristics of Flight Simulator 98 and instrument flight simulations in general that work in our favor:

1. Flight Simulator 98 has many graphics options so there is some middle ground for those of us who don't have the fastest machines on the planet.

2. Because instrument flight will be the primary focus of the flights discussed in this book, ground textures and other graphical "eye candy" will become less important.

Although feel is often judged according to personal preferences, there are times when things are just so out of whack that criticisms about "poor flight modeling" or "bad programming" are simply incorrect. In actuality, the sim's performance trouble is a result of hardware and/or configuration problems. In either case, the end result is an aircraft that is deemed unflyable and vastly unsuitable for precision instrument flight. This is why we must focus on optimizing Flight Simulator 98's performance and feel for instrument flight. There's much to discuss; let's start at the beginning.

Flight Simulator 98 Installation Tips

Obviously, before playing Flight Simulator 98, you'll need to install it. But rather than consume time and text with step-by-step installation instructions, we'll limit our installation discussion to many less obvious items and devote more space to covering instrument flight. For more in-depth installation and

setup directions, please see the *Microsoft Flight Simulator 98: Inside Moves* strategy guide (ISBN 1-57231-635-7), also from Microsoft Press.

Minimum System Requirements

Before installing Flight Simulator 98, you should confirm that your system meets the minimum system requirements. If you don't meet these requirements, Flight Simulator will not work satisfactorily and all the optional optimizing in the world won't preclude problems. By the same token, just as there is no such thing as having too much money or hard disk space, it's impossible to have a computer that's too fast for Flight Simulator 98.

Flight Simulator 98's minimum system requirements are:

- Multimedia PC with 486DX/66 MHz or higher processor (Pentium recommended)
- Microsoft Windows 95 operating system or Windows NT workstation 4.0 or later
- 8 MB of memory (16 MB recommended)
- 105 MB of available hard-disk space
- Double-speed or faster CD-ROM drive
- Super VGA, 256-color monitor
- Microsoft Mouse or compatible pointing device (joystick recommended)
- Sound card with speakers or headphones required for audio

General Installation Tips

Read the README.TXT file in the Flight Simulator 98 folder and the Installation section of Flight Simulator 98's game manual. Additionally, here are some tips to help you with the installation of Flight Simulator 98.

- Close all running applications before attempting to install Flight Simulator. Setup cannot install system files or update shared files if they are in use during the setup process by other applications.
- Flight Simulator 98 requires DirectX version 5.0 or later and it must be installed before Setup will allow you to proceed with Flight Simulator installation.
- If your hard disk size is four gigabytes or greater and you are unable to install Flight Simulator 98, Microsoft has released a Flight Simulator 98 software upgrade patch to correct this error. At the same time it also

provides an upgrade tothe DirectPlay component of DirectX 5.0a to improve performance on the Internet Gaming Zone. The patch is available from the Microsoft Flight Simulator web site at: http://www.microsoft.com/games/fsim/news.htm or can be directly downloaded by clicking the following link:ftp://ftp.microsoft.com/ deskapps/games/public/flightsim/FS98ptch_USOnly.

Control Patrol

On May 30th, 1997, the Federal Aviation Administration (FAA) released an Advisory Circular (AC 61-126) specifying how to qualify a PC-ATD (Personal Computer-Aviation Training Device) for instrument instruction. Under this new AC, student pilots are now allowed to log ten hours of training flight time with an approved PC-ATD under the guidance of a flight instructor.

Although the FAA has approved the use of PC-ATDs in instrument flight training, as this book went to press, none of the mainstream PC-based flight simulators had become PC-ATD certified. The PC-ATD is a new category of FAA-approved training devices. Prior to PC-based programs like Flight Simulator 98, the only other simulators currently certified for flight credit have been expensive, single-purpose flight simulators and flight training devices (FTD).

PC-ATD approval requires specific hardware like a self-centering yoke and other various physical cockpit controls. This hardware is seen as an integral part of the training package. Although it's possible to fly Flight Simulator 98 solely by keyboard (or mouse), a genuine realism buff demands nothing less than a joystick or flight yoke controller (the FAA's preference) to simulate primary flight controls (ailerons and rudder). Regardless of the FAA's reasoning and requirements, there are more compelling reasons for considering one of these controllers than the aesthetics alone.

Elevator trim (a "back-pressure" force) is one good example of what you'll forfeit if you use Flight Simulator 98 with a keyboard. If we were just out to fly around for sheer amusement, unconcerned about precision flight or landings, the keyboard or mouse might suffice. But because instrument flight is our goal, with an emphasis on precision, the keyboard and mouse simply fail the versatility requirements. Although elevator and aileron control input can be adequate with a mouse or keyboard, you lose the precision afforded by a flight controller when you need to apply both inputs at the same time (diagonal movements).

Yokin' Around

New desktop pilots usually find adjusting to a joystick or flight yoke to be easy. Certainly all of the real versions of the aircraft modeled in Flight Simulator 98 use either a flight stick or flight yoke, and not a mouse or keyboard for flight control. More specifically, all of the airplanes (except for the Sopwith Camel, the Schweizer 2-32 sailplane, and the Extra 300) use flight yokes in real life.

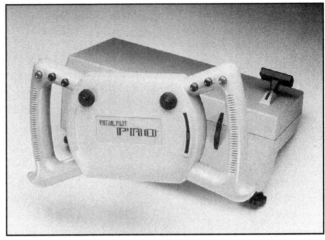

A reasonably priced, quality flight yoke is the Virtual Pilot Pro from CH Products. It features throttle control, elevator trim wheel, six buttons, and two view hats.

Stickin' It

On the other hand, the real Bell 206B JetRanger helicopter uses a cyclic stick. For helicopter flight only a joystick will suffice. Attempting to use the mouse or keyboard to fly the JetRanger will prove nearly impossible. Helicopter flight is a demanding activity (centered around three axes) that's pretty tough without any control handicaps. If you're serious about flying the whirlybird, therefore, you'll need a joystick.

Caution: for helicopter flight, you may want to stay away from those joysticks that are stiffly sprung or are control-pressure resistant. Like an airplane, flying a helicopter requires precision control, but controlling a helicopter that's hovering requires smooth stick movements that quickly shift from one direction to another. The cyclic in a real helicopter doesn't center itself. If your joystick is too stiff, control movements (ones that are easy with a non-centering stick) will be more difficult to perform with precision.

The Microsoft SideWinder 3D Pro combines many of the most sought-after features such as programmability, throttle slider, twist action rudder control, and view hat all in a neat package.

Instrument Flight Techniques
For Microsoft Flight Simulator 98

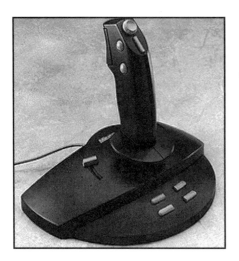

The SideWinder 3D Pro from Microsoft combines many of the most sought-after joystick features into one neat package.

Shake a Stick

Flight Simulator 98 supports force feedback joysticks through DirectX 5.0. But the only driver currently available is for the Microsoft SideWinder Force Feedback Pro. (As of this writing, a beta driver for the CH Products Force F/X was available at http://www.force-feedback.com.) Although you may need to get past the philosophical differences between flight yokes and joysticks for some of the aircraft in Flight Simulator 98, the benefits of a force feedback joystick really add to the Flight Simulator 98 flight experience.

Through the force feedback feature you'll be able to literally feel the shaking of oncoming stalls, the bumping of turbulence, appropriate control stiffening when airspeeds increase, and the contrasting control easing as airspeed decreases. You can't feel with your body what your Flight Simulator aircraft is doing while you sit in front of your computer, but force feedback can help supplement this deficiency. A force feedback joystick is truly a pleasure to use with Flight Simulator 98.

Pedal Pushers

The need for a set of rudder pedals or rudder controller really is governed by two criteria of flying PC-based aircraft. It depends on your Aircraft Flight Realism setting and whether you have Auto-coordination set in Aircraft Settings. If you fly Flight Simulator 98's airplanes at the more user-friendly difficulty settings, the keyboard will be more than adequate for rudder control.

However, when it comes to piloting the JetRanger, just as a joystick is essential, you'll have a very difficult time using the keyboard for anti-torque control. It's said that flying a helicopter is like walking, chewing gum, patting the top of your head, and rubbing your stomach all at the same time. Actually, hovering is harder than that—and even more difficult on a computer. Therefore, the best recommendation for flying the helicopter is to get

a set of rudder pedals, or at the very least, a joystick that twists for rudder control.

The second criteria is philosophical and a matter of personal preference. Using rudder pedals in real airplanes or anti-torque pedals in helicopters is all part of the experience of flying. For some people, though, using a twisting joystick over a set of pedals just may not seem realistic. So that's another personal preference you'll have to identify and consider.

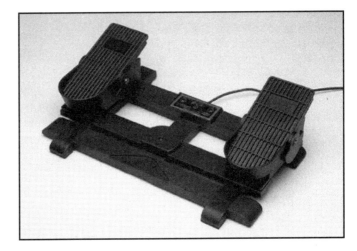

ThrustMaster's RCS is a solidly constructed set of rudder pedals.

If you decide pedals are the way to go, both ThrustMaster and CH Products produce excellent rudder pedal controllers. Made from aluminum and plastic, the RCS from ThrustMaster is a solid piece of equipment. The Pro Pedals from CH Products feature dual pedal action that will work for both driving games and flight sims.

Throttle Jockey

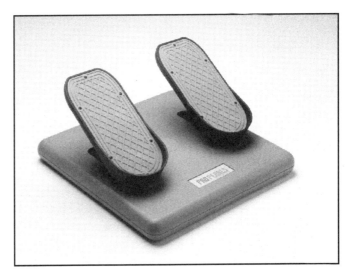

The Pro Pedals from CH Products work well for both driving games and flight sims.

Flight Simulator 98 allows you to use the keyboard, mouse, or throttle controller (whether it's a dedicated throttle controller or the throttle wheel on a joystick) to control the throttle or

Tip: *Aircraft Settings are only saved with individual flights. If you want to use rudder pedals while in-flight and/or fly at the Difficult Flight Realism setting with the saved situations, you'll need to open and reset each individual situation. Then you'll need to save each with the new settings if you want them to remain that way.*

helicopter collective. The keyboard is fine for airplane throttle control, but it's rather lacking when it comes to using it as a helicopter collective. Airplanes don't require quick throttle adjustments, but the keyboard simply won't cut it for hovering a helicopter. Nevertheless, despite the philosophical differences, the throttle wheel feature on some joysticks will work very well for collective control.

The old Joystick icon in Control Panel has been replaced with a new icon called Game Controllers in DirectX 5.0.

Controller Setup Tips

In order use a joystick, flight yoke, rudder device, or throttle device in Flight Simulator 98, it must first be installed and calibrated in the Windows 95 Control Panel. DirectX 5.0 replaces the old familiar Joystick icon in Control Panel with a new icon called Game Controllers. Although the look may have changed, it generally operates the same way as the old Joystick version.

Here are some tips for setting up controllers:

• See the Windows 95 manual and your joystick manufacturer's documentation for specific instructions about installing your particular controller.
• Once you have the proper controller drivers installed, you'll need to calibrate your joystick. The calibration routines are found on the Game Controller Properties tab found by clicking on the Game Controllers icon.
• If you have rudder controllers don't forget to click on the Rudder/Pedals check box to enable them.

Common Calibration Problems

Most every computer sold today has a game port either built into the motherboard, located on a multi-function card, or on a soundcard. Unfortunately, not all of these work correctly with some of the higher speed computers—and this can cause calibration problems. So, if you experience

calibration problems, don't overlook the game card as a possible cause. A dedicated, speed-adjustable game card is by far the best for the high-end games of today's PC environment, but they aren't always necessary.

Sensitive Nature

Once your controllers are installed and calibrated, you'll need to enable them in Flight Simulator 98. The place where controllers are configured in Flight Simulator 98 is located under the Options menu selection in the Custom Controls submenu.

In the upper left corner of the Custom Controls Sensitivities tab is the Joystick Enable box. The first thing you need to do is click on the Enable Joystick check box to enable any controller other than the keyboard or mouse. (You can also toggle the joystick on and off while in the cockpit by pressing the K key.) When the Enable Joystick box is checked, flight control capabilities for the mouse and keyboard are disabled.

Below the Enable Joystick Box is the Control Device list box that cites each installed controller. To the right is an Axis drop-down box. The controller/device selected in the Control Device list will determine which axes will be available in the Axis drop-downbox.

Directly below the Axis drop-down box are two slide controls. One is flight control sensitivity, and the other controls the Null Zone. Just as the name suggests, sensitivity means how sensitive that control will be. Sliding this control toward High will make your airplane more responsive to control movements, while sliding the sensitivity control towards Low will do just the opposite. Depending on which device you've chosen in the Control Device box, the Null Zone slide control may be grayed out. That's because Null Zones only apply to joystick axes. In any case, the slider controls below the Axis box reflect the controller options for the axis currently selected.

Don't overlook the game card as a possible cause of calibration problems. A dedicated, speed-adjustable game card like this ACM from ThrustMaster will work correctly in a high-speed computer.

Joystick Troubleshooting

If you have problems getting Windows to recognize your joystick or if your joystick refuses to calibrate, here are a few solutions to common problems:

- *There may be more than one game card or game port installed in the system. If there are, only one should be enabled. See your game card or soundcard manual for details on how to disable any extra game cards/ports.*

- *If one or more of your game ports are Plug and Play types, Windows 95 sometimes has trouble determining which to keep activated. One solution is to power down the system and then remove all game cards. Install the one you want to use, and set it up in Windows 95. Next power down the system again, re-install the remaining cards, and tell Windows 95 to disable/ remove any new game port devices.*

- *The Windows 95 joystick driver may be missing or the Windows 95 joystick driver may be installed improperly. See your Windows 95 manual or joystick manufacturer instructions for details on proper installation.*

If you can't calibrate your controllers in the Windows 95 Game Controller Properties Test tab, they won't be calibrated in Flight Simulator 98, either.

- *The Windows 95 Game Controllers configuration may not be selected properly. Make sure the type of joystick you select has the required number of axes for your setup. The "4-button flight yoke w/throttle" configuration works with a four-button joystick and analog throttle. Selecting the check box enables rudder pedals.*

Tip: *Many controller problems are not hardware related. In fact, most of the time the controllers are just set up incorrectly. If you have a programmable joystick such as a ThrustMaster FLCS and currently have the view hat or buttons programmed for digital operation (mimics key presses), the calibration routines will not recognize these as joystick signals.*

- *The calibration of the Windows 95 driver is incorrect. If you can't calibrate your controllers in the Windows 95 Game Controller Properties Test tab, they won't be calibrated when you run Flight Simulator 98. If you have the proper driver and joystick selected, any problems may mean your joystick or game card is malfunctioning. Find out for sure by swapping them out with ones known to work properly.*

Naturally, if you haven't been flying yet or have little experience in the cockpit, there's no way to tell if your control sensitivities are right for you. You may want to leave these settings as they are until you feel a need to change them. This is another matter of personal preference; knowing when something isn't responsive enough or is totally uncontrollable. If you find that you can't turn or get off the ground, you'll want to increase the offending axis' sensitivities. Conversely, if

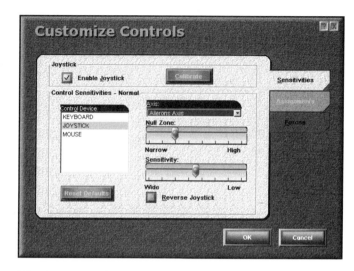

The Customize Controls box is where controllers are enabled and configured.

you find the slightest movement of your joystick causes your airplane to overreact, slide the offending axis' sensitivities down.

Null Zone refers to the amount of dead space around the neutral point of the controller. If you find that your aircraft unintentionally maneuvers with the slightest control movement while still in the neutral position (joystick centered), consider widening the Null Zone. Such problems are usually caused by joystick or game card problems, but this adjustment can help alleviate a hardware problem through software. Note that the Null Zone setting in the Preferences window will adjust the null zone for all controller axes, and all settings made here will affect all flights.

Below the slider controls is a Reverse Joystick check box. Enabling this option will reverse the operation of the selected axis. Not only will this help with non-standard controller operation, it can let you easily alter the operation of a throttle controller to work in the same direction as a helicopter collective lever. (The collective on a helicopter increases lift as you pull on it, as

> **Tip:** *You can enable the mouse for flight control and use it simultaneously with a joystick by clicking the right mouse button and selecting Mouse As Yoke. You'll be able to use the mouse for flight control, but once you move the joystick, it will override any mouse control inputs.*

Instrument Flight Techniques
For Microsoft *Flight Simulator 98*

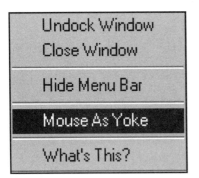

> Undock Window
> Close Window
> ――――――――――
> Hide Menu Bar
> ――――――――――
> **Mouse As Yoke**
> ――――――――――
> What's This?

A right mouse button click will bring forth a pop-up menu that lists the Mouse As Yoke option.

Tip: *The Reset Defaults button in the lower left-hand corner of the Custom Controls window will reset all of the Sensitivity and Null Zone settings back to their default positions. Be aware, however, that the Enable Joystick setting will be disabled as well.*

opposed to an airplane throttle control that increases power as you push it.) But because this option is a global setting (one affecting all flights), you'll have to remember to change it back for airplane throttle use.

Advanced Adjustments

Although these tips apply to all of the aircraft used for instrument flight in Flight Simulator 98, for the sake of simplicity we'll use the Cessna 182S in our examples. On the 182S, just to the left of the throttle control knob are the control position indicators. The real 182S (and non fly-by-wire aircraft) doesn't have anything like this, basically because it doesn't need them. Your flight controls are directly tied to the control surfaces. On a computer, however, your control movements correspond to virtual aircraft control movement—which is not connected. In other words, the control of your virtual aircraft is managed through software, and depending on how that software is set up, it will result in proper or improper control of your virtual aircraft. Just as the name suggests, the control position indicators are graphical representations of where your control surfaces are located at any time within their range of movement. The center vertical index represents your elevator. The horizontal index on the top portrays your ailerons, and the horizontal index on the bottom depicts your rudder.

Earlier we mentioned that there is little need to adjust your controller parameters until you know where to start. Now that you're in the cockpit, this is the time. The first thing you should look for is whether the pointers are centered when your stick is centered. If they aren't, you may need to adjust your joystick's trim wheels (if they have them), or recalibrate the offending controller(s).

The next thing you want to check for is proper movement in both axis and direction. Move your controllers and watch the control movement indexes.

What you are checking is that the aileron control moves the aileron index, and so on. Furthermore, you want to make sure that control movement moves the corresponding index in the correct direction. For ailerons and rudder, left control index movement corresponds with left controller input and vice versa. The elevator index moves up for up elevator controller input and your downward input should move the same index downward. If you have a problem here, you may have the Reverse Joystick box enabled in Custom Controls.

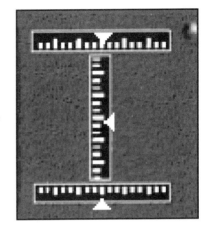

These control position indicators are just to the left of the throttle control knob on the C-182S.

Control travel should be checked next. The entire length of a control position indicator box represents 100 percent control deflection in both directions. The middle represents the neutral position. Slowly move one control axis as you watch the corresponding index on your instrument panel. If the index never reaches the ends of the position indicator box, you need to increase the sensitivity of this axis, unless you've already adjusted this axis down to suit your preferences.

On the other hand, if the controller index reaches the end of the indicator box long before your controller reaches the end of its travel, the sensitivity on this axis is too sensitive. If an axis' sensitivity is too high, your aircraft will be over-responsive and hard to control. However, if the sensitivity is too low, the aircraft will be tough to maneuver. You'll get the feeling that you're flying through molasses.

Naturally, controller sensitivities are a matter of preference and everyone is different. A good starting point for most people is a setup where the sensitivity setting moves the index to meet the end of the control position at the same time your controller physically meets its travel limit. This will net you 100 percent control movement and no dead spots. The only exception you may want to consider is rudder travel. Most pilots will probably feel more comfortable with a rudder sensitivity setting that nets less than 100 percent indicator travel.

As for Null Zone adjustments, that's really something that should be adjusted in the air. Gross problems, however, can be identified and corrected during the ground check. Look for spikes when your controller is in its centered position. Spikes are erratic, non-intentional control inputs, and are generally caused by hardware-related problems such as dirty potentiometers in your controller, or game card problems. Nevertheless, adjusting Null Zones can help. It's worth a try—besides, it's free!

After all of that discussion, you should have your controllers all set up properly. This is important, since a sharp pilot may be able to fly with a poorly adjusted controller, although he or she will know something is wrong. Sadly enough, though, a new pilot usually won't be able to tell if there is anything wrong and may just blame poor performance on their lack of piloting skills (when it could really be an improperly setup controller). The best part of all of this: once you've adjusted your controllers properly, you shouldn't have to do it again until you change controllers, or reinstall Flight Simulator 98 without backing up your FLTSIM98.CFG file from the Flight Simulator 98 folder.

Controller Positioning

When discussing flight simulators, one aspect of controller configuration that usually goes unaddressed is controller placement. That means the location of each controller in relation to where you sit and what you sit on. When you sit inside the cockpit of an airplane in-flight, the only way to maintain precise control of your aircraft is to have steady hands, even when the aircraft is moving and bouncing around as well. The way you keep steady hands under such conditions is by resting or bracing your arms or elbows against something. When your elbows are supported against something solid, it gives your hands the required stability for good aircraft control.

Naturally, you don't need to worry about turbulence or other jarring movements while sitting in front of your computer, but the technique used in real airplanes can be beneficial to computer pilots just the same. Moving your controls to an exact position is really difficult to do without stability. What you can use as bracing varies from pressing your back into a sturdy chair, to resting the edge of your palm or wrist against the base of your joystick as you control it.

In the cockpit you can generally rely upon your body as being a fairly stable place to brace your elbow against because you're strapped in your seat firmly. Pressing your elbows against your rib cage can give you the support you desire, but it can become tiresome after a while. Another popular bracing point is the cockpit armrest. Of course, such decisions are matters of personal preference, but the armrest works the best for many pilots. Now that you know what to consider, see what works best for you.

Helicopter pilots develop what is known as helicopter hunch. The cyclic stick is positioned between the pilot's legs and using the armrests for bracing would be impractical (unless you have some extraordinarily long forearms). What most pilots do is rest their forearms on the top of their legs for stability. This creates that helicopter hunch body positioning.

Although this is the way it's done in real life, computer joysticks are not designed for use between the user's legs. Rely on one of the airplane bracing methods mentioned earlier instead. Again, even though you aren't faced with outside forces affecting your controller stability, bracing your hands will increase the precision of your controller movements.

Setting Preferences

Preferences are usually a matter of personal taste, but not always. As we touched on earlier, the specific activity in Flight Simulator 98 you wish to participate in can influence which preferences are more suitable. Preference settings not only stipulate what you'll see and hear, but also how well they are seen and felt.

Feel for Graphics

Of course, everyone wants to run simulations at the highest resolution possible with silky smooth frame rates. The importance of graphics quantity and quality is dependent on what you plan to do in Flight Simulator 98. If you're into sightseeing, you'll probably be willing to accept a loss in frame rate for prettier scenery. Because we'll be flying instrument approaches, if you have to make a choice between graphics or feel (and most of us do), you'd be better off without the scenery while keeping faster instrument updates instead.

"Frame rate" is a phrase that refers to the amount of times your screen (or frame) is redrawn within a second. The faster your screen is redrawn, the smoother the animation/flight/scenery (or whatever) will appear. But when it comes to simulations, a low frame rate will affect how the simulation feels as well. For example, if screen updates are too slow, everything will be too choppy to fly comfortably and control inputs will be delayed and inconsistent.

When you get down to it, this is another subjective area that can only be left to personal taste. What's comfortable for one person may not be comfortable for another. The best we can do is offer some guidelines.

Instrument Flight Techniques
For Microsoft Flight Simulator 98

Anything you do to Flight Simulator 98's display settings will affect your graphics performance. This includes the amount of detail specified, screen resolution, traffic, weather, the number of windows, and window sizes. Because we'll pursue precision flying instead of sightseeing, we want detail and resolution settings that make your airplane feel instantly responsive and update your instruments smoothly and quickly. If your system isn't able to keep up with your current detail and resolution settings, you'll always be playing catch-up and you'll never fly your aircraft well.

Although people have different opinions on the subject, most people find that frame rates under 15 frames-per-second are too choppy for serious flight. Flight Simulator 98 has a frame-rate display that can help you determine your tolerances and assist with your graphics detail balancing. Pressing Shift + z on your keyboard will cycle through the coordinate display and frame-rate counter in the upper left corner of your current window.

Display Preferences

Now that you know what you want, let's look at what you can change to reach those goals. The Display Preferences window is under the Options menu and Preferences selection. Display Preferences are global settings. In other words, changes made here will affect all flight situations. As mentioned earlier, display options affect graphic performance. If you're not yet keen about setting your own graphics options at this point, the drop-down box labeled Performance Mode (at the top of the window) lists some suggested basic configurations. From there you can tweak your settings (cross-checked with the frame-rate display) to match your needs.

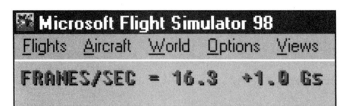

Shift + Z will cycle through the coordinate display and frame-rate counter.

Tip: *Anytime you adjust any display options on the Display Preferences window or any of the Display Options sub windows, the Performance Mode box will automatically switch to User Defined.*

There are three criteria used in the suggested configurations: machine type, performance preference, and graphics

resolution. Here are some recommendations and suggestions to aid your quest for perfection in graphics and feel:

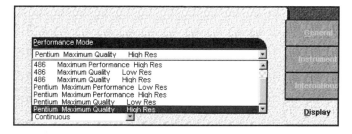

The Performance Mode drop-down box lists some suggested configurations based on machine type, performance preference, and graphics resolution.

- Begin your selections based upon your machine type or lower.
- Select Maximum Performance for more serious flying. Maximum Quality is for sightseeing or running Flight Simulator 98 on fast machines.
- Choose between High Res and Low Res based on frame-rate preferences.

3D on the PC

The DirectX 5.0 specification includes Direct3D (D3D), which is supported by all mainstream graphics board vendors. Therefore, Flight Simulator

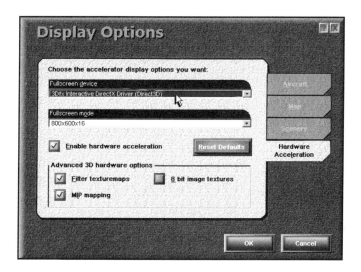

The Hardware Acceleration tab is where you select and configure Flight Simulator 98's Fullscreen devices.

98 will work with most 3D-accelerator cards to and through D3D. However, 3D capabilities (such as fog and haze effects) as well as overall D3D performance vary by chip set, and sometimes by manufacturer. If you're in the market for one of these visual marvels, shop the market before spending your money. With any 3D purchase, the performance gain over a 2D video card will be noticeable. You'll be able to run Flight Simulator 98 with more detail and at good or better frame rates.

Below are a few notes and tips on purchasing, installing, and configuring a 3D graphics cards.

- You must have D3D compatibility in order for it to work with Flight Simulator 98, but that's usually a given.
- To see transparent clouds in 3D mode, make sure the Cloud Thickness options are turned off (Options: Preferences: Display Tab: Display Options Button: Scenery tab: Cloud Thickness).
- 3Dfx Voodoo-based cards only support 3D acceleration in Fullscreen mode. Furthermore, you must enable the 3Dfx driver as your Fullscreen device. To do this, set Hardware Acceleration to On in Options: Preferences: Display: Display Options: Hardware Acceleration. Then, under Fullscreen Device, select 3Dfx Interactive DirectX Driver (Direct3D) and set Fullscreen Mode to 00x600x16. To enter Fullscreen mode press Alt + Enter.
- Flight Simulator 98's menu bar can't be displayed while in D3D mode when using a 3Dfx Voodoo-based graphics card.
- Windowed 3D acceleration only works in 16-bit color screen modes.
- "Bubble" lighting effects on runway lighting with 3Dfx Voodoo-based graphics cards can be fixed with updated drivers. The reference Voodoo drivers (from http://www.3dfx.com) fix this problem on most systems.

Sounds Abound

Although they won't affect your graphics performance as much as settings made in Display Preferences, depending on the speed of your computer, you may need to tinker with Sound Preferences. In most cases the small performance gain you'd obtain isn't worth the tradeoff of lost realism in your Flight Simulator 98 experience. Also be aware that certain sound options will aid instrument flight procedures.

General Sound Operation

Sound Preferences settings are also globally applied, but the choice of whether to hear any sounds at all (e.g. totally on or totally off) is situation-based (saved with each flight). Because this overall sound setting is saved when you save a Flight, you have the option of using, ignoring, or overriding this setting.

All sounds can be toggled on or off by pressing the Q key on your keyboard. On the General Preferences tab (click Options, then select Preferences...), Start Up options has a drop-down box in the middle of the window named Sound. From this drop-down box you can choose from three sound selections: Off, On, and Based on Flight.

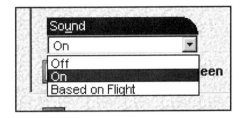

The three sound selections (Off, On, and Based on Flight) are configured on the General Preferences tab under Start Up options.

Off disables all sounds by default. This means any time you start Flight Simulator 98, you will not hear any sounds regardless of the sound state you opted for in the saved Flight. Conversely, On enables all sounds regardless of whether sounds were enabled or not. The Based on Flight option sets overall sound to the saved Flight settings. There are two points you should note; pressing the Q key will override any of these settings, and turning the sound Off in the Start Up options will not disable the sound in the opening introduction film.

Sound Advice

The Sound Preferences tab is under Options on the menu bar. On the left side of the Sound Preferences window there are five categories of sounds that you have control over. Directly to the right of each are volume slider controls. To disable a particular group of sounds, just un-check the appropriate box. To adjust the volume of each sound group, slide the corresponding volume control bar. Just as you'd suspect, High increases the sound volume, and Low decreases it.

The five sound groups and what they encompass are:

Engine: This affects only the sound of your engine. Being able to turn this down or off can come in handy during those marathon cross-country trips. However, enabling this option is a splendid way to instantly be clued-in to engine performance states or problems.

Cockpit: Cockpit sounds include stall warnings and message beeps while in multiplayer mode. You'll probably want to keep this one enabled as stall warnings and message beeps are fairly important. The only thing you may want to adjust is the volume.

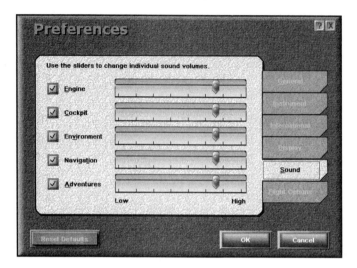

The Sound Preferences window lists the five categories of sounds in Flight Simulator 98.

Environment: The Environment group of sounds includes crashes, splashes, landing skids, and bumps. Although these sounds may not seem to serve any purpose other than to satisfy some warped masochistic yearnings, they *can* help you. Well, maybe not the crash and splash stuff, but knowing (through an audio cue) the very instant that your wheels touch the ground during a landing can help you stay more fully aware of your current situation.

Navigation: Navigation sounds are limited to radio navigation sounds such as marker beacons for ILS landings. You definitely want to keep this enabled.

Adventures: If you disable these sounds you'll really be missing a treat. This option enables ATC (Air Traffic Control) radio instructions and co-pilot voices.

Chapter Two

AIRCRAFT

While Microsoft Flight Simulator 98 comes with eight aircraft, not all of them are suitable for instrument flight, either because of the lack of certified instrumentation or inherent limitations (such as the sailplane's lack of "user operated" propulsion). Even among the IFR-capable aircraft in Flight Simulator 98, not all are suitable for primary instrument flight training. This is principally due to two factors: aircraft complexity, and the somewhat-related factor created by the higher speeds that some of the aircraft must be flown at.

When you're in the cockpit—and flying solely by referring to instruments—your workload is pretty high. Matters are only compounded when you have to complete the same number of procedures (or more) in the shorter interval of time you have when you fly in one of the faster aircraft. It's a double-edged sword; because the aircraft is more complex, you'll have more procedures to complete. Also, because the aircraft is faster, you'll have less time in which to complete all your required tasks.

On the other hand, there are those who believe the sophistication of autopilot systems in the more complex aircraft in Flight Simulator can make them perfectly acceptable aircraft in which to learn instrument flight. While it's probably true that someone with even the most rudimentary piloting skills could be taught to flip on the autopilot in the 737—and thus achieve success in making an instrument flight—the autopilot really should be viewed as a tool and not a substitute for pilot proficiency. Anyone who believes otherwise would probably really be better served with a book titled something like *Autopilot Flight Training* rather than *Instrument Flight Training*.

With that said, it's strongly recommended that you begin with one of the more conventional trainers—in particular the Cessna 182S or the Cessna 182RG (although you should note that the C-182RG is considered a *complex* airplane due to its retractable landing gear). As your proficiency increases, feel free to advance to some of the other aircraft Flight Simulator 98 offers.

The following pages contain short histories, specifications, and airspeed limitations of the fully instrument-flight-capable aircraft in Flight Simulator 98. Note that although some specifications (such as interior dimensions) are strictly for academic purposes, other information such as airspeed limitations can be extremely useful for purposes of flight planning and flight configuration. The order of presentation of aircraft has been arranged according to our suggested primary instrument flight training suitability.

Trainers

While it's debatable whether any single flight characteristic classifies an airplane as a trainer, there's no question that the performance and speed of a trainer must be high enough to keep the pilot busy. At the same time, performance and speed mustn't be so high that they overwhelm inexperienced aviators. In Flight Simulator 98, just as in the real world, both the Cessna 182S Skylane and the Cessna 182RG Skylane clearly fit the bill. Their combination of relatively slow speed, maneuverability, power, and forgiving nature make them ideal for primary pilot training. Because the same company manufactures both of the Skylanes, let's discuss them jointly.

Cessna Skylane: History

Clyde V. Cessna founded the Cessna Aircraft Company in 1911. In 1927, the company began producing aircraft at its factory in Wichita, Kansas. The model 182 first went into production in 1956 (as did the Model 172, which was later dubbed the "Skyhawk"). In 1958, the deluxe version of the 182 line received the title designation Skylane.

In 1962, the model 182 received a new sportier body featuring a larger cabin and a new rear window. Except for some internal structural changes, today's Skylane is very similar to the version produced back in 1962.

Skylanes remained in continuous production until the end of 1987 when the volume of liability suits against U.S. light plane manufacturers made it impossible to continue production. Eventually, with changes in the law, more protection has been given to light plane manufacturers to reduce liability suits. In 1996, as a result, production of Skyhawks and Skylanes resumed. Cessna's newest model was introduced—the 182S, first featured in Flight Simulator 98.

Skylane Characteristics and Comparisons

Although the most obvious difference between the 182S and the 182RG is the 182RG's retractable landing gear (hence the designation RG—Retractable Gear), performance-wise they're really quite similar. The only performance differences you're likely to experience (other than the added complexity of having to retract and extend the landing gear) is the 182RG's slightly faster cruise, top

Cessna 182S Skylane.

speed, and climb rates. The other performance numbers remain virtually the same. However, inside the cockpit you'll notice other differences.

Even though the 182RG's engine has a 5hp. advantage over its fixed-gear cousin, the added weight of the landing gear retraction system basically offsets this minute power advantage. Reducing aerodynamic drag by getting the landing gear cleanly out of the way of the oncoming airflow produces small gains.

The 182RG and the 182S are equipped with different instrument panels. While the 182S features the latest single-engine panel produced by Cessna, the 182RG is equipped with an older model. While most of the instruments and radio stack are the same, the 182RG is equipped with only one VOR receiver and indicator head. The RG also lacks a cylinder head temperature and EGT (Exhaust Gas Temperature) gauge, has slightly different fuel and oil gauges, and, of course, adds a landing gear indicator.

Cessna 182S Skylane: Specifications

Engine:	Textron Lycoming
Model Number:	IO-540-AB1A5
Max. Power:	230 BHP rating
Propeller:	McCauley, 2-Bladed
	Constant Speed
Landing gear:	Fixed tricycle,
	steerable nosewheel

Cessna 182S Engine Instrument Markings

Instrument	Red Line (Minimum)	Green Arc (Normal Operating)	Red Line (Maximum)
Tachometer	—	2000-2400 RPM	2400 RPM
Manifold Pressure	—	15-23" Hg.	—
Cylinder Head Temperature	—	200-500° F.	500° F.
Oil Temperature	—	100-245° F.	245° F.
Oil Pressure	20 PSI	50-90 PSI	115 PSI
Fuel Quantity	E (2.0 gal. Unusable each tank)	—	—
Fuel Flow	—	0-15 GPH	—
Suction Gauge	—	4.5-5.5" Hg.	—

Crew:	1
Seats:	4
Length:	29 ft.
Height:	9 ft. 3 in.
Wingspan:	36 ft.
Wing area:	175.5 sq. ft.
Max. ramp weight:	3110 lbs.
Max. takeoff weight:	3100 lbs.
Max. landing weight:	2950 lbs.
Std. empty weight:	1882 lbs.
Useful load:	1228 lbs.
Wing loading:	17.8 lbs./sq. ft.
Power loading:	13.5 lbs./hp.
Max. fuel capacity:	92 gal.
Max. usable fuel:	88 gal.
Max. rate of climb (SL):	924 ft./min.
Service ceiling:	18,100 ft.
Max. operating speed (SL):	145 knots
Cruise (75% power):	140 knots
Best cruise altitude:	8000-10,000 ft.

Interior:

Cabin length:	11 ft. 1 in
Cabin max. width (centerline):	3 ft. 6 in
Cabin width (floor level):	3 ft.
Cabin height:	4 ft. 0.5 in.

Cessna 182S Skylane Airspeeds and Airspeed Limitations

Vne	175 KIAS	Never Exceed Speed
Vno	140 KIAS	Max. Structural Cruising Speed (never exceed, unless in smooth air)
Va at 3100 lbs.	110 KIAS	Maneuvering Speed
at 2600 lbs.	101 KIAS	
at 2000 lbs.	88 KIAS	
Vfe(1)	10 deg. <140 KIAS	Max. Flap Extension Speeds
Vfe(2)	20 deg. <120 KIAS	
Vfe(3)	Full <100 KIAS	
Vr	50-60 KIAS	Rotation Speed
Vx at SL	63 KIAS	Best Angle of Climb
at 10,000 ft.	66 KIAS	
Vy at SL	80 KIAS	Best Rate of Climb
at 10,000 ft.	72 KIAS	
Max. glide (flaps up)		Best Glide Engine Out, Flaps Up
at 3100 lbs.	75 KIAS	
at 2600 lbs.	60 KIAS	
at 2000 lbs.	62 KIAS	
(flaps down) at 3100 ft.	70 KIAS	
Approach no engine (flaps up)	70 KIAS	
(10 deg. flaps)	65 KIAS	
Vs	54 KCAS	Stall Clean
Vso	49 KCAS	Stall Landing Configuration
Vref	Approx. 60 KIAS until flair	Landing Speed
Max. demonstrated crosswind velocity (takeoff and landing)	15 Knots	

Cessna 182RG Skylane.

Cessna 182RG Skylane: Specifications

Engine:	Avco Lycoming
Model Number:	O-540-J3C5D
Max. Power:	235 hp.
Landing gear:	Retractable tricycle, steerable nosewheel

Cessna 182RG Engine Instrument Markings

Instrument	Red Line (Minimum)	Green Arc (Normal Operating)	Red Line (Maximum)
Tachometer	—	2000 - 2400 RPM	2400 RPM
Manifold Pressure	—	15-23" Hg.	—
Oil Temperature	—	100-245° F.	245° F.
Oil Pressure	20 PSI	60-115 PSI 1	15 PSI
Fuel Quantity	E (2.0 gal. Unusable each tank)	—	—
Fuel Flow	—	0-15 GPH	—
Suction Gauge	—	4.5-5.5" Hg.	—

Crew:	1
Seats:	4
Length:	28 ft. 7.5 in.
Height:	8 ft. 11 in.
Wingspan:	36 ft.
Wing area:	174 sq. ft.
Max. ramp weight:	3112 lbs.
Max. takeoff weight:	3100 lbs.
Max. landing weight:	3100 lbs.
Std. empty weight:	1782 lbs.
Useful load:	1330 lbs.
Wing loading:	17.8 lbs./sq. ft.
Power loading:	13.2 lbs./hp.

Max. fuel capacity:	92 gal.	
Max. usable fuel:	88 gal.	
Max. rate of climb (SL):	1140 ft./min.	
Service ceiling:	14,300 ft.	
Max. operating speed (SL):	160 knots	
Cruise (75% power 7500 ft.):	156 knots	

Cessna 182RG Airspeeds and Airspeed Limitations

Vne	178 KIAS	Never Exceed Speed
Vno	157 KIAS	Max. Structural Cruising Speed (never exceed unless in smooth air)
Va @ 3100 lbs.	112 KIAS	Maneuvering Speed
Vfe(1) 20 deg. < 120 KIAS Vfe(3)	10 deg. < 140 KIAS Full < 95 KIAS	Max. Flap Extension Speeds Vfe(2)
Vr	55 KIAS	Rotation Speed
Vy @ SL	80 KIAS	Best Rate of Climb
Max glide (flaps and gear up) @ 3100 lbs.	83 KIAS	Best Glide Engine Out, Flaps Up
Approach no engine (flaps up) (10 deg. flaps)	70 KIAS	65 KIAS
Vs	54 KCAS	Stall Clean
Vso	50 KCAS	Stall Landing Configuration
Vref	~60 KIAS until flair	Landing Speed
Max. demonstrated crosswind velocity (takeoff and landing)	15 Knot	

Transports

Besides having the ability to carry more passengers than a trainer, the main differences between what we'll classify as *transports* and trainers are size and speed. But don't think that faster means more nimble. Although the Boeing 737-400 is much faster than a trainer, it *drives* like a proverbial bus. (Considering that the 737 is virtually a bus that just happens to fly, this driving characteristic isn't all that surprising.)

Transport characteristics and comparisons

In Flight Simulator 98 there are two aircraft that can be classified as transports: the Learjet 45, and the aforementioned Boeing 737-400. Besides being much larger than the Skylanes, these two aircraft are multi-engine turbine-powered jet transports. Although it won't matter to your virtual pilot's physiology in Flight Simulator 98, these transports feature pressurized cabins as well. Both turbine power and cabin pressurization make these aircraft more suited for high-altitude flight than the piston-powered, single-engine, non-pressurized Skylanes.

As you'll see, takeoff and landing speeds of the transport class of aircraft are much higher, and as mentioned at the beginning of this chapter, this makes them less suitable for primary instrument flight training. But if you're set on trying your skills, keep in mind that the 737 is a little more forgiving. Due to its size, it tends to take over-controlling a little better than the Learjet 45. To complete an analogy, if the 737 is a flying bus, the model 45 could be considered to be a Ferrari limousine.

Inside the cockpit, both transport aircraft feature *glass cockpit* electronic displays (although the 737-400 features a mixture of electronic and advanced analog instruments). Most pilots find that electronic readouts simplify recognition and reduce viewing effort. Although this would seem to reinforce the instrument flight training with transport aircraft argument, the increased speeds of these aircraft generally negate any instrument recognition benefits for beginning pilots—of course, if you refrain from using the advanced autopilots.

Boeing 737-400.

Boeing 737-400: History

William E. Boeing founded the Boeing Company in 1917. Right from the very start, Boeing was interested in producing aircraft for the military. Although the Boeing Company produced a successful airliner called the Model 247 in the 1930s, the long line of Boeing commercial jet transport aircraft owes its origins to their military cousins. Perhaps the most famous bomber of World War II

was a Boeing aircraft—the B-17 Flying Fortress. Over the years Boeing continued the tradition of creating big airplanes with other notable military bombers such as the B-29 Superfortress, the B-47 Stratojet, and the awe-inspiring B-52 Stratofortress.

The third incarnation of the highly successful "7" series, the Boeing 737 has become the best-selling commercial jetliner of all time. (Over 700 737s are in the air...at *all* times!) First introduced in 1967, the 737 line of short- and medium-range jet transports has evolved through several different incarnations to fulfill the needs of Boeing customers. Currently there are only three versions of the 737 being produced. The smallest being the 737-500, seating 108 passengers; the slightly larger 737-300, which accommodates 128 passengers; and the 737-400 (modeled in Flight Simulator 98), which is the largest version, capable of carrying 146 passengers, all in two classes.

The first 737-400 entered service on September 15, 1988 and is currently available in basic and long-range versions. The "next generation" of 737s (the 737-600, 737-700, and 737-800) will fly faster, higher, and farther than current models. They'll also feature improvements in operating costs, noise, fuel burn, and thrust.

With more than 3000 737s in service around the world and hundreds more on order, the Boeing 737 is often the first jet transport that new airline pilots fly.

Boeing 737-400: Specifications

Engines:	2 CFM International
Model Number:	CFM56-3B or CFM56-3C high-bypass turbofans
Max. Power:	22,000 lbs. (97.86 kN) or 23,500 lbs. (105 kN) each
Crew:	2
Passengers:	Up to 188 (basic U.S. configuration is 146)
Length:	119.7 ft.
Height:	36.6 ft.
Tail height:	36.5 ft.
Wingspan:	94.9 ft.
Wing area:	1135 sq. ft.
Aspect ratio:	7.91

Max. takeoff weight:	138,500 lbs. (150,000 lbs. high-gross-version)
Usable cargo volume:	1373 cu. ft.
Wing loading (138,500 lbs.):	132.2 lbs./sq. ft.
Max. usable fuel:	36,114 lbs. (5311 U.S. gal.)
Max. pressurization differential:	8.65 lbs./sq. in.
Max. operating speed:	Mach 0.82
Range:	2390 statute miles (146 passengers)
High cruise speed (FL 370)	0.74 Mach
Normal cruise speed:	0.745 Mach (441 knots)
Runway required for takeoff (balanced-field length, sea level, standard conditions, max. weight):	7730 ft. (8740 ft. high-gross-version)

Interior:

Cabin width:	11ft. 7in

Boeing 737-400 Airspeeds and Airspeed Limitations

Vne	Mach .82	Never Exceed Speed
Vno		Max. Structural Speed
Va		Maneuvering Speed
Vfe(1)	1-5 deg. < 250 KIAS	Max. Flap Extension Speeds
Vfe(2)	10 deg. < 215 KIAS	
Vfe(3)	15 deg. < 205 KIAS	
Vfe(4)	25 deg. < 190 KIAS	
Vfe(5)	30 deg. < 185 KIAS	
Vfe(6)	40 deg. < 162 KIAS	
Vfs	175 KIAS	Flap Retracton Speed
Vr	151 KIAS	Rotation Speed
Vx		Best Angle of Climb
Vy	280 KIAS	Best Rate of Climb
Max. glide		
V13		
Vmc	Min. Controllable Airspeed	1 Engine
Vs		Stall Clean

Boeing 737-400 Airspeeds and Airspeed Limitations, continued

Vso		Stall Landing Configuration
Vref	~140 KIAS	Landing Speed
Vlo	270 KIAS	Max. Gear Operation
V1	150 KIAS	Takeoff Decision Speed
V2	160 KIAS	Takeoff Safety Speed
V2+30	190 KIAS	Single Engine Cruise

Learjet 45: History

In the late 1950s, William P. Lear, Sr. (who, incidentally, was the inventor of the now-obsolete, but fondly remembered (eight-track tape player), predicted the need for a small, private jet airplane for business travelers that would equal the performance of commercial jetliners. His basic concept was to create a small transport jet with "near-fighter-jet performance."

To achieve this goal, Lear put together a team of engineers in Switzerland to design an airplane loosely based on a Swiss fighter known as the P-16. The airplane they came up with and built in Wichita, Kansas in 1962 became the Lear Jet 23. (Note the spelling. More about this in a minute.) In addition to being the first small jet to reach the market in volume production, the Lear Jet 23 set a number of speed and time-to-climb world records that sealed its reputation as the ultimate in business jet travel.

Due to a competitive marketplace causing profitability problems, in 1967 Lear sold the company to Gates Rubber Company in Denver and the company name was changed to Gates Learjet Corporation. A number of successful years followed until 1982, when the entire industry entered a market slump. Five years later (in 1987), Gates sold its stock in the company to Integrated Acquisitions. This subsidiary of Integrated Resources later filed Chapter 11 and sold the company to Bombardier Inc. of

Learjet 45.

Montreal, Canada, which has operated the company since 1990, under the name of Learjet, Inc..

Under Bombardier, Learjet created the all-new Learjet 45 as a replacement for the successful Model 35 series to offer midsize comfort and capability at light-jet costs. This advanced aircraft took to the air October 7, 1996 and received FAA-type certification in September 1997.

Learjet 45: Specifications

Engines:	2 AlliedSignal/Garrett
Model Number:	TFE 731-20 turbofans
Max. Power:	3500 lbs. st (15.6 kN) each
	Takeoff thrust flat-rated to
	88° F (31° C) 3650 lbs.
	(APR rating) each
Crew:	2
Passengers:	Up to 9
Length:	58 ft.
Height:	14.1 ft.
Wingspan:	47.75 ft.
Wing area:	311.6 sq. ft.
Max. ramp weight:	20,450 lbs.
Max. takeoff weight:	20,200 lbs.
Max. landing weight:	19,200 lbs.
Max. zero fuel weight:	15,500 lbs.
Spec. basic operating weight:	12,850 lbs.
Max. payload (D.E.):	2650 lbs.
Payload full fuel (A.E.F.):	1600 lbs.
Full-fuel payload:	1500 lbs.
Fuel with max. payload:	4950 lbs.
Wing loading at 20,000 lbs.:	64.2 lbs./sq. ft.
Max. usable fuel:	6000 lbs. (882 U.S. gal.)
Service ceiling:	51,000 ft.
Max. operating speed:	Mach .81
Range: (NBAA IFR Reserve, NMSMKMISA, with 4 pax/2 crew):	1710 nm
High cruise speed:	0.78 Mach (445 knots)

Normal cruise speed:	0.77 Mach (441 knots)
Long-range cruise speed:	0.76 Mach (434 knots)
Fuel consumption per hour at cruise:	186 gal. (1265 lbs.)
Runway required for takeoff (balanced-field length, sea level, standard conditions, max. weight):	4580 ft.
Runway required for landing (standard conditions, max. weight):	2990 ft.
Avionics:	Honeywell Primus 1000 four-tube EFISEngine Instrument/Crew Advisory System (EICAS)Honeywell Primus 650 weather radarDual Primus II nav/comm systems

Interior:

Cabin length (cockpit divider to end of pressurized compartment):	19 ft. 9in.
Cabin max. width (centerline):	5 ft. 1 in.
Cabin width (floor level):	3 ft. 4 in.
Cabin height:	4 ft. 11 in.
Floor area (excluding cockpit):	65.8 26.1
Total volume (cockpit divider to end of pressurized compartment):	410 ft.

Learjet 45 Airspeeds and Airspeed Limitations

Vne	Mach .81	Never Exceed Speed
Vno		Max. Structural Speed
Va		Maneuvering Speed
Vfe(1)	8 deg. < 200 KIAS	Max. Flap Extension Speeds
Vfe(2)	20 deg. < 185 KIAS	
Vfe(3)	40 deg. < 150 KIAS	
Vx		Best Angle of Climb
Vy		Best Rate of Climb
Max glide		
Vmc	104 KIAS	Min. Controllable Airspeed 1 Engine

Learjet 45 Airspeeds and Airspeed Limitations, continued

Vs @ 16,500 ft.	119 KIAS	Stall Clean
Vso @ 16,500 ft.	101 KIAS (20 deg. flaps) 92 KIAS (40 deg. flaps)	Stall Landing Configuration
Approach speed (recommended)	~125 KIAS @ 14,000 lbs.	
Vref	113 KIAS	Landing Speed
Vle	260 KIAS	Max. Gear Extension
Vlo	200 KIAS	Max. Gear Operation
V1	109 KIAS	Takeoff Decision Speed
V2	134 KIAS @ 16,900 lbs.	Takeoff Safety Speed
V2+30	164 KIAS @ 16,900 lbs.	Flap Retract/Ringle Engine Cruise
Vsse	146 KIAS	Intentional One-Engine

Other Instrument Flight Aircraft

Due to the lack of a better way to classify the remaining two instrument-flight-capable aircraft in Flight Simulator 98, we've grouped the Extra 300S and the Bell 206B JetRanger in an "others" classification. One of these aircraft is a purpose-built aerobatics monoplane while the other is a helicopter. On one level, the only thing they have even remotely in common is their unsuitability for primary instrument flight. Let's talk about why.

Characteristics and comparisons

Manufactured in Dinkslaken, Germany and featuring a welded-tube fuselage covered with composite panels and an all-composite wing, the Extra 300S can withstand G loads (±10G) and roll performance (>400 degrees per second) exceeding that of most military fighter aircraft. To say that the Extra 300 is nimble would be a gross understatement. In the hands of an untrained pilot, it can be downright twitchy.

On the other hand, the Bell 206B helicopter behaves more like a C-182S than any other aircraft in forward flight (besides the C-182RG). However, when it comes to instrument flight, there's no mistaking the Bell 206B for anything other than a helicopter. One common assumption pilots make is thinking if they ever got into trouble when flying through a thick fog, they could always just hover out of the cloud and into safe skies. As you'll see when you moving through this book, it's nearly impossible to hover by instruments alone.

In terms of instruments, the 300S and the JetRanger are equally equipped, the only exception being that the JetRanger is also equipped with a single HSI (Horizontal Situation Indicator). As you'll see later, although the HSI is not the same as a VOR (VHF Omnirange Radio) receiver and indicator head, it does provide the same information.

Extra 300S: History

In 1987, aerobatic pilot and aircraft designer Walter Extra developed the Extra 300. Taking the basic layout of the Extra 230 and adding a more powerful 300 horsepower six-cylinder engine and a second seat, the Extra 300 was born. Although there were other sleek, unlimited aerobatic monoplanes around, it was the huge canopy used to cover the two-place cockpit that made the 300 special.

Up until the time the Extra 300 was introduced, unlimited monoplanes (single-wing airplanes) were all single seaters, so there was no way to receive training in them with an instructor onboard. Although the Pitts Special biplane was a two seater, biplanes were losing their dominance in aerobatic competition. The Extra 300 was assured a place in history as the world's first unlimited aerobatic monoplane trainer.

In 1993, the Extra 300 was type certified by the FAA in both normal and aerobatic categories. Because of its certification and relatively large size (compared to most aerobats) the Extra 300 is suitable for cross-country flights when outfitted with full IFR gear, comfortable seats, and even a three-axis auto pilot.

The Extra 300S derivative was first introduced in 1992 to compete with the incredible Russian Sukhoi Su-26 monoplane. To gain a performance edge, the 300S version has only a single seat, but retains the same engine as the original 300. Other changes include a lowered wing to provide better visibility.

Extra 300S.

Extra 300S: Specifications

Engine:	Lycoming
Model Number:	AEIO 540-L1B5
Max. Power:	300 BHP rating
Landing gear:	Fixed taildragger
Crew:	1
Seats:	1
Length:	21.82 ft.
Height:	8.6 ft.
Wingspan:	24.6 ft.
Wing area:	112.38 sq. ft.
Max. landing weight:	2095 lbs.
Aerobatic weight:	1810 lbs.
Std. empty weight:	1343 lbs.
Max. usable fuel:	42.3 U.S. gal.
Max. cruise:	185 knots
Max. maneuvering speed:	158 knots
Max. roll rate:	400+ deg./sec.

Extra 300S Airspeeds and Airspeed Limitations

Vne	220 KIAS	Never Exceed Speed
Vno	158 KIAS	Max. Structural Cruising Speed (never exceed unless in smooth air)
Va	112 KIAS	Maneuvering Speed
Vr	70 KIAS	Rotation Speed
Vy	80 KIAS	Best Rate of Climb
Max. glide	80 KIAS	Best Glide Engine Out
Approach no engine	70 KIAS	
Vso	55 KIAS	Stall Landing Configuration
Approach speed	90 KIAS	
Vref	~70 KIAS until flair	Landing Speed

Bell 206B JetRanger: History

In 1935, Lawrence Bell founded what was to become the Bell Aircraft Corporation. Although most people today associate the Bell name with helicopter manufacturing, its roots have a long and honored history in airplane design. Just a few years after its beginnings, Bell already had built a reputation creating distinctive and innovative designs for conventional aircraft, such as the P-39 Aircobra.

Bell 206B JetRanger.

Later successes are too numerous to recount here, but just to skim the top, Bell built the P-59 (America's first jet-powered airplane), the X-1, (the world's first super-sonic plane, flown into the history books by Chuck Yeager), and the X-2 (the first airplane to attain Mach 3.0).

In 1941, just before the U.S. was drawn into World War II, Larry Bell set up Arthur Young, a mathematician and inventor, in a small shop in Gardenville, New York. Developed from models that Young used for demonstrating the viability of helicopters, the Bell Model 30—a single-seat, open-cockpit machine powered by a 165-horsepower engine soon became a reality. The Model 30 experimental helicopter first flew untethered in June 1943.

After a rapid succession of improvements and refinements, similar to the third prototype of the Model 30, the newly designated Bell Model 47B was awarded the world's first helicopter license in 1946. Two months later, the Civil Aeronautics Board (forerunner of the Federal Aviation Administration), awarded Bell the first helicopter certification ever granted.

The Model 47 family established Bell as a major manufacturer and as a result, Bell began supplying helicopters to the U.S. armed forces. By 1951, Bell helicopters were in service around the world and breaking records. Because Bell Aircraft Corporation's reputation for helicopters began to rival its reputation as a builder of conventional aircraft, the company created a separate helicopter division (Bell Helicopter Corporation) in 1956.

Headquartered in Fort Worth, Texas, the company was acquired by Textron Inc. in 1960. By 1976, Bell Helicopter had become Textron's largest division, and in 1982 the company became an incorporated subsidiary of Textron. From then on, the innovative rotary-wing company started in that small shop back in New York state became Bell Helicopter Textron Inc..

In 1960, Bell designed the Model 206 to meet the U.S. Army specifications for a light observation helicopter (LOH). Although the 206 lost the competition, Bell used the technology developed during the LOH contest as the basis of a new commercial helicopter, the Model 206A. This model, named JetRanger, first flew in December, 1965 and was certified in October, 1966. Benefiting from a cost miscalculation suffered by the winner of the LOH competition, Bell eventually became a supplier for the Army LOH with a military version of the Model 206A (designated OH-58A Kiowa). Deliveries of the OH-58A began in May, 1969 and were deployed to Vietnam for both LOH and transport duties.

The direct descendant of the 206A, the Model 206B JetRanger III was introduced in 1977. Featuring the lowest operating costs of any helicopter in its class, the five-place 206B is the world's most popular helicopter with more than 8000 in service worldwide.

Bell 206B JetRanger: Specifications

Engine:	Allison
Model Number:	250-C20B or 250-C20J turbine
Max. Power:	420 SHP flat-rated to 317 SHP (236 kW)
Max. Continuous Power:	85% Torque (270 hp.)
Max. Power (five minutes):	100% Torque
Max. Takeoff Power:	100% Torque (317 hp.)
Normal Cruise Power:	80% Torque
Max. Rotor RPM (power on):	100%
Min. Rotor RPM (power on):	97%
Max. Rotor RPM (power off):	107%
Min. Rotor RPM (power off):	90%
Crew:	1
Seats:	5
Length:	31.29 ft.
Height:	11.63 ft.
Rotor Span:	33.33 ft.

Skid Width:	6.28 ft.
Max. Gross Weight:	3200 lbs.
Empty Weight:	1750 lbs.
Useful Load:	1450 lbs.
Fuel Capacity:	91 gal.
Average Fuel Consumption	260-285 lbs./hr. (38-42 gal./hr.)
Max. Rate of Climb:	about 1300 fpm
Max. Operating Altitude:	20,000 ft.
Max. Speed:	130 knots
Normal Operating Speed:	0-130 knots

Bell 206B JetRanger Airspeeds and Airspeed Limitations

Vne	130 KIAS	Never Exceed Speed
Vy (also least sink)	52 KIAS	Best Rate of Climb
Max. glide (distance)	69 KIAS	

Information Sources

1997 Cessna 182S Skylane Information Manual

Boeing Aircraft Corp. at http://www.boeing.com/commercial/737.html

Learjet, Inc. at http://www.learjet.com/45_stat.html

Pilot's Help: Flight Simulator 98

Pilot's Handbook: Flight Simulator 98

Chapter Three

Instrument Flying Basics

The Federal Aviation Administration (FAA) is a department in the U.S. government that's charged with the dual role of regulating and promoting aviation. To fulfill this mission, the FAA sets regulations that all pilots must follow when flying in the U.S. Fortunately, the FAA doesn't want to over-regulate pilots flying in clear weather or low traffic areas.

This is precisely why two distinct sets of regulations called Visual Flight Rules (VFR) and Instrument Flight Rules (IFR) have been created. Each set of rules specifies pilot training requirements and operational procedures a pilot must follow. Weather conditions are a major factor in determining which set of rules to apply to a flight. Unfortunately, it'd be physically impossible to cover every aspect of the FAA regulations within the pages of this book and still have room to talk about actually flying Microsoft Flight Simulator 98. Although this limitation may seem like a drawback, quite frankly, as advanced as Flight Simulator is, there are many aspects of FAA regulations and regulated flight that are not modeled yet. So it's with these considerations in mind that we devote this chapter to taking you through only those regulations that affect your ability to learn and enjoy instrument flight with Flight Simulator 98.

Rules of the Game

As mentioned, the FAA uses Federal Air Regulations (FARs) to define VFR and IFR flight rules. Basically, the FARs are the gospel of aviation regulation for operation within U.S. airspace. In addition to defining VFR and IFR procedures, FARs regulate all aspects of aviation including aircraft maintenance, commercial operations, and aircraft instrument inspections.

As you might imagine, the FARs manual is not light reading material. Luckily, Flight Simulator 98 has extracted many of the FARs applicable to VFR and IFR flight and included them in Pilot's Help. Choose Help from the main menu and select Index from the drop down menu. Search for "FAR" and you

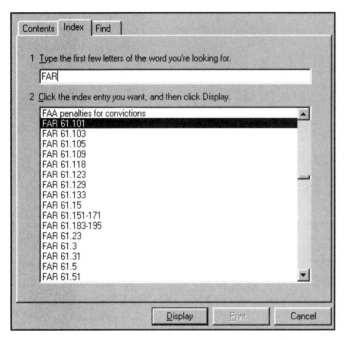

This numbering system is utilized by Federal Air Regulations (FARs) to reference individual regulations.

will come across several topics called "FAR" followed by a "61" or "91". These numbers refer to the numbering system utilized within the FARs to reference individual regulations or what is commonly referred to as FAR "Parts."

If you click on one of the "61" titles, you find information contained in FAR Part 61. FAR Part 61 is a FARs subsection which outlines pilot certification. Here you'll find information on pilot training requirements for all types of pilot licenses, including the instrument rating (FAR 61.65). An instrument rating allows a pilot to operate flights under either IFR or VFR regulations. Without this rating, a pilot can only adhere to VFR regulations. The FAR 91 titles in the Index refer to FAR Part 91. FAR Part 91 contains information on VFR and IFR general operating procedures which you will find useful in planning your flights. It includes details on flight plans, altitudes where your aircraft can fly, and fuel reserve requirements. FAR Part 91 also defines various classes of airspace and levels of Air Traffic Control (ATC) in each type of airspace. ATC is, of course, the program in the U.S. responsible for guiding air traffic.

Tip: *Not included in Flight Simulator 98 are FARs Part 135 and Part 121. These sections are additional regulations which apply to air carriers. If you want to make your journeys in the B-737 and follow regulations to the letter, you may want to study the complete FARs document on the Internet at http://www.faa.gov/AFS/FARS/far_idx.htm.*

Airspace

Because some areas of the US have more air traffic than others, various levels of airspace have been defined to efficiently control airspace and provide aircraft separation. Controlled airspace refers to airspace that requires an ATC clearance before the pilot can enter it and/or requires that a pilot operate by IFR regulations when an IFR environment exists. The definition of IFR and VFR flight conditions will be presented later in this chapter.

Controlled airspace is categorized as either Class A, B, C, D, or E. Depending on the type of airspace, different requirements exist regarding ATC communication, aircraft speeds, and pilot qualifications. Except for Class A airspace, controlled airspace is depicted on government aeronautical charts.

Class A airspace is the airspace located above 18,000 MSL (Mean Sea Level) and below Flight Level 600 (approximately 60,000 MSL). Above 18,000 feet, all altitudes are abbreviated as FL (Flight Levels). For example, to be at FL310 is to fly at 31,000 MSL. Only traffic using IFR procedures are allowed to fly in this area. Class B airspace is located around busy airports and a pilot must receive a clearance from ATC before entering, whether VFR or IFR skies are present. Its bottom layer begins at the surface around a primary airport and increases in increments as it moves away from the primary airport. This allows aircraft to fly and avoid rigid regulations under the airspace. The top boundary is located at 10,000 MSL and has a diameter of about 30 nautical miles (NM). Even if you fly under Class B airspace and if you're located within this 30 NM ring, you need to have a working transponder, which is explained later in this chapter.

Class C airspace exists at airports with control towers and radar approach control facilities. These areas are busy, but not saturated enough to warrant Class B's rigid control. Radar

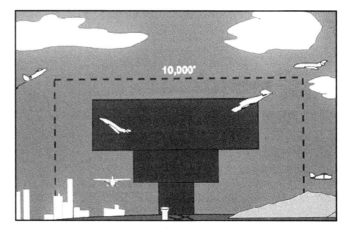

The bottom cloud layer starts at the surface around a primary airport and increases incrementally as it moves away from the primary airport.

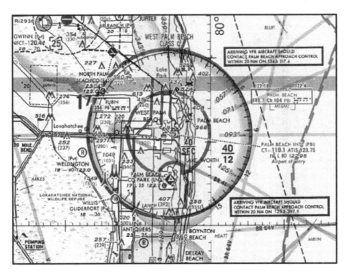

Class C airspace is usually busy, but not burdened with so much traffic that it needs Class B controls. This U.S. Aeronautical Charts depicts Class C airspace.

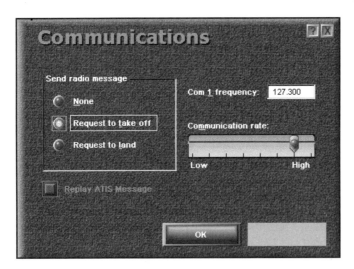

If you want to get official go-aheads from Air Traffic Control, use the Communications dialog box.

approach control monitors aircraft passing in or out of a control tower's area of responsibility. Like Class B airspace, rings with varying top and bottom boundaries are used to define Class C airspace. The inner ring begins at the surface and extends to 4000 feet above the surface. The outer circle begins 1200 feet above the surface.

Class D airspace is located at airports with a control tower. Control towers oversee traffic taxiing on the ground, taking off, and flying through an area around the airport. This ring-shaped area has a radius close to five miles and extends vertically to 2500 feet. You must have a clearance from the tower to operate in this area. Flight Simulator 98 provides the functionality to receive a clearance to depart and land from an ATC-controlled airport. This versatility is described in the next section of this chapter. Any controlled airspace not classified as Class A, B, C, or D is called Class E

airspace. This includes IFR routes where a clearance is required when IFR conditions exist. Uncontrolled airspace is any area where ATC does not need to provide a clearance to a pilot regardless of the weather conditions. If IFR skies exist in uncontrolled airspace, a pilot can fly using IFR skills if he has an IFR rating. However, the pilot must be sure not to enter controlled airspace without a clearance.

Air Traffic Control In The Real World

If you were flying on a genuine IFR flight plan, ATC would monitor your entire flight. Your flight might be extended if ATC needed to steer ("vector") you around other aircraft. Hopefully, ATC could give you headings to follow that would lead you directly to your destination.

ATC's primary mission is to provide IFR traffic separation. They will, however, provide additional services if they are not overloaded with VFR air traffic separation and issuing weather updates to pilots. In the U.S., ATC guides aircraft primarily by using radar. However, in many countries and in some parts of the U.S., this radar coverage is not available. Then, pilots are obligated to give accurate position reports enabling ATC to track the position of the aircraft in question.

Two types of radar track aircraft, and they are called primary and secondary radar. Primary radar transmits a beam of radio waves from a parabolic dish antenna. If the radio wave is reflected, a "blip" or target will show up on the air traffic computer display. This beam is slowly rotated in a circle so that all parts of the sky are scanned by the beam. A problem with primary radar is that it is prone to "clutter." That is, the beam may be reflected by rain, mountains, or other ground obstacles. In addition, the bigger the object hit by the beam, the more intense the radar return on the CRT (Cathode Ray Tube, the TV screen used by ATC). This means that a Cessna Skylane will be much harder to track than a Boeing 737. Another problem is that the radar energy can't penetrate obstacles, and blind spots are created by mountains and other large, solid obstacles. Additionally, the beam may be focused at too high or too low an angle to capture all aircraft in an area of the sky.

Secondary radar is used to supplement primary radar, enhancing the radar coverage of an area. If the aircraft has a transponder (a radar beacon) on board, it will respond with a high-energy pulse when the radar "interrogates" or strikes it. The controller can track a small piston aircraft as accurately as a large jet. The signal will not by affected by "clutter" or weather interference. When you set your transponder with a "squawk code," that code will be transmitted along with the pulse sent by the transponder, which is discussed later in this chapter.

ATC

Using radar (or a pilot's position reports in remote areas), ATC personnel keep air traffic operating under IFR rules, with individual aircraft maintaining safe distances from one other. When you receive ATC instructions on Flight Simulator 98's adventures and lessons, you will be shielded from any mid-air mishaps. However, once you take off on an IFR flight of your own design, there is a slight risk you may encounter traffic. To minimize the chance of your aircraft mixing metal with a passing LearJet, you can set the weather conditions to meet VFR definitions and heed the see-and-avoid principle.

In Flight Simulator 98, ATC is simulated in many lessons and adventures. ATC will audibly give you a clearance to take off or tell you what direction in which to fly. This information may also be presented to you as text on the screen. When you take off or land from an airport with a control tower, Class C airspace, you can simulate receiving a clearance from ATC. Summon the Communications dialog box by selecting Aircraft of the main menu. Choose the Communications submenu and activate the Request to Take Off or Request to Land options.

A flight plan form tells ATC who and what you are, as well as where and how you intend to fly to your destination.

Flight Plans

Pilots flying under VFR rules are not required to file a flight plan. A flight plan is the information a pilot provides ATC so that they have a record of the flight. A flight plan form includes flight details such as aircraft number and color, estimated time of departure and arrival, pilot's name, the number of people on board the aircraft, fuel on board, and routing. If

you choose to use VFR rules, you can select any route of any length you might enjoy. Pilots who file IFR cannot be quite so flexible. In addition to having to file a flight plan unless flying in uncontrolled airspace, the route of flight must use approved IFR routes and altitudes. IFR routes exist to ensure an aircraft will stay above obstacles during periods of poor visibility and will be explained in detail in Chapter Five. To realistically fly using IFR rules in Flight Simulator 98, you should determine your flight plan before takeoff. This process is outlined later in this chapter.

IFR Routings

Because an IFR route is so clearly defined, pilots using IFR rules are allowed to fly at altitudes up to and above 18,000 feet. Above FL180 is occupied by fast flying aircraft. ATC has to know where planes are located at all times. Pilots using a VFR flight plan are not allowed in this positive (full-time) control area. It may be discrete and economical to use IFR rules if you are taking the Boeing-737 out for a jaunt.

Additionally, regulations define restrictions on what altitudes VFR and IFR rules traffic can occupy in uncontrolled airspace. On an easterly heading, all flights should cruise on odd altitudes. Flights operating under IFR should remain on the "000" ("cardinal") altitudes such as 5000 and 7000 ft MSL. VFR flights add 500 feet to cruising altitudes. The same principle is applied to west-bound IFR flights but at even altitudes such as 6000 and 6500 MSL. VFR flights would be found at 5500 and 7500 feet MSL.

Alternate Airports

The one item of information that may appear on an IFR flight plan, and is not required on a VFR flight plan, is the alternate airport. The "1-2-3" rule determines whether or not you are required to specify an alternate or contingency airport on an IFR flight plan. This rules states that from one hour before to one hour after the ETA (Estimated Time of Arrival), the weather report or forecast for the intended destination airport must indicate that the cloud ceiling will be 2000 feet above the airport elevation and the visibility will be at least three statute miles (one hour-2000 feet-three miles). If the destination city is not forecasted to have these conditions, an alternate airport must be designated. The assumption is that with less than these conditions, completion

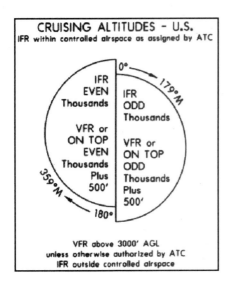

CRUISING ALTITUDES - U.S.
IFR within controlled airspace as assigned by ATC

0°

IFR EVEN Thousands

IFR ODD Thousands

179° M

VFR or ON TOP EVEN Thousands Plus 500'

VFR or ON TOP ODD Thousands Plus 500'

359° M

180°

VFR above 3000' AGL
unless otherwise authorized by ATC
IFR outside controlled airspace

VFR and IFR rules and regulations govern how flights are assigned different altitudes within an airspace.

of the flight as planned will be questionable. Things might be worse.

If an alternate airport is required, it also must meet certain criteria. The weather conditions at the alternate airport for the ETA varies depending on what kind of instrument landing aid is available at the airport. Instrument landing aids provide guidance to a pilot landing at an airport during periods of poor weather. If no instrument landing guidance exists at the alternate airport, the forecast must indicate that a descent can be made from the en-route altitude through to the landing and remain in visual conditions throughout. If a landing facility does exist at the airport, the airport is to have a forecasted ceiling of at least 600 feet and visibility of at least two miles or at least an 800 foot ceiling and two miles visibility depending on the type of landing instrumentation available. Chapter Six will provide more data on the various landing systems and how to determine which weather minimums to apply to each.

Fuel Requirements

To plan an IFR flight, you need to consider a few other requirements. On an IFR flight plan, you must have a 45-minute fuel reserve rather than the 30 minutes required during VFR rules flights. To mimic the same rule in Flight Simulator 98, go to Aircraft on the main menu and select Aircraft Settings. Go to the Realism tab and slide the realism bar to Real. Then activate the Engine Stops When Out of Fuel option. You'll be sure to know when you have planned poorly!

You need to know how much fuel you have to determine whether or not you meet the 45-minute reserve requirement. Go back into Aircraft Settings and select the Fuel tab. A dialog box will appear. This shows how much fuel (in gallons) the left and right wing tanks hold. On the Lear 45, fuel can also be held in auxiliary tanks. The Bell 206B JetRanger holds fuel in its center tank.

You can specify the amount of fuel to fill in each tank or a percentage to fill. Flight Simulator 98 will automatically determine how many gallons this

equals. If you go to Help on the main menu and select Aircraft Handbooks, you can click on the Lear 45 option located at the bottom of the text. If you click on the Performance specifications, you will see that the Lear 45 burns about 186 gallons of fuel per hour. Fuel burn is not given for the other aircraft types. You can use 13 gallons per hour when flying one of Cessna Skylarks and 1000 gallons per hour in the Boeing 737.

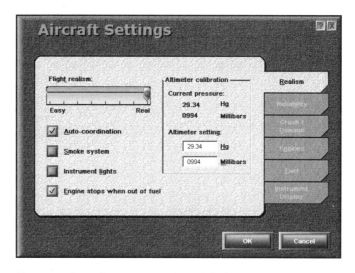

How much realism can you handle? If you want your plane to realistically run out of gas, use the Realism tab under Aircraft Settings.

Flight Clearance

A clearance must be received from ATC before entering controlled airspace during IFR weather. A typical clearance is found in the Dallas to Denver: Boeing 737-400 adventure. Go to Flights on the main menu and click on Adventures. Click on the Dallas to Denver: Boeing 737-400 option.

ATC (on Ground Control or a dedicated clearance delivery frequency) will audibly transmit the following clearance to you: "Bluesky 737 is cleared to the Denver International

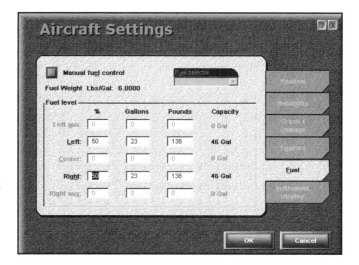

Tank capacity is no mystery; this dialog box shows how much fuel your plane's tanks can carry.

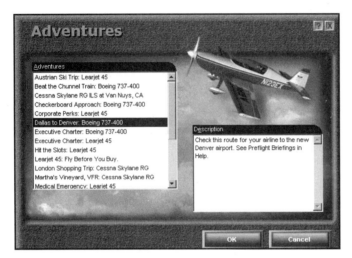

Airport via direct Wichita Falls, J168 Lamar, J20 Falcon, direct, Denver maintain flight level 350. Squawk 3327." This is spoken at the rapid rate ATC usually uses in actual flight operations. If you miss a piece of the clearance (which is easy to do with so many numbers included in it), simply press CTRL + M to repeat it.

The first part of the clearance identifies to whom the clearance is issued. In this case, the aircraft has the

The Adventures section of Flight Simulator 98 lets you pilot a 737 from Dallas to Denver, among many other flights.

call sign Bluesky 737. This is followed by the destination of the clearance. The aircraft in this adventure is cleared to Denver International. The next part of the clearance states the route of the flight. Flight routes will be explained in detail in Chapter Five. The aircraft will be flying at FL35, which is approximately 35,000 feet MSL.

Transponder

The final part of the clearance is the transponder squawk code. ("Squawk" originated in World War II when original transponders responded to radar interrogation with a shrill parrot-like sound.) We dial this code (3327) into the transponder's digital windows. This code allows ATC to specifically identify your aircraft on a computer display (independent of other aircraft) and track your location. You can set the transponder code two different ways. You first option is to choose Aircraft off the main menu and select Navigation. Click on the Transponder/ADF tab and manually fill in the transponder code field to the four-digit squawk code.

Alternatively, you can set the code directly on the transponder. Bring your radio stack up by selecting Views on the main menu and choosing Instrument Panel. Select Radio Stack for the B-737 airplane or Bendix/King Radio Stack if flying one of the Cessnas. Click your cursor on each transponder digit display

to increase its value. On the Lear 45, the transponder is located on the main instrument panel, which simplifies changing the code. On VFR flights where you are not receiving guidance from ATC, the transponder is set to 1200 (the standard VFR code).

Dallas to Denver Flight Plan

This section shows you what a sample IFR flight plan for the run from Dallas to Denver looks like. Notice how each field of the flight plan is determined.

Type: You use the same flight plan form whether you are following VFR or IFR rules. You indicate what set of rules you will be obeying in this box.

Aircraft ID: In this field, you give the registration number of the aircraft. This is usually written on the tail of the aircraft. In the US this is referred to as the "N" number. All U.S. registration numbers start with the letter N.

Type/Special equipment: The first field of this box asks for the type of aircraft you will be flying. The second box asks what type of navigation equipment is on board. The IFR equipped aircraft in Flight Simulator 98, except for the Sopwith Camel and the Schweizer 2-32 sailplane, are type "A". This means that the aircraft has a DME and transponder with altitude encoding capability.

DME will be explained in Chapter Five. Chapter Four will discuss why the Sopwith Camel and sailplane should not be used on IFR flights.

True Airspeed: True airspeed is how fast you expect the aircraft to cruise en-route. Go into Help on the main menu and choose Aircraft Handbooks. Chose the aircraft type at the bottom of the display. From this display, choose performance specifications to find the

DEPARTMENT OF TRANSPORTATION — FEDERAL AVIATION ADMINISTRATION							Form Approved OMB No. 04-R0072	
FLIGHT PLAN								
1. TYPE	2. AIRCRAFT IDENTIFICATION	3. AIRCRAFT TYPE/ SPECIAL EQUIPMENT	4. TRUE AIRSPEED	5. DEPARTURE POINT		6. DEPARTURE TIME PROPOSED (Z) ACTUAL (Z)	7. CRUISING ALTITUDE	
X VFR IFR DVFR	BLUESKY 737	737A	500 KTS	DFW		1500	FL35	
8. ROUTE OF FLIGHT								
DIRECT WICHITA FALLS - J168 LAMAR - J20 FALCON - DIRECT DEN								
9. DESTINATION (Name of airport and city)	10. EST. TIME ENROUTE HOURS MINUTES		11. REMARKS					
DEN	1 12							
12. FUEL ON BOARD HOURS MINUTES	13. ALTERNATE AIRPORT (S)		14. PILOT'S NAME, ADDRESS & TELEPHONE NUMBER & AIRCRAFT HOME BASE CAPT J. SMITH ON FILE WITH BLUESKY AIRWAYS				15. NUMBER ABOARD 100	
4								
16. COLOR OF AIRCRAFT	CLOSE VFR FLIGHT PLAN WITH_____FSS ON ARRIVAL							
FAA Form 7233-1 (8-72)							FAA AC 72-830H	

This graphic representation shows what an IFR flight plan from Dallas to Denver looks like.

cruising speed of the aircraft you're using. The temperature you set in Flight Simulator 98 will affect this airspeed. Chapter Four will explain how to let Flight Simulator 98 determine your true airspeed for you during flight.

Departure Point: This is the three-character code of the airport from which you are departing (in our example, DFW).

Departure Time: The departure time in box 6 is in Universal Mean Time also referred to as "zulu" time. To determine Greenwich Mean Time, first convert the time to a 24-hour clock. One PM converts to 1300 hours. Next, use the table below to determine how many hours to add to this figure. Let's say Dallas is using Central Daylight Time. To depart at 1500 Zulu, the current time in Dallas must be 10:00 AM.

Conversion to Greenwich Mean Time

Time Zone	Hours to Add for Greenwich Time
Eastern Standard	5
Eastern Daylight Savings	4
Central Standard	6
Central Daylight Savings	5
Mountain Standard	7
Mountain Daylight Savings	6
Pacific Standard	8
Pacific Daylight Standard	7

Cruising altitude: This is the initial altitude you requested.

Route of Flight: This is the route you plan to follow to get to your destination. IFR routings will be explained in Chapter Five.

Destination: This is the three character code of the airport you plan to land at (in our example, DEN).

Estimated Time En-route: To estimate the total time en-route, you have to know the distance between DFW and DEN. You could take the straight line distance between these two locations. One way to do this is to get a map and a ruler, converting the map measurement to the mileage value of the map. This can be cumbersome, especially if you are planning a long flight. A more

efficient way is to find an Internet site that will do the measuring for you. You may want to try the distance calculator located at www.thd.nl/aviation.

A real problem using straight-line distance is that IFR routes generally won't provide a direct course between your departure point and your destination. Luckily, IFR routes on U.S. Aeronautical charts list the length of individual route segments. You can then list and add these segments to find the total route length. You will find the distance between DEN and DFW to be roughly 600 miles.

Certainly you need to determine what effect winds aloft will have on your speed. The section on weather describes how to determine weather conditions. If you will encounter a direct headwind, subtract the velocity of the wind from true airspeed to get your actual speed over the ground. This is called ground speed. If you will encounter a direct tail wind, add wind speed to true airspeed. If the wind affects the aircraft track at an angle rather than directly, only add or subtract half the wind speed from true airspeed. If the wind affects the aircraft track as a direct (90 degree) cross-wind, subtract a quarter of the wind speed from your true airspeed. Divide distance by this ground speed to determine estimated time en-route.

Remarks: A request or special note can be placed in this area, such as "Request customs service."

Fuel on board: You would divide your estimated time en-route by your aircraft's fuel consumption rate.

Alternate airport: If your destination airport does not meet the requirements of the "1-2-3" rule, you will need to specify what your alternate landing site is.

Pilot name: Pilot details so ATC can get information on the pilot if the need arises.

Number on Board: This number includes both crew and passengers.

Weather Watch

Weather conditions are a major factor in determining if VFR can be followed or IFR rules must be implemented. The weather minimums needed to operate under VFR rules are more strict than requirements for operating under IFR rules. There are two reasons for this rigidity. When operating under VFR rules, you are responsible for seeing and avoiding other traffic. The more clear the skies, the better chance of conflicting traffic. During flights using IFR rules, Air Traffic Control (ATC) provides additional protection against midair collisions. VFR flight, therefore, has cloud separation and visibility requirements to assure you can see and avoid.

Determining IFR Weather Conditions

It seems simple to determine if the conditions you set in Flight Simulator 98 are within VFR minimums, but it can actually be confusing. FARs define VFR weather conditions differently depending on several factors, like the type of airspace you're flying within, your altitude, and whether it's day or night time. VFR flight is permitted in Visual Meteorological Conditions (VMC).

Concisely stated, the weather conditions needed to fly under VFR regulations are flight visibility greater than three statute miles and a cloud ceiling greater than 1000 feet above the surface. However, you need to be careful in applying this generality. If you're flying at an altitude between 18,000 feet MSL and FL600, Class A airspace, VMC does not exist—according to FARs—no matter how pleasant the weather. Above FL180 only IFR, ATC-cleared operations are permitted. As mentioned above, various levels of VFR minimums are established to insure there is plenty of time for pilots to see and avoid each other.

Basic VFR Weather Minimums

Airspace Type	Flight Visibility	Distance from Clouds
Class A	Not applicable	Not applicable
Class B	3 SM	Clear of clouds
Class C	3 SM	500 ft. below
		1000 ft. above
		2000 ft. horizontal
Class D	3 SM	500 ft. below
		1000 ft. above
		2000 ft. horizontal
Class E	3 SM	500 ft. below
Less than 10,000 ft. MSL		1000 ft. above
		2000 ft. horizontal
At or above 10,000 ft. MSL	5 SM	1000 ft. below
		1000 ft. above

Basic VFR Weather Minimums, continued

Airspace Type	Flight Visibility	Distance from Clouds
Class G = 1200 ft., or less above the surface, regardless of MSL altitude		
Day*	1 SM	Clear of clouds
Night*	3 SM	500 ft. below
		1000 ft. above
		2000 ft. horizontal

*An airplane may be operated clear of clouds at night below 1200 ft. AGL when the visibility is less than 3 SM but more than 1 SM in an airport traffic pattern and within 1/2 NM of the runway.

Airspace Type	Flight Visibility	Distance from Clouds
Class G = More than 1200 ft. above the surface, but less than 10,000 ft. MSL		
Day	1 SM	500 ft. below
		1000 ft. above
		2000 ft. horizontal
Night	3 SM	500 ft. below
		1000 ft. above
		2000 ft. horizontal
Class G = More than 1200 ft. above the surface and at or above 10,000 ft. MSL		
	5 SM	1000 ft. below
		1000 ft. above
		1 SM horizontial

When the weather conditions do not meet basic VFR ceiling-visibility minimums, IFR flight conditions exist. IMC (Instrument Meteorological Conditions) are usually described as flying in clouds, rain, haze, fog, snow, and smog. However, IFR flight skills may be demanded even when the current conditions are well within the FAA's definition of VFR skies. They must be available any time the pilot cannot use visual references to control and navigate the aircraft. Control means the ability to keep the aircraft in straight and level flight. Navigation is flying the path, tracking the route to your destination. For example, it is difficult to fly above the Great Lakes or the Everglades at night, even without a cloud in the sky, because in those locations there are no lights on the ground and no distinguishable horizon line to help you keep you oriented. Fortunately, Flight Simulator 98 generously provides enough moonlight for you to see the horizon.

Although defined as VMC, flying with flight visibility between three-five statute miles can be stressful, if not hazardous. It might be legal, but unwise to enter "marginal VFR." It's essential to have some IFR skills before

*Paris is known as the City of Lights, although this view—
with three-miles visibility—really doesn't do it justice.*

venturing too far from your home base in these "marginal" conditions. Visual operations become demanding with minimal visibility.

"VFR On Top" is a special type of clearance that can be requested by the pilot. An IFR-rated pilot is allowed to enter IFR conditions in order to get on top of a cloud layer. Once on top of a cloud layer, the pilot continues to fly following IFR rules with an ATC clearance and altitude requirements. If you choose to simulate an "VFR On Top" clearance in Flight Simulator 98, you should cruise at VFR altitudes, avoiding clouds and obeying VFR regulations. It is rarely wise to abandon all the protection and services of an ATC-monitored IFR flight for VFR liberties. Perhaps proceeding toward clear skies and perfect VMC means you have no need for ATC, other than the IFR clearance to depart.

Weather Generation in Flight Simulator 98

As soon as you learn how to control the aircraft using IFR skills, you should set Flight Simulator 98's settings to IMC. Learning to handle the aircraft confidently and completely under challenging circumstances is the essence of piloting aerial machines. Flight Simulator 98's weather conditions can be set using either the standard or advanced dialog box. The standard dialog box only allows you to set one cloud ceiling and has a limited selection of visibility settings. Your challenge is to use the Advanced Weather dialog instead. On the Main Menu bar, select Options. From the drop down menu, select Preferences. Click on the General tab display and highlight the Advance Weather Dialog option.

When you get back to the Main Menu, select World. From the drop down menu select Weather. Click on the Clouds tab. From this dialog box, you can set a cloud base. This is the altitude where you will first enter the cloud as you climb. The cloud top is the altitude where you will exit the cloud as you continue the climb. Because clouds are usually ragged and not perfectly flat, you can also factor in a deviation figure to increase flight realism. If you use the deviation option, you will not enter the cloud at the exact altitude input in the cloud base field. Instead, you will enter it at some point between the input value and the deviation amount. Deviation can be set at up to 656 feet.

You can also set the type of clouds you will encounter on your flight using the Advanced Weather dialog box. Clouds differ in the altitudes where they're found and by the amount and type of precipitation contained within. In addition, the stability of the air forming

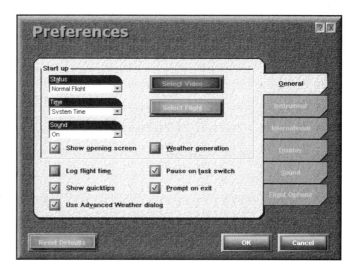

Flight Simulator 98 lets you use a standard weather setting, or you can test your mettle via the advanced weather setting. Are you up to the challenge?

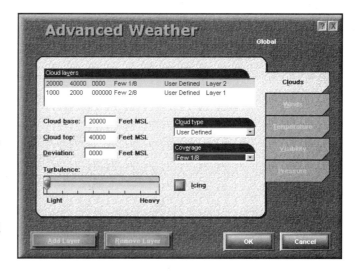

You can even determine how realistic your cloud cover is, as set in this dialog box.

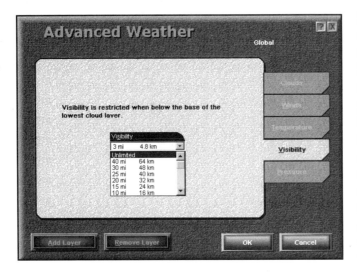

The Visibility tab lets you preset how clear the skies are, and how far you can see—anywhere from 1/16th of a mile to unlimited range.

Weather Areas (accessed under the Worlds menu) lets you set specific weather conditions within a certain geographic region.

the clouds has a great effect on the turbulence you will find when you fly in or below them. If you scroll through the Cloud Types, you will notice Flight Simulator 98 defaults the turbulence, icing, cloud coverage, and altitude fields to a realistic standard. You can, however, overwrite these defaults. You can also select two layers of clouds when using the Advanced Weather option. For instance, you could have one layer with a cloud base at 1000 MSL and a cloud top at 2000 MSL. You could then create a second layer with a base at 20,000 MLS and top at 40,000 MSL.

Clicking on the Visibility tab allows you to select visibility between 1/16th mile and unlimited. A visibility of one half mile demands your best IFR skills. You will alter visibility depending on the IFR activity being pursued. The practice exercises in this book will recommend cloud ceiling and visibility.

You can also choose Weather Areas under the

World menu. This screen allows you to set specific weather conditions within a defined geographic region. For example, you may want to have VFR skies en-route to check out the scenery. When you get to your destination, you may want the weather to deteriorate so you can practice an IFR landing. You have the ability to set two weather areas. IFR weather conditions refer to cloud ceilings or visibility rather than the base of clouds. A low ceiling, about 600 feet above ground level (IFR environment), will allow you to enter clouds and instrument flight soon after takeoff. You should set the thickness of the layer to at least 2000 feet so that you have room to practice instrument-controlled climbs and descents.

Before taking off into the wild blue yonder on an IFR flight, you should check the weather at the destination airport.

Weather Conditions at Alternate Airports

Whenever you choose to fly using IFR rules, you should go to Weather Areas under

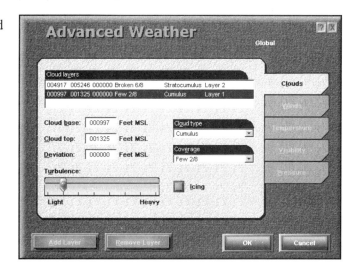

Checking the cloud cover is the key step in determining visibility.

the World option on the main menu to determine if your intended destination meets the requirements of the "1-2-3" rule. Using the longitude and latitude coordinates of your destination airport, determine what weather area is active for that location. If you don't know the coordinates of your destination airport, click World on the main menu and select Airport/Facility Directory from the main menu. On the global map, click on the location of your destination airport. Scroll through the list until you find your airport.

You also need to consider the speed and movement of the weather area to determine if it will still be at your destination at your ETA (Estimated Time of Arrival) or if another weather system will be moving in soon. Once you have determined the correct weather area, go to back into the World menu and select Weather. Under the Clouds tab, look at the data lines contained in Cloud Layers. If you wish to change the weather area where your destination airport is located, read the weather section included in this chapter.

To determine if the destination meets the requirements of the "1-2-3" rule, you need determine how high any ceiling is above the airport. You can not use the altitude of any low cloud base to calculate the ceiling. Cloud layers that are classified as "scattered" or "few" do not constitute a ceiling. Only a cloud layer that is spread over 5/8ths of the sky (or greater than 50 percent) is called a ceiling. A ceiling will be described as a "broken" or "overcast" layer. Cloud ceilings are measured in mean sea level (MSL) which is height above sea level. Therefore, to determine the actual distance between the airport and cloud ceiling, you would need to subtract the airport elevation from the cloud base. Airport elevation can be found in the Airport/Facility and also uses MSL as a measure. Use the Airport/Facility Directory to determine elevation the same way the latitude and longitude search was performed.

For example, suppose an airport with an elevation of 1000 feet MSL had a weather system in which two cloud layers existed at one destination. One layer is composed of cumulus clouds that begin at an altitude of 997 feet MSL. This altitude is referred to as a cloud base. If you were at the airport and were looking up, you would estimate that 2/8ths of the sky was filled with this cloud type. This amount of coverage is classified as "few." Therefore, this layer of clouds does not constitute a ceiling. A second layer exists above this layer. This layer is composed of stratocumulus clouds with a base of 4917 feet MSL. These clouds fill 6/8thsof the sky and are thus classified as a "broken layer." The base of any "broken" or "overcast" layer is a ceiling. An overcast layer covers the entire sky. In our example, a ceiling is calculated by subtracting the

airport elevation from the MSL cloud layer. We need to determine how high the ceiling is above the airport. Therefore, the cloud ceiling is 4917 feet MSL and is located 3917 feet above the airport. This cloud condition meets the 2000 foot requirement specified in the "1-2-3" rule. You can then click on the Visibility tab to determine the visibility you can expect at the airport. This information is important to determine if VFR visibility exists at your airport of landing.

Flight Training and Skills

Controlling an aircraft in VMC involves the same sampling of your senses. You use outside references to determine if the aircraft is right side up, turning, or climbing. The most informative reference point, both in Flight Simulator 98 and in the real world of aviation, is the view of the horizon line in relation to the cockpit window. To perceive the needed changes in aircraft

PCs and the Instrument Rating

Pilot training requirements are different in VFR and IFR licensing regulations. Different skills are required of a pilot who will fly in IMC. The IFR pilot will need many additional control and interpretation talents to fly safely through poor weather.

Until recently, a licensed VFR pilot, however familiar with the instruments, couldn't take the IFR flight test until having logged 125 hours of total flight time. The FAA recently changed the requirements for the instrument rating. Pilots can now be IFR-rated after earning their private pilot license and receiving an added 40 hours of training specifically for the IFR flight test.

The FAA allows for 20 hours of the 40 necessary hours to be completed in a ground trainer with an instructor. These non-PC-based simulators can be costly for a flight-training center to purchase. Due to the efforts of organizations like the Aircraft Owners and Pilots Association (AOPA), the FAA has recently issued an advisory circular approving the use of PC-based aviation training devices. Now, ten of the 20 hours in a ground trainer can be acquired on a PC-based training device.

Research reflects that instrument flying skills can be transferred from the PC to the aircraft. The FAA stipulates standards for the aircraft controls for a PC. Jeppesen is the only company which currently has begun to manufacture this approved control device. It probably won't be long before other manufacturers begin to roll them off the assembly line.

PC-based simulators have become increasingly popular with students over the years. They allow a pilot to practice a greater amount of IFR training exercises in a given period of time than in the air. They lose time in the air fitting in with other traffic. In addition, a lot of things are happening during IFR operations, so it is nice to take a time-out by pressing pause. Students will now be able to apply this PC-type of practice toward their training requirements.

You instinctively understand the orientation of a turn, like the 30-degree banking maneuver being performed here.

Just like driving a car in heavy rain or fog, your ability to use visual references during flights in IFR skies is severely limited. Here's what a left-hand turn looks like in IMC.

attitudes, you also use visual clues for guidance to determine the required control inputs.

For instance, if you want to make a left-hand turn at 30 degrees of bank, you have a concept about how the "picture" of this orientation looks. That is, how high the nose should be raised and where the horizon line should divide the windshield. Using vision is the VFR skill. With good VFR skills, you have subconsciously gathered these "pictures" through experiences on past Flight Simulator journeys.

A pilot cannot rely on VFR skills to control the aircraft in IMC weather. With the required instrumentation in the cockpit and adequate training, you can meet this problem with IFR piloting skills. Instrument flying skills is control of the aircraft solely by reference to the instruments. You will no longer need to see out the window to determine "the picture" of aircraft performance. Instead, you have the ability to gather the same type of data from the aircraft instruments. Chapter Four explains these IFR skills in detail.

AVIATION FUNDAMENTALS

The weather conditions you set in Microsoft Flight Simulator 98 may cause you to lose your visual bearings during a flight. When that happens, the cockpit instruments are the only references you have to determine if the aircraft is climbing, turning, or descending. Aircraft instruments are used to gather data on what the aircraft is doing just like car instruments are used to determine how an automobile is performing. For example, you have an instrument to tell you how fast you are going and one that helps you determine when it's time to stop for gas. Even with these aids, a driver must keep an eye out the windshield to avoid crashing. Aviation is even more complex—with a tricky third dimension (altitude). Because there is so much occurring when you fly, your ability to gather information must be quick and precise.

The instruments provided in most of the aircraft in Flight Simulator 98 allow you to fly the bulk of your journeys without depending on outside visual information. Developing an IFR (Instrument Flight Rules) skill is known as attitude instrument flying. Attitude instrument flying is often referred to as "precision flying" because it allows you to achieve the exact performance required of the aircraft. You'll be right on your desired heading, altitude, speed, and climb or descent rate. This chapter will present the aviation fundamentals needed to become proficient at these tasks.

The Primary Instruments

Before you can attitude instrument fly, you'll need a firm understanding of the cockpit instruments. There are six instruments, called the *primary instruments*, that provide the most crucial information: the heading indicator, attitude indicator, altimeter, turn indicator, airspeed indicator, and vertical speed indicator. Each of these instruments will be explained in detail.

Tip: *You may notice that the Lear 45 and Boeing 737 (B-737) do not have turn indicators. A turn indicator is not a requirement to fly under IFR rules when using sophisticated instrument systems.*

Federal Air Regulation 91.205 defines what equipment must be present and functioning in the cockpit before the aircraft can operate under IFR procedures. This required equipment includes a two-way radio for communication with ATC, rate-of-turn indicator (except on large airplanes that have advanced instrument systems), slip/skid indicator, altimeter, clock, attitude indicator, and heading indicator. We'll discuss those instruments later in Chapter Five.

All of the aircraft in Flight Simulator 98 are equipped with these required instruments except for the Sopwith Camel and Schweizer 2-32 sailplane. These aircraft do come with an altimeter and airspeed indicator, and the Schweizer 2-32 sailplane also has a vertical speed indicator. However, the lack of a complete IFR panel (and power for the sailplane) would not make them viable for trips where you might encounter IMC. Besides failing to meet Federal Air Regulations (FARs), it would be virtually impossible to control attitude, performance, and navigate with only two of the six primary instruments.

The Attitude Indicator

The attitude indicator (AI) is also called the artificial horizon because it provides you the same information as the actual horizon line during VMC. At a glance, you can determine if the aircraft's nose, called "pitch" or vertical attitude, is pointing up or down. You can also quickly determine if the wings are level with the horizon.

Check your attitude (your vertical attitude, that is) with a quick glance at your attitude indicator.

Pitch and Bank
When the nose of the aircraft is raised or lowered, the aircraft moves about its lateral axis. You can visualize the lateral axis by drawing a line from one aircraft wingtip to the other. Another way to "see" the lateral axis is to imagine yourself holding a model airplane. To demonstrate pitch, you'd grasp each wing tip of the model and rotate the nose up or down. The line between our fingers is "lateral"

and stationary, therefore, the movement is occurring around that stable axis.

An aircraft can get off the ground and fly through the air because of the angle air meets and flows over the wings. As an aircraft accelerates, air meeting the wing splits. Some of this air will flow over the upper half of the wing and some will flow underneath it. The air flowing across the top half of the wing must travel a greater distance than the air on the underside of the wing, if they arrive at the trailing edge at the same time. Applying a physics concept called Bernoulli's Principle, it can be calculated that the air on top of the wing will create an area of lower pressure above the wing than the air below the wing. This low pressure "lifts" or vacuums the wing (and airplane) upward. To fly, therefore, is a function of "lift."

When you turn the aircraft left or right, the aircraft is actually rolling about its longitudinal axis. You can visualize the longitudinal axis by drawing

The angle the aircraft nose is raised or lowered in comparison to the horizon line is called the pitch angle. This aircraft, for example, is pitched down.

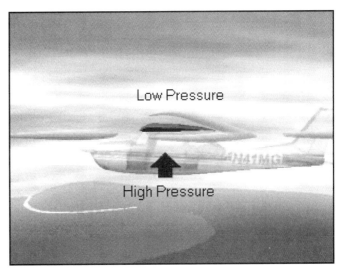

When a wing cuts through air, it creates two areas of pressure—and the lift that moves the plane upward.

Aircraft turns are the results of shifting an aircraft on its longitudinal axis.

When making a turn, extra lift must be applied or some altitude will be lost.

a line from the tail of the aircraft to the nose. For example, if you turn the aircraft to the right using KEYPAD 5, the wing on the right side of the aircraft will dip down and the wing on the left side will rise. The aircraft will roll right around the longitudinal axis. The degrees from level that the wing is lowered (in relation to the natural horizon) is called *bank angle*.

Notice that a turn is not caused by moving the aircraft nose to the right or left. The bank of the wings is what starts the turn. When the wing banks, the lift on the wing is canted or leaned horizontally. Instead of vertically, the lifting force is tilted. Therefore, some of the lift is working to pull the plane up vertically and some is horizontal, pulling the aircraft around the turn. Because a portion of the lift is diverted to the turn, less lift is acting upwards. This usually may require you to pull (pitch) the nose up slightly during a steep turn to maintain altitude. Added pitch creates added lift, compensating for that which

is forfeited in the turn. To remain level, we must retain the same value of the vertical component of lift, even while allocating some lift to effect a turn.

Reading the Pitch and Bank on the AI

The easiest way to think of the AI is that the top half is painted blue and represents the sky, while the bottom half is painted brown and represents the earth. Where the two colors divide represents the earth's horizon. That is the *artificial* horizon. When you look at the AI in level flight, you will notice a set of wings or a small depiction of an airplane overlaying the artificial horizon line. This representation is called the "miniature aircraft wings." In the Cessna Skylane 182S (C-182S) and Cessna Skylane 182 RG (C-182RG), these miniature aircraft wings are displayed as a solid red bar. The Lear 45 and B-737 have attitude indicators with an electronic display like a television.

Both types of miniature wings, except for the display on the Lear 45, have a solid "dot" at the center used for pitch measurement. When the dot is located on the artificial horizon, the nose is level with the actual horizon. Keep in mind that the background moves—not the representation of the airplane. These "wings" are fixed to your aircraft and duplicate your movement. When the nose is pitched up, the miniature wings will remain stationary in their current position while the colored background moves down. The miniature wings will now overlay the blue area of the AI and will have risen above the artificial horizon line just like the actual aircraft wings did. How much the nose was raised can be measured using the dot or the width of the miniature wings. You would count how many dots you could stack between the artificial horizon line and the dots' current position. This is used as a reference point for the next time you want to

The attitude indicator gives a fast and realistic picture of aircraft performance, in this case a left turn in the making.

The attitude indicator in a Boeing 737 has calibration marks at ten-degree intervals.

pitch the nose the same number of degrees to repeat the same performance.

Instead of using dots, some pilots prefer to use the bar width of the miniature aircraft wings. Pilots count how many bar widths separate the miniature wings and the horizon line. You will use the bar width method when flying the Lear 45 since its AI does not have a dot.

Several horizontal markers on the AI are also used for reference purposes. On the Lear 45 and B-737, these marks are calibrated in degrees to measure the pitch angle of the aircraft. The mark just above the artificial horizon line is five degrees of pitch. The next three calibration marks represent 10, 15, and, 20 degrees, respectively. If the aircraft nose is pitched below the horizon, the AI display will rotate up. Now the miniature wings overlay the brown area of the AI and have descended below the horizon line.

The AI is also calibrated to show bank angle. The bank bar marks bank angles and remains fixed along the top of the AI. When the miniature wings are level, the sky pointer will point at the zero-bank calibration mark. When the aircraft turns to the left, the AI display rotates. The sky pointer always points "up." The bank angle marks depict how many degrees from "vertical up" the airplane has been rolled or banked. With some back pressure to add lift, the miniature wings will rise a bit into the brown area of the display. Both bank and pitch are simply and vividly represented.

On the C-182RG and C182S, the bank calibration marks are located at 0, 10, 20, 30, 60, and 90 degrees. The 0-degrees calibration mark is found on top of the AI, at the 12 o'clock position. Two index lines on each side of the AI identify 10- and 20-degree bank angles. This area is referred to as a shallow bank. The next three calibration marks have longer index lines. The first represents a turn with a 30-degree bank angle. Turns made between 20- and 35-degree roll angles are called medium banks. The next calibration mark is at 60 degrees. Turns made between 35 and 60 degrees are steep turns. Steep turns in a C-182S are usually made at 45 degrees of bank. It is a line you would imagine between the 30-degree mark and the 60-degree mark. The 90-degree calibration mark is located at the three o'clock and nine o'clock positions. On the Lear 45 and B-737, you'll find that marks are located every ten degrees.

By observing the degree of bank and pitch, you can obtain a fast and realistic picture of aircraft attitude. When the miniature wings are level with the artificial horizon line and the dot is centered on the artificial horizon, this is called *straight and level flight*.

Turn-rate Indicators

An aircraft can also move about its vertical axis. This axis can be imagined as a line from top to bottom of the aircraft. Movement around the vertical axis is

A third axis of movement extends vertically through the center of the aircraft, running from top to bottom.

called *yaw*. Yaw means the aircraft nose has moved right or left. The turning efficiency is measured by compass degrees traveled per second. This is the *rate of turn* or *turn rate*.

The instruments in Flight Simulator 98 displaying turn rates are the turn indicator (TI) and the turn coordinator (TC). The turn indicator measures rate of turn as a change of compass heading over time. The TC also factors in the roll rate of the banked wing. For example, when the wings are first banked, the nose of the aircraft may not start to change headings immediately. Therefore, the TC may register the roll or bank before the TI reflects the progress of the turn in degrees of change.

The Turn Indicator

The turn indicator (also commonly called the heading indicator) is used in the Extra 300S and Bell 206B JetRanger. When the aircraft nose is turning to the right, the indicator will deviate to the right. If the aircraft nose turns to the left, the indicator will turn to the left. You will notice a calibration

Two instruments show turn rate; one of them is the turn indicator.

Pick a calibration mark and stick to it for two minutes, and your aircraft will complete a 360-degree circle.

mark on each side of the instrument display. If the aircraft indicator points to one of these calibration marks and is held for exactly two minutes, the aircraft will complete a 360-degree circle. Dividing 360 degrees by 120 seconds (two minutes) reveals that an aircraft turns three degrees per second in a standard rate turn.

The bank angle required for a standard rate turn varies with the aircraft's speed. A fast plane tracks a bigger circle or less turn per distance traveled. To complete the turn in two minutes, the pilot must steepen the bank angle for fast airplanes. Conversely, the slower the airspeed, the shorter the radius of the circle flown and the pilot must decrease the bank angle to not finish the turn early. One formula for calculating the bank angle is bank angle = (aircraft speed/10) + (aircraft speed/10) X 1/2. Indicated airspeed, explained later in this chapter, is shown on the airspeed indicator. Since the C-182S cruises at 120 KIAS, the bank angle required to make a standard rate turn is 12 + 5 = 17 degrees. During instrument flight, all turns should be made at standard rate or less to maintain greater control of the aircraft. Another formula, perhaps an easier one, involves dropping the last digit of the indicated speed and adding five to that number. Therefore, 100 is figured as 10 + 5 or 15 degrees of bank. (60 knots is 6 + 5 or 11 degrees required.) The bank should not exceed 25 degrees in very fast planes, since so often a standard rate is not feasible.

The Turn Coordinator

The turn coordinator is used in the C-182S and C-182RG. As mentioned above, the TC shows rate of roll in addition to rate of turn. The TC display is similar to the TI display. Instead of using a straight indicator needle, miniature aircraft

wings are used to illustrate the turn. The wings turn in the same direction as the turn.

Making Coordinated Turns

At the bottom of the TC and TI is the *inclinometer*, also called the *slip/skid indicator* or simply "the ball." It indicates the balance of forces at work in a turn. When the ball rolls toward the inside of the turn (the same direction the wings are banked in), the result is a "slipping" turn. This means the angle of bank is too steep for the rate of turn.

If the ball moves toward the outside of a turn, you are in a "skidding" turn. This means the rate of turn is too great for the bank angle. To maintain a coordinated turn, keep the ball in the center of the inclinometer by adding or lessening rudder pressure on the side where the ball has deviated. Rudder (like it is in a boat) is a control that yaws, slews, or moves the nose to the left or right. Use KEYPAD ZERO to apply left rudder and KEYPAD ENTER for right rudder.

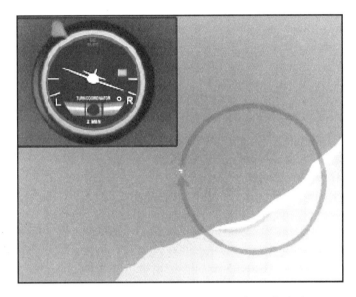

Standard rate turns, like this one, are used regularly because they provide the pilot with greater control of the aircraft.

When the angle of bank is too steep for the rate of turn, a slipping turn results (like this one).

If the rate of turn exceeds the bank angle, a skidding turn will occur.

Because rudder pressure varies and often requires the subtle control of a variety of forces, Flight Simulator 98 can be instructed to automatically control rudder pressure for you. To choose this option, select Aircraft from the main menu and go to Aircraft Settings. On the Realism tab, activate the Auto-coordination field.

Airspeed Indicator

The airspeed indicator shows how fast the aircraft is moving through the air, measuring how fast air molecules are flowing past the plane. It does *not*, however, measure how fast the aircraft is moving over the ground. The effect of wind does have a bearing on the speed of an aircraft over the ground. In a 20-knot head wind, the airspeed indicator may read 100 knots (how fast air molecules are moving past the plane), but in reality your ground speed is only 80 knots. Your forward travel is impeded by a headwind, like a boat affected by a river current.

It's not a speedometer; the airspeed indicator in the Cessna 182S measures how fast air molecules flow past the aircraft, not how quickly the aircraft is traversing the ground.

Airspeed is measured in knots or nautical miles traveled per hour. You can convert knots to miles per hour. To calculate miles per hour, multiply knots by 1.15. For example, if your airspeed indicator reads 100 knots, you are traveling at approximately 115 miles per hour (100 knots X 1.15).

Indicated Airspeed vs. True Airspeed

The airspeed needle points to the aircraft's indicated airspeed in knots (KIAS). Pilots use this value to determine acceptable

performance speeds for takeoff and landing, for example. KIAS is an accurate reflection of the aircraft's actual airspeed. Variation in the atmosphere and the way the instrument's probe is installed can cause this number to be imprecise. The actual speed the aircraft moves through space is called true airspeed. (TAS). Pilots use true airspeed to compute navigation or travel time expectations. TAS increases whenever air density decreases (and there is less density or air resistance), such as during a climb or when flying into warmer air. IAS is converted to TAS by multiplying IAS by double the altitude where the aircraft is cruising. For instance, at 5000 feet MLS, you would multiply IAS by ten percent. Flight Simulator 98 can do this calculation for you. To cause your airspeed indicator to display TAS rather than IAS, select Options from the main menu and select Preferences. Click on the instruments tab and deactivate the Display indicated airspeed option. True Airspeed is a more accurate reflection of your ground speed. You use this value in flight to estimate your time of arrival at your destination airport. Once you know how long it will take you, you can determine if you have sufficient fuel on board.

The airspeed indicator in a B-737 is centered around a color-coded "barber pole."

Markers on the Airspeed Indicator

The color coding on the airspeed indicator in the C-182S provides important information. The green arc represents the normal airspeed operating range. The yellow arc represents the caution range, and the red line is a "never exceed" limit. If you are flying at airspeeds in the yellow or red range, turbulence or vigorous control inputs could cause the aircraft to suffer structural damage. The white arc is the range wherein you can extend the flaps. The bottom of the white arc is the stalling speed with flaps down, and the bottom of the green arc is the stalling speed with the flaps up. A stall occurs when the air flowing over the top of the wing is disrupted and is no longer laminated in flow to produce enough lift to keep the aircraft aloft. If stalled, you quickly lower the nose and add power (if you're not already at full power) to get the air flowing smoothly and efficiently over the wing.

The airspeed indicator in the B-737 does not have color coding. The critical speeds in jet aircraft depend on the operating altitude. The maximum speed permitted is lowered at high altitude and must not exceed the red and white

Although imprecise and slow in some of its measurements, the vertical speed indicator (VSI) is useful for identifying trends.

indicator called the "barber pole." You will notice in climbs that the value of the barber pole decreases. However, remember that the barber pole is pointing out indicated airspeed. The corresponding TAS is actually increasing. The aerodynamics of the airplane only respond to indicated airflow, the molecular flow over the wings. You *will* go faster to maintain the same speed, and the same molecular flow, if the molecules get farther apart, as they do in less dense air. IAS is the aerodynamic molecules you need to fly. TAS is how fast you're really going to collect them.

Vertical Speed Indicator

The vertical speed indicator (VSI) shows how fast you are climbing or descending and is calibrated in feet per minute. Most climbs and descents during attitude instrument flying are made at a particular airspeed and you accept whatever rate of change you get.

The VSI instrument case is filled with air obtained through a vent on the outside of the aircraft. Thus, the air pressure in the case is the same as the air pressure outside of the aircraft. This is static pressure. A bellows in VSI around the case is also filled with ambient air from outside the aircraft. When case pressure and inner bellows pressure are equal, the airplane is level and the rate of change is zero. However, the bellows has a "calibrated leak." The VSI can measure the difference in rates of climb and descent by the direct and immediate change in case pressure, weighted against the delayed (and leaking) pressures within the bellows.

Because of the calibrated leak, the VSI may lag behind climb or descent changes by about six to nine seconds. The VSI needle also tends to fluctuate when turbulence is encountered. Because of these limitations, you should use the VSI to identify trends. For example, you would use it to determine if you are climbing at an increasing rate or to determine if your rate of climb has begun to level off.

Altimeter

The altimeter is used to show how high the aircraft is above mean sea level (MSL). Height above MSL is the aircraft's distance above sea level. Since you

cannot see outside during instrument conditions, you will find yourself governed by this instrument. You want to stay well above any obstacles in the area and at your assigned altitude.

It's important to understand that the altimeter measures height above mean sea level and not height above *ground* level (AGL). If the ground elevation is above sea level, often the case beyond coastal areas, the aircraft will be closer to the ground than is evident. Your height above the ground (AGL) is found by subtracting the elevation of terrain below you from your indicated altitude above sea level. If you're high enough to be safely above obstacles or at an assigned altitude, this is only academic and not a practical consideration.

To properly provide altitude information, the altimeter must be set with the current barometric pressure in your area. Go into Aircraft on the main menu and select Aircraft Settings. On the Realism tab, you can change the Altimeter setting using either Hg or Millibars measurement units. The current local pressure is displayed above the Altimeter setting field for you to use as a reference. To change the current local pressure, select World on the main menu and then select Weather. The Pressure tab allows you to change the current settings.

When your flight altitude is above 18,000 MSL, you should set the altimeter to a pressure setting of 29.92 HG. At this altitude, you do not have obstacle worries. There are, however, other fast-flying aircraft cruising at these altitudes. When all pilots are using a common pressure setting, it enables ATC to issue altitude assignments that guarantee separation and safety.

To do its job correctly, the altimeter must be set according to the barometric pressure of the area in which you're flying.

The Heading Indicator

The heading indicator, also called the directional gyro (DG), shows which compass heading the aircraft is tracking. You fly using the DG rather than the erratic and free-floating magnetic compass. The compass is difficult to read during flight. We initially set the DG to agree with the compass heading. On the ground this is easy with a stable, undisturbed magnetic compass. A DG slowly loses its calibration or heading accuracy over time. This is called *gyro drift* and you can set Flight Simulator 98 up with or without this option. Go to

The heading indicator (or directional gyro) shows what compass heading you're tracking.

Aircraft and select Aircraft Settings. On the Reliability tab, activate the Gyro drift option. If you select this option, press D to recalibrate the DG about every 15 minutes. About that time you should assure that the DG and magnetic compass still agree. The DG is stable (even in turbulence) and is your primary heading display.

Around the face of the heading indicator you will see a moveable marker with two red lines on it called a heading bug. This is set upon any heading assigned to you or one you've determined to fly. You place it on a heading value using the red knob on the bottom right-hand corner of the HI. Place your cursor on the knob and press on the mouse until it spins onto the proper course.

Aircraft Control Using the Instruments

Aircraft control in attitude instrument flying is making control inputs based solely on the information that the aircraft instruments provide. Sudden changes in the aircraft's altitude, erratic instrument changes, and even inner-ear maladies can cause confusion and loss of aircraft control when flying in IMC. Therefore, you make small control inputs and determine what effect the change has on aircraft performance. Once you make a control input, you must wait for the instruments to stabilize before you determine if the single input is sufficient or other inputs are needed.

For example, if you overshoot your desired altitude, you should level the plane and assess the value of the error. This determines the amount of correction you will need to return to your assigned altitude. Big corrections will simply overshoot your desired altitude in the opposite direction. With calculated and appropriate control inputs, you "make things happen," not simply "watch them happen."

Instrument Interpretation

Instrument interpretation is the process of understanding and responding to the information that the instruments convey. You must fully understand instrument indications and how they interact. By scanning and comparing the instruments, you determine what the aircraft is doing, despite the absence of an outside view.

For example, let's say you're in straight and level flight and you notice your airspeed begins to decrease. This could be caused by either the aircraft nose pitching up or by decreasing the power. To determine which, you would

look at other instruments to determine if they indicate a climb or a decrease in power.

Instrument interpretation also involves seeing the relationships between various instrument data. This includes recognizing trends in the movement of your instrument needles. For instance, you need to recognize not only that your VSI is showing a climb at 500 feet per minute but also that your rate of climb has increased dramatically in the last ten seconds and is *still* climbing. Your interpretation of this situation would vary depending on the aircraft you were flying and on the maneuver you were executing. If you were attempting straight and level flight in a C-182S, you would realize the aircraft in our example would be close to overstressing from the climb. On the other hand, if you were trying to climb in the Lear 45, you would realize that the climbing stresses would be well within the tolerances of the aircraft.

Instrument Cross Check

During IFR flight, one continually scans and interprets instrument indications and smoothly applies control pressures to fly a predetermined route at a set altitude. The ability to scan quickly and assimilate information, for whatever change may be necessary, is the essence of instrument flight. The primary instruments to monitor are the attitude indicator, heading indicator, airspeed indicator, and altimeter. It's also a good idea to regularly check the turn coordinator and VSI. An organized scan pattern keeps your eyes moving to check *all* the primary instruments at regular intervals.

You can use any comfortable scan pattern or frequency so long as you view each instrument systematically. During your

The "T-Scan" is a popular scanning method, easy to remember because of its "shapely" name.

Instrument ID

To test your understanding of instrument interpretation, identify what the aircraft in each illustration is doing.

A.

B.

C.

D.

Answers: A. *Straight climb* **B.** *Left-hand descending turn* **C.** *Straight and level flight* **D.** *Right-hand climbing turn*

scan, do not fixate on any one instrument. You may find yourself doing this when confused about the functioning of some instruments, instead relying too fully on one or two instruments that you have completely mastered.

Another common scanning error is omitting an instrument in the pattern. Adhere to your scan pattern. It's wise to develop a scan pattern that systematically flows around the control panel. You will find that maintaining the scan can become physically exhausting. However, without it the aircraft will deviate from the performance

Even though the cockpit of the B-737 is loaded with equipment, the basic IFR instruments also form a T-shaped pattern (if your cockpit is laid out like this).

you want. The more deviation permitted, the more difficult it will be to return to assigned headings and altitudes.

The most common scan used is the "T-Scan". The T-Scan begins with the attitude indicator followed by this sequence: heading indicator, attitude indicator, altimeter, attitude indicator, airspeed indicator, attitude indicator. About every third pattern you should include the VSI and turn coordinator. You may modify this scan depending on the maneuver you're executing. For example, if you're in a turn, you will pay attention to the turn coordinator. To assure a standard rate turn, cross-check the HI to determine how you've progressed to the new heading. In a climb, airspeed indicates the proper altitude, the VSI shows the rate and the altimeter shows the value of your progress to a new altitude. (The same holds true in a descent.)

The T-Scan revolves around the attitude indicator. This instrument provides the most immediate perspective during attitude instrument flying and should be the center of any scan you develop. It immediately reveals the aircraft's pitch and bank. You should also not neglect your engine instruments. Your engine instruments should be reviewed for all the things you would normally check during VFR flight: power settings, fuel quantity, engine temperature, and voltage readings. The last thing you want when you're up in the soup is an in-flight engine emergency.

Aircraft Control by the Numbers

To efficiently control the aircraft, it is imperative to understand Power + Altitude = Aircraft Performance. Attitude refers to the combination of pitch and

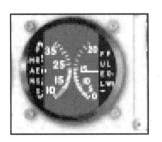

F3 and F2 are used to increase and decrease the power setting on the manifold pressure gauge.

bank. What this equation illustrates is that at a given power and attitude in a particular aircraft, the same aircraft performance will be observed each time. This *no surprises* formula allows you to "fly by the numbers."

Power is set on the C-182S using throttle. Use F3 and F2 in increase and decrease the power setting on the manifold pressure gauge. You need to also set your propeller speed to the proper revolutions per minute (RPM). Use CTRL + F3 to increase RPM and CTRL + F2 to decrease RPM.

For simple flight, Flight Simulator 98 can automatically set the propeller RPM for you. Go to Aircraft and select Aircraft Settings. Go to the Engines tab and set Prop Advance to automatic.If you want to control RPM, set Prop Advance to Manual.

You'll need to set the prop advance to manual if you want to control RPM, which is measured by this gauge.

Let's suppose you're flying the C-182S and set full power and 2,500 RPM. You raise the nose until the attitude indicator shows pitch at eight dots high (right above the second pitch line). Because the nose is raised, the plane will begin to climb and the airspeed will begin to decrease. You should hold this attitude and wait for the instruments to settle down. After a few moments, the airspeed will cease decreasing and stabilize at 80 knots. Meanwhile, the aircraft VSI will also show a climb. This needle initially decreased until it stopped at about 700 feet per minute.

The next time you choose this aircraft and set full power to 2500 RPM, pitch eight dots up, and hold the wings level,

you can expect the instruments to stop moving when the airspeed shows 80 and the VSI a 700-foot per minute climb under similar atmospheric conditions.

How Instrument Flying Translates into Flight Simulator 98

To attitude fly, there are six basic power/attitude concepts you will need to learn. They are cruise level, cruise descent, cruise climb, approach level, approach descent (precision), and approach descent (non-precision). The cruise positioning is used when you are traveling from one location to another. The approach conditions are used when you are making an instrument landing.

C-182S Flight Configurations

	Manifold Pressure	RPM	Pitch	Airspeed	VSI	Flaps
Climb	2500	2500	+1 dot above the second calibration mark	80	+700	Up
Cruise	2350	2350	0	120	0	Up
Cruise Descent	2000	2000	- 2 dot	120	-700	Up
Approach Level	2000	2000	+1/2 dot	90	0	Up
Approach Descent (precision)	2000	2500	-1/2	90	-500	Down 10 degrees
Approach Descent (non precision)	1900	2500	-1 dot	90	-700	Down 10 degrees

B-737 Flight Configurations

	Percent Power	Pitch	Airspeed	VSI	Flaps
Climb	90 below 18,000 MSL 110 above 18,000 MSL	+ 5 degrees	250 below 18,000 MSL 220 above 18,000	+6000	Up

B-737 Flight Configurations continued

	Percent Power	Pitch	Airspeed	VSI	Flaps
Cruise	85	0	300	0	Up
Cruise Descent	60 above 18,000 MSL 50 below 18,000 MSL	- 2 dot	220	-2500 above 18,000 MSL and -1800 below 18,000	Up
Approach Level	55	+ 5 degrees	180	0	Down 10 degrees
Approach Decent (precision)	55	- 1 dot	140	-500	Full
Approach Decent (precision)	50	-1 dot	140	-1,000	Full

Lear 45 Flight Configurations

	Percent Power	Pitch	Airspeed	VSI	Flaps
Climb	Full below 20,000 MSL Gradually educed until 84 above 20,000 MSL	+ 10 degrees	250 below 20,000 MSL .6 Mach above 20,000 MSL	+4700	Up
Cruise	84	0	.71 Mach	0	Up
Cruise Descent	80 above 10,000 MSL Gradually reduce until 28 below 10,000 MSL	-3 degrees above 10,000 MSL -5 degrees below 10,000 MSL	220	-1800	Up Above 10,000 MSL. Down 8 degrees below 10,000 MSL
Approach Level	45	0	180	0	Down 8 degrees
Approach Descent (precision)	50	-2 1/2 dot	140	-700	Full
Approach Descent (non-precision)	30	-2 1/2 dot	140	-1800	Full

Attitude instrument flying requires you to control pitch, bank and power. It is important to understand the role of control instruments and performance instruments. Control instruments allow you to make a control input to effect a desired performance. You are establishing a condition such as setting the throttle to 22 inches or positioning the horizon bar on the altitude indicator to two dots nose high.

Performance instruments let you know how well you did at setting this condition. For example, the VSI showed a rate of climb of 500 feet per minute, the airspeed indicator displayed a decrease in airspeed of ten knots and the altimeter showed a climb after the AI was set nose high two dots.

Let's suppose you were climbing at 500 feet per minute but really wanted to fly at 550 feet per minute. You would use your control instrument, the attitude indicator, and smoothly set a higher pitch value. Then you would scan your instruments to determine how the performance instruments had changed. Hopefully, you would see that you have increased your rate of climb to 550 feet per minute. If you did not, you would need to use your control instrument again to reset the conditions. Once you found the control positions that work, you would memorize them for the next time you wanted to achieve a 550-foot climb per minute at the specified airspeed.

The instruments used as control and performance instruments depend on the type of maneuver. The attitude indicator and power control are always used as primary instruments. The attitude indicator is used to control the combination of pitch and bank. This is why the attitude indicator is such a vital and informative factor in your scan pattern. The throttle is also used as a control instrument for power in piston aircraft; thrust levers perform this same function in turbines. The power setting tends to remain constant during attitude instrument flying and does not need to be scanned as often.

The performance instruments can be further classified into direct and indirect performance instruments. In the example demonstrating the control and performance instruments used in achieving a 550-foot per minute climb, the direct performance instrument is the VSI indicator. It informs you if the desired performance, a 550-foot-per minute climb, has been established. The drop in airspeed and increase in altitude indirectly validates that a 550-foot-per-minute climb has been established.

Straight and Level Flight

Now that you understand the aviation fundamentals involved in attitude instrument flying, let's talk about how to put it all into practice. This section will provide some tips to improve your flying technique and warn you of some common pitfalls to avoid.

Holding Pitch

The pitch attitude required to hold straight and level flight varies with the speed of the aircraft. As you may have noticed during slow flight exercises, pitch altitude increases cause airspeed to decrease and vice versa. The attitude indicator is the control instrument used to set pitch in straight and level flight. You will set the aircraft wings so that they are lined up correctly on the horizontal bar. This will be right on or just below the horizon line with cruise power set.

To verify you have achieved your desired level altitude, use the altimeter, VSI, and airspeed indicator as performance instruments. The altimeter should show no change in altitude. If it does show a deviation, note how fast it is deviating. If it is showing a slow change in altitude, you will need to make only a small pitch correction on the AI in the direction opposite the movement. If you are rapidly changing altitude, you will need to make a greater pitch correction.

If you are off altitude by less than 100 feet, you want to make a pitch correction of about 1/2 dot in a C-182S. If you are off by more than 100 feet, you may want to use a correction of about one dot and also increase your power setting. You should apply just enough pressure to slow the rate of needle movement on the altimeter, but not aim to stop it abruptly. Then add a little more pressure to stop the needle's movement completely. At this point you will be back to level flight. If the needle starts moving past your desired altitude in the opposite direction, you'll know that you've overcompensated.

The vertical speed indicator also tells you about your pitch attitude. It shows the trend in your aircraft's vertical movement. Suppose your altimeter showed that you were below your specified altitude by 50 feet. When you increased your pitch, the altimeter would take a moment to show a significant change in altitude. Therefore, you will not be able to determine immediately from this instrument that you are beginning to climb. On the other hand, the

VSI will show a change in vertical movement. This can and should be used as an early alert for detecting changes in pitch altitude. You must wait for the aircraft to settle before getting rate changes from the VSI. Making small control changes will help minimize this lag.

The airspeed indicator is also a performance instrument. At constant power and altitude setting, your airspeed will remain constant. If you see your airspeed increasing without adding power, check to see if you are nose low and are losing altitude. If your airspeed is decreasing, check if the nose is high and you're climbing.

Bank Instrumentation

The attitude indicator is the control instrument to initially bank the airplane or assure level flight. In level flight, the wings should be parallel with the horizontal bar. The primary instrument to determine straight and level flight is the heading indicator. If you are flying at a magnetic heading of 090 and your heading indicator shows that you are drifting toward 095, check your altitude indicator to ensure the wings are level. To correct for the deviation, you should make a turn back to 090 at a bank angle no greater than the number of degrees to be turned. Remember, you should strive for small, deliberate control movements. In this case, your bank would be five degrees or less.

The turn coordinator also acts as a bank instrument in straight and level flight. When the miniature airplane is level, the aircraft is flying straight. If the wings are banked, the aircraft is also turning in the same direction. To return to level flight, bank the aircraft in the opposite direction using the attitude indicator. Use the ball on the turn coordinator to ensure you are in coordinated flight. If the ball is right of center, apply right rudder pressure until it centers. If the ball is left of center use left rudder until the ball centers. The wings on the miniature airplane should become level when you have returned to a level altitude.

Setting Power

The approximate power setting is usually known and used to achieve certain operating performance such as fuel burn. It is not generally reset during flight except for transitioning between cruise and climb flight. However, if you want to increase your airspeed while maintaining your altitude, you should increase your power setting. You will notice the nose begin to rise when the power is applied and the plane try to climb. Increased speed is increased lift. To compensate, lower the pitch of the nose and re-trim the aircraft to maintain level flight. To decrease airspeed without entering a descent, pull back on the throttle. The aircraft will initially try to descend at the same airspeed it was at in level flight. Pull the elevator back to increase the pitch so that level altitude is maintained. The airspeed will begin to bleed off and stabilize at a lower speed (assuming you still have adequate power to continue flight).

Common Problems in Straight and Level Flight

Late Pitch Corrections: Don't accept being off your desired attitude by "only" 20 feet. This can quickly become a larger deviation and harder to correct if not resolved immediately.

Chasing the VSI: The VSI should be used as a trend instrument. Cross check the VSI against the altimeter, altitude indicator, and airspeed indicator. (It may fluctuate, but you shouldn't.)

Excessive Pitch Correction: When you need to make small changes in pitch, raise or lower the nose of the aircraft no more than one dot at a time.

Failure to maintain pitch correction: After you set pitch on the AI, scan the other instruments to see how the change effected air craft performance. Don't forget to also scan the AI to make sure you are still holding the correct pitch altitude. Trim it for hands-free operation.

Late Heading Corrections: Don't accept deviating from your desired heading by three degrees. Like pitch, it is easier to correct such deviations sooner than later.

Omission: This is failure to scan the heading indicator, especially when making changes to power or pitch.

Remembering Heading: It's easy to forget what heading you're supposed to track, especially when you are correcting your heading to compensate for wind. Making use of the heading bug can help eliminate this problem.

Climbs

To begin a climb, set your control instrument (the altitude indicator) to climb pitch by gently pulling back on the elevator. This pitch attitude will be around three dots high in the C-182S. You should then apply climb power, which is full power and full RPM on most complex airplanes. In climbs, the airspeed indicator is the primary performance instrument for pitch and the AI is the primary performance instrument for bank. The manifold pressure gauge is monitored for the power setting.

The VSI is a performance instrument for pitch. It will show an upward trend and will stop at around 600 feet-per-minute. The airspeed will begin to decrease and level off at around 80 knots. If the aircraft is flying faster than 80 knots, we would use the attitude indicator to slightly raise the nose of the aircraft. This would initiate a greater rate of climb. If we were slower than 80 knots, we would lower the nose decreasing the rate of climb. Usually in IFR, we climb and descend at a specific airspeed rather than a specific rate of climb. If you wanted to climb at 500 feet-per-minute, you would set the altitude indicator to achieve the desired rate of climb and then accept the corresponding airspeed.

When you are cruising in straight and level flight, you use pitch to correct small altitude deviations. You essentially trade airspeed for altitude in changes of less than 100 feet. You may have noticed during slow flight and landing, you control airspeed with pitch and descent rate with power. You will apply the same principle when performing instrument landings.

You lessen climb or descent rates before you arrive at your desired altitude. Otherwise, you will overshoot it. A good guide to lead your desired altitude by ten percent of the vertical airspeed. Thus, if climbing at about 500 feet-per-minute, begin to level out about 50 feet before reaching your new altitude.

To stop the climb, pressure the yolk forward until the pitch is level on the attitude indicator. Let the airspeed build to cruise climb before reducing power. Verify that you're flying level by making sure the altimeter is not moving from your desired altitude and the VSI is level and stable. Once airspeed is at cruise speed, reduce the power to cruise and follow your straight and level procedures.

Descents

You should begin descents by reducing your power to descent power and lowering the nose by setting the altitude indicator to the proper pitch position. Prevent the aircraft from turning by keeping the attitude indicator's miniature wings parallel to the horizon line. If you're trying to make a constant airspeed descent, control airspeed using the attitude indicator and accept the resulting rate of descent. A constant rate descent is made at a predetermined VSI value rather than a specific airspeed. The VSI is the primary performance instrument. You accept whatever airspeed you get.

Begin to level off about 50 feet before your desired altitude. To descend and level at 3000 feet, raise the nose to level flight approaching 3000 feet and follow straight and level flight procedures.

Common Problems During Climbs and Descents

Over-controlling pitch on entry: If you don't know the pitch/power setting to reach the performance you want, make small changes in pitch and cross-check the other instruments before making another control input.

Failure to learn pitch/power combinations: Use the flight attitudes presented earlier in this chapter or discover others so you can efficiently control the aircraft.

Failure to maintain pitch correction: After you set pitch on the AI, scan the other instruments to see how the change affected aircraft performance. Don't forget to also scan the AI to make sure you are still holding the correct pitch altitude.

Ignoring rate of climb for level offs: You should scan the VSI to determine when you should begin to level off from your climb or descent.

Turns

All turns in IFR should be made at standard rate. On the C-182S, use the altitude indicator to establish a turn of approximately 18 degrees bank. You may need to raise the pitch to counteract for the loss of lift acting vertically. You will also need to add a little power to maintain your airspeed. Use the turn coordinator to verify you are making the turn at standard rate.

To recover from the turn, apply opposite aileron and rudder. Return the power to cruise and set pitch to level flight. Lead the roll out by one-half the degree of bank. For example, if your bank angle is 18 degrees, you should roll out about nine degrees before your desired heading. If you had turned to the right from a northerly heading to 090 degrees, your roll out would begin on a heading of 081 degrees.

Common Problems in Turns

Bank fixation: Try to not fixate on the bank instruments when you roll into and out of a turn.

No anticipation of turning forces: As discussed in the beginning of this chapter, an aircraft turns because some lift is diverted into the turn. Therefore, the pitch of the aircraft will need to be increased to maintain the same altitude. You should anticipate this.

Straight and level procedures: Not following straight and level techniques after making a turn. Most often forgotten after making a well-executed turn and roll out.

Turning in the wrong direction: Before you start your turn, take a minute to determine which direction you should turn to get to your new heading in the shortest arc.

Making Life Easier with Trim

Trim reduces the pressure the pilot needs to hold on the control to keep the aircraft nose in a desired altitude. Trim will reduce your workload. Do not use trim to make changes in pitch but only to relieve control pressures. It will lessen the amount of workload and allow you to maintain control during distractions. Use KEYPAD 1 to trim up and KEYPAD 7 to trim down

Once trim is set, it should not need to be adjusted unless you are changing airspeed. If you pull off power for a decent, the airspeed will initially rise as the nose drops but if no change in trim is made, the aircraft will stabilize at the original airspeed. When flying straight and level, turbulence may prompt a need for you to make small control inputs. But once the trim is set, you should not need to reset it unless you are changing airspeed.

Practice Exercises

Instrument flying is precision flying. But perhaps nothing will emphasize it better than some actual flight maneuvering. During these exercises, try to stay as close as you can to your desire heading, altitude, airspeed, and VSI. Don't compromise, allowing yourself to deviate "only" 20 feet above altitude.

The FAA allows a pilot to be within 100 feet of altitude, ten degrees of heading, and ten percent of airspeed in the IFR flight test. However, strive to stay within 20 feet of altitude and five degrees of bank to improve your flight skills. Remember to constantly scan your instruments. The earlier you recognize deviation in your performance, the easier it will be to correct it. Remember the keys to successful altitude instrument flying: scan, interpret, control.

Practice Exercise 1

For the first exercise, let's go to Meigs Field. If you haven't just started up Flight Simulator 98, click on Flights from the main menu and choose Select Flights. Pick the Default Flight, which is at Chicago's Meigs Field. You will be lined up on runway 36 in the C-182S. Next let's set some IFR conditions. Go to World and select Weather on the sub menu. Click on the Clouds tab and set the base to 2000 feet and the cloud top to 4000 feet. Set the deviation to 40 feet. Make this a stratocumulus layer with 7/8ths coverage. Next go to the Visibility tab and set it for one mile.

You will have enough visibility to take off and get established. After takeoff, maintain runway heading and set your cruise climb attitude. You should climb at 80 knots and the AI should be located just above the second calibration mark. Continue on this climb until you arrive at 2500 feet. Around 2450 feet, you should begin to lower the nose. Don't reduce power until the airspeed builds up to 120 knots. Practice level flight until you can hold it pretty well. Next, make a left-hand turn to a heading of 360 using a standard rate—about 18 degrees of bank. At the completion of the turn, begin a descent down on the runway heading and descend to 2000 feet.

Exercise 2—Advanced Maneuvers

This maneuver uses one of the VFR lessons contained in Flight Simulator 98. You can pause anytime by pressing P and selecting some IML weather. This lesson makes steeper turns and combines turns with climbs and descents. Additionally, the flight instructor in this lesson will point out when you are not keeping up with the speed of the lesson.

Choose Flights on the main menu and select Lessons. Select Climbs, Turns, Descents from the list. As soon as the program finishes loading, press P to pause the lesson. Go to World and select Weather on the sub menu. Set the base to 4000 MSL and the cloud top to 6000 MSL. Set a user-defined cloud type and choose Haze for coverage area. Next go to the visibility tab and select a visibility of 1/16th of a mile. Press P to resume the lesson. If you miss any instruction when you go back into the lesson, hit CTRL + M to have the information repeated.

Lesson begins: Fly heading 270 and altitude 5000 feet

Maneuver 1: Left turn to 270 using 30 degrees of bank

Maneuver 2: Right turn to 270 using 30 degrees of bank

Maneuver 3: Left turn to 360 using 30 degrees of bank and descend to 4000 MSL

Maneuver 4: Right turn to 180 using 30 degrees of bank and descend to 3000 MSL

Maneuver 5: Left turn to 180 using 30 degrees of bank and climb to 4000 MSL

Maneuver 6: Right turn to 090 using 30 degrees of bank and climb to 5000 MSL

Maneuver 7: Left turn to 090 using 45 degrees of bank

Maneuver 8: Right turn to 090 using 45 degrees of bank

Maneuver 9: Left turn to 180 using 45 degrees of bank descend to 4000 MSL

Maneuver 10: Right turn to 180 using 45 degrees of bank descend to 3000 MSL

Chapter Five

Navigation Basics

In the last chapter, we discussed how to control the aircraft during IMC (Instrument Meteorological Conditions) using just the aircraft instruments. The question now is how to find your final destination when IMC exists. The answer is *procedural instrument flying*.

Procedural instrument flying is the set of IFR rules pertaining to radio navigation. Radio navigation allows you to determine your position above the ground with radio signals. These signals may be picked up on an aircraft receiver or picked up by ATC (Air Traffic Control) who would then relate the information to you.

If you've used the radio navigation equipment available in Microsoft Flight Simulator 98 on your VFR flights, you won't find procedural instrument flying to be much different. On those VFR flights, you may have used this equipment to backup your pilotage—finding your course using landmarks. During IMC, there is no backup system for radio navigation because you can't see what you're flying over. Therefore, procedural instrument flying is very particular about what altitudes a pilot can cruise and the routes that can be flown. This chapter will show you how to simulate procedural instrument flying in Flight Simulator.

Radio Waves Explained

A radio wave is a form of electromagnetic radiation. This energy travels in a substance by means of vibration from particle to particle in a wave pattern. For example, dropping a rock in a pond will create an energy wave. Waves can be seen travelling away from the spot the rock hit the water. It is the energy wave that is moving outward, not the water.

A cycle describes one complete oscillation of the wave. You need to define a reference point on the wave to measure the interval of a cycle. In the rock example, you could use the very top of a wave as a reference point. The cycle would begin at the tip of one wave and end at the tip of the very next wave. You will hear the term frequency often when discussing the differences between radio navigation aids. Frequency is a measure of how many of these cycles are completed in a unit of time. Hertz (Hz) is the unit of measurement used to describe frequency in a second as the unit of time.

Some waves can pass through any medium. X-rays waves can even travel through us. Other types of waves are reflected by certain substances. ATC relies on radar radio waves being reflected by aircraft in order to track them.

To create a radio wave, a high-frequency alternating current is passed through an antenna. This wave travels at a speed of 186,000 miles per second! The frequency of the wave is equal to the frequency of the alternating current used to create it.

What's in a Frequency?

For those of you who just remembered why you hated physics class, don't panic. The key concept to understand is that frequencies in different ranges have specific properties that effect the way you use them in Flight Simulator. The following table describes the frequency bands used in aviation.

Frequency Ranges

Band	Frequency Range
Low-frequency (L/F)	30 - 300 kHz
Medium-frequency (M/F)	300 - 3000 kHz
High-frequency (H/F)	3000 kHz - 30 MHz
Very high frequency (VHF)	30 - 300 MHz
Ultra high frequency (UHF)	300 - 3000 MHz

Low (L/F) and medium frequency (M/F) waves travel into the sky until they hit one of Earth's outer most atmospheric layers—the ionosphere. The wave is then reflected back down to the ground. Therefore, the distance these waves can be received varies on the height and density of the ionosphere and the angle the wave hits the ionosphere.

High frequency waves also reflect off the ionosphere. However, once they return to the ground, then are reflected back up toward the sky. Therefore, they can usually be received over longer distances than L/F and M/F waves.

Very high frequency (VHF) and Ultra high frequency (UHF) waves do not reflect off the ionosphere. The only way a receiver will pick up the wave is to lie directly in its path. This limitation is called "line of sight" reception. The reception range of line of sight signals increases with altitude and can be calculated using the formula (in nautical miles) in which range equals the square root of aircraft altitude times 1.5.

For example, let's say you're flying at an attitude of 11,000 feet MSL. The line of sight signal you might be using is being broadcast from a transmitter located at an elevation of 1000 feet MSL. Thus, you are 10,000 feet above the transmitter. You would multiply 10,000 by 1.5 to arrive at a value of 15,000 feet. The square root of 15,000 is 122.47. Therefore, you can expect to be able to pick up this signal when you are within 122 nautical miles of the ground-based transmitter. Flight Simulator incorporates line of sight reception using a similar model.

The Need for Radio Navigation

Radio navigation was developed by necessity after World War 1 ended. Commercial aviation was still in its infancy. However, the surplus of aircraft produced for the war, now lying idle, attracted entrepreneurs and the U.S. government to the prospects of commercial aviation. The government did its best to promote this industry by passing legislation which subsidized air carriers with mail delivery contracts. Postal contracts still contribute significantly to the profits of airlines today.

The problem these fledging airlines encountered were the same as today—navigating at night and in low-visibility conditions. These daring pilots often braved these conditions using low-tech solutions such as routes marked by bonfires and spotlights. When the visibility was very low, these primitive guidance methods were ineffective. Nevertheless, the mail must be delivered—"Neither rain nor sleet nor snow ." This led to the sophisticated navigation methods used today.

The VOR Explained

The VOR (Very high frequency Omni-directional Radio range) is the most commonly used en-route navigational aid in the United States. It's found in abundance in the U.S., giving pilots a wide variety of options when planning an IFR flight.

The VOR is a ground-based transmitter that broadcasts signals with frequencies between 108.0 and 118.0 MHz. The "omni-directional" reference in the name refers to the fact that the VOR wave is transmitted in all compass directions. As shown in the accompanying figure, these signals radiate out from

VOR navigation is the most common method of navigation in the United States.

The VOR is used to determine the aircraft's position over the ground.

the VOR like spokes on a wheel. This means you will be able to pick the wave up whether you're north, south, west, or east of the VOR. Keep in mind you'll also need to be in range of the VOR to pick it up. VOR range in Flight Simulator 98 will be discussed later in this chapter.

A VOR transmitter actually broadcasts two signals. One is called the *reference phase* and the other the *variable phase*. At a position of magnetic north, the reference and variable signals are in phase with one another. When the two signals are in synch like this, you could place one on top of the other and it would look as if only one wave existed. The phase of the variable signal gradually changes as it rotates around compass headings. If you were to place one pattern on top of the other at any position other than north, you would be able to see the patterns of two distinct waves.

A VOR receiver located in the cockpit picks up both signals and compares the two patterns. This receiver can calculate the electrical phase angle between the two signals. This difference can be used to determine an aircraft's position in relation to the VOR. The pilot uses the information to determine the aircraft's magnetic course to the VOR transmitter.

Radials

As we just mentioned, the VOR transmits a differently phased signal in each compass direction. Therefore, each of these signals is essentially its own course which can be tracked. Each course is called a radial. A radial is defined according to its magnetic direction *from* the station. The course that begins at the VOR and heads due east is called the 090 radial (R-090). If you were flying a heading

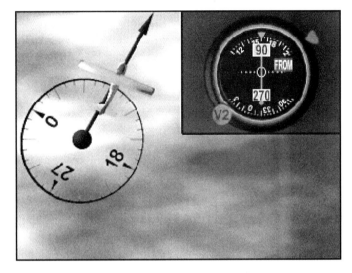

Tracking Radial 090.

of 090 on the 090 degrees radial from the VOR, you would be east of the VOR and flying away from it.

If you were flying a heading of 270 on the R-090, you would be flying inbound to the "station." Station is a term used to refer to a ground-based navigational aid—in this case the VOR. The term "NavAid " is also used to describe ground-based navigational transmitters.

The Cockpit Receiver

All the IFR-equipped aircraft in Flight Simulator 98 come with a VOR receiver. In fact, the Cessna Skylane 182S (C-182S) and Bell 206B JetRanger are equipped with two VORs. The standard VOR instrument is comprised of a VOR receiver, Omni Bearing Selector (OBS), Course Deviation Indicator (CDI) and a receiver flag. The Lear 45 and B-737 are loaded with a special type of VOR display called a Horizontal Situation Indicator (HSI) which will be described later in this chapter.

The VOR receiver in the Cessna Skylane S.

The VOR Receiver

The VOR receiver allows you to tune in the transmission frequency of the VOR you wish to track. You can set the receiver two ways in Flight Simulator 98. First, you could select Aircraft from the main menu and choose the Navigation option. Click on the Navigation Radios tab to get the input window. In this window, you have the option to enter a frequency for NAV1 and NAV2 (if NAV2 is available). NAV1 refers to the top VOR display and NAV2 to the bottom display. In the Frequency field, type the desired frequency. Tab out of this field and Flight Simulator 98 will determine if a VOR with this frequency is in range. If so, it will populate the name of the VOR next to the frequency field to help you determine if you have typed in the correct numbers. You can also manually dial in the frequency, should you prefer to do so. On all the aircraft except for the Lear 45, you will need to bring the radio stack into view. Select Views from the main menu and choose Instrument Panel on the submenu. Click on Bendix/King Radio Stack (or in the case of the B-737, on Radio Stack).

Click your cursor on each digit in the frequency display to change its value. The figure to the left shows NAV1 in the C-182S being set to a value of 117.95. The cursor will display an "+" sign if it will rotate the value up, and a "-" sign if it decreases the value of the digit.

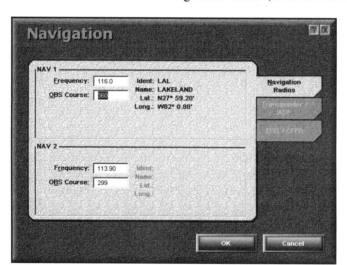

Using the menu to tune the VOR.

The OBS

The OBS allows you to rotate the compass direction, selecting a specific radial or course, shown at the top of the VOR display. The VOR internally calculates the aircraft's position in relation to the radial on this compass heading. The OBS can be set two ways. First, you can select Aircraft from the main menu and select Navigation. Go to the Navigation Radios tab and enter the OBS setting in the OBS field. The second method is to manually rotate the OBS knob located on the lower left-hand side of the VOR. To rotate the OBS clockwise, put your cursor on the left side of the knob so that a "-" appears. Then click on the cursor. To rotate the OBS counter-clockwise, place the cursor on the right side of the knob until a "+" appears.

Using the cursor to turn the VOR will save time.

The CDI

The CDI will let know where you are in relation to the radial set by the OBS. It will be centered (straight up and down) if you're located on the radial. If not, it will deflect to one side displaying which side of the course you are on. From this orientation, you can determine which way you should turn. You should be careful *not* to assume that if the CDI is deflected to the left that you need to turn to the left. Interpreting the CDI will be discussed in detail in an upcoming section.

The Receiver Flag

The receiver flag affirms that a signal is being picked up by the VOR receiver. This flag is located in the bottom center of the VOR display. When a signal is being received by the VOR, the receiver flag becomes active and will display a "TO" or a "FROM" flag.

If a FROM flag is displayed, the aircraft is on the same side of the VOR as the radial you have selected in the OBS. The FROM flag looks like an upside-down triangle. If your OBS is set to R-270 and you see a FROM flag, you are located west of the VOR.

The FROM flag resembles an upside-down triangle.

The TO flag is a right-side-up triangle.

You can't use the VOR when it doesn't pick up a signal.

Setting the stage for reverse sensing.

If a TO flag is displayed, you're on the opposite side of the VOR as the radial selected in the OBS. The TO flag looks like a right-side-up triangle. With an OBS set at 270 and a TO flag, the aircraft is located east of the VOR.

When the VOR receiver does not register a signal, this flag will change to a red and white striped rectangle. Our figure shows a VOR receiving no signal. This flag will also appear when the receiver has trouble interpreting a signal when it is directly above a VOR or when it's about to reverse the FROM/TO indication. These signal problems will be described below.

Reverse Sensing

If your heading matches your OBS selection, you can track your course using the following principle. If the CDI deflects to the left, turn left to intercept your course. If the CDI swings to the right, turn right to intercept your course. When the OBS and heading indicator are in synch, you also know exactly which way you need to turn.

It gets trickier when you have your OBS set to the opposite value as your heading. The concept of *reverse sensing* comes into play. For example, suppose you were flying inbound on R-270. You are flying a heading of 090 but set the OBS to 270. The needle will center when you are on course whether reverse sensing exists or not.

The confusion begins as soon as the CDI drifts off-center. Let's say the CDI drifted to the left as shown here. You may be tempted to turn the aircraft to the left if you haven't determined reverse sensing to exist. You actually need to turn to the *right* to get back on course.

First, let's acknowledge there is no practical value in ever flying reverse sensing. It makes no sense to set one course or heading and then fly another. There is one exception, called a "back course" instrument approach, which we'll describe later. But for now, there are two ways around this. The first is to reset your OBS to a heading of

090. As soon as you reset the OBS, the VOR display will look like that shown in the figure. The second option is take a few moments and think about compass directions. You would look at the compass directions where CDI has deflected. Looking back at the figure showing CDI drift, the CDI has deflected towards southern values. Therefore, you need to turn toward southern values. Looking at your heading indicator, southern values are found toward the right.

Don't be fooled by reverse sensing.

The HSI

The B-737 and Lear 45 use a sophisticated type of VOR display called the *Horizontal Situation Indicator* (HSI). The HSI is essentially a heading indicator with a VOR placed on top. The OBS is represented by an arrow that points to the OBS selection. The tail of the OBS represents the CDI. Since the compass card moves as the aircraft heading changes, it automatically displays the aircraft's current position in relation to the course you've selected. Therefore, you never need to worry about reverse sensing. If the CDI is deflected to the left, you will know that you need to turn to the left.

Notice the second arrow located below the OBS arrow. This arrow replaces the TO/FROM flag used on conventional VORs. It always points to the station. Instead of mentally determining your position in relation to the VOR, you know exactly which way the VOR is located just by glancing at this indicator.

Turn the OBS to your heading to prevent reverse sensing.

VOR Range

There are three classes of VORs used for navigation. In real-life aviation, the published minimum range a signal can be received is different for each class of VOR and is shown in the next table. Notice in the table that terminal class VORs broadcast on a distinct set of frequencies.

The HSI combines the heading indicator and the VOR displays.

VOR Range

Class	Range (NM)	Frequency Band
H	40 (any altitude)	112.00-118.00
	100 (above 14,500 ft.)	
	130 (above 18,000 ft.)	
L	40 (below 18,000 ft.)	112.00-118.00
T (Terminal)	25 (below 12,000 ft.)	108.00-112.00

Determining VOR Range in Flight Simulator

Flight Simulator models the three classes of VORs. To determine the range of a particular VOR you are using, the first thing you need to do is determine the class of the VOR. If you are using a map from your Pilot's Guide, notice that the legend on page seven indicates terminal VORs will be designated with a "(T)". No special designation is placed next to H or L.

When you journey to locations outside the areas contained in the Pilot's Guide, you must apply more of your knowledge. First you must find the frequency of the VOR you want to use. Go to World and select Airport/Facility Directory on the menu. When the map of the world appears, click on the section your VOR is located in. Another map will appear asking you to refine your selection. Flight Simulator will display a list of airports for that area. To get to the navigational aids, click on the Navaids option in the upper right-hand corner. A list will appear like the one shown at left. Search the list for your desired navaid and note its frequency and elevation.

Notice that the Airport/Facility Directory did not

VOR details can be found in the Airport/Facilitiy Directory.

specify the class of VOR. If the VOR frequency is between 108.00 and 112.00, you are using a terminal- class VOR. Otherwise, you're using either an H- or L-class VOR. Since L-class VORs are found so infrequently in the United States, you can guess that the VOR is most likely an H-class. The Airport/ Facility Directory published by the National Oceanic and Atmospheric Administration specifies H- or L-class VORs. To obtain this data, this directory can be ordered by calling 800-638- 8972 or on the Internet at www.nos.noaa.gov/aaa/welcome.html.

Let's say you wanted to depart from Melbourne International and head down towards Miami Beach. You looked up the Melbourne VOR in the Airport/Facility Directory and found it has a frequency of 110.00 and an elevation of 30 feet. Since 110.00 is between 108 and 112, you are using a T-class VOR.

Go to World and select Go To off the main menu. Select Airports and choose Melbourne International in Florida. Before take off, set your NAV1 to the Melbourne VOR. Set the frequency to 110.00 and the OBS to 180. After take off in the Cessna 182S, depart to the south and climb to 3000 feet. Notice that Nav 1 is just about centered and the FROM flag is active. Keep heading south to find out where you lose the signal.

On the top center panel is an instrument called DME (Distance Measuring Equipment). The DME will be explained in detail later but a general knowledge off it will benefit this exercise. It displays how far away you are from the VOR. Keep an eye on this value to get a good feel for how much VOR reception Flight Simulator will give you.

When you get to a DME reading of 40.5 NM, you lose the signal. Since you are flying at an altitude of 3000 feet and the VOR is located at an elevation of 30 feet, you know terminal VORs have a range of 40.4 nautical miles at an altitude of 2970 feet above the VOR. If you were to climb into higher altitudes, you would find that reception range is the same at all altitudes when dealing with T class VORs in Flight Simulator.

In real-life aviation, the VOR signal is not automatically lost at 40.4 nautical miles. Instead, reception range varies at different altitudes. In addition, the signal may be lost for a few moments but then come back in again. Microsoft has put a patch on the Internet that will more realistically simulate these features. This VOR patch (along with fixes for scenery and adventures problems) is included in the converter called the Converter for Flight Shop Aircraft and Adventures. You can download this path from the Internet site www.microsoft.com/games/fsim/news.htm.

With the converter installed, the signal in the above example will not be lost until 43.0 NM at 3000 feet and 48 NM at 6000 feet. At 9000 feet, the signal will be lost at 53 NM but then come again at 54.5 NM. The signal is finally lost again at 57 NM.

Now let's go to Lakeland Linder Regional Airport in Florida. The frequency at Lakeland is 116.00 and the elevation of the VOR is 130 feet. Since 116.00 is above 112.00, this is an H-class VOR. Set the OBS to a heading of 180 degrees and fly a heading of 180 after take off. Climb to 1000 MSL and keep an eye on the DME. You will notice that the DME reads 52 NM when you lose the VOR reception.

If you were to climb to a higher altitude, you will notice that you will start picking up the signal again. At 5000 MSL, the signal is good to 79 NM. If you climb again to 10,000 feet, you will receive the VOR for 110 NM. If you keep climbing to 18,000 MSL, you will get the VOR until 130 NM. Reception is lost after 130 NM no matter what your altitude.

An example of an L-class VOR is the Monroe VOR. Go to Monroe Regional Airport in Louisiana and set NAV1 to the Monroe VOR (MLU) on a frequency of 117.2. Take off and track the R-180. The signal will be lost at 48.6 NM at 3000 feet. At 10,000 feet, the signal is lost temporarily at 54.0 NM. It then comes back in at 56.3 NM and is lost for good at 57.0 NM.

Identifying the Frequency

There are lots of VORs out there so it's very easy to type (tune) in the wrong value (digits) and still receive a VOR signal. If you aren't careful, you could end up following a signal 100 miles away from where you wanted to go. Before you navigate using a VOR, you should properly identify the station.

The best way to do this is to match the VOR's three-letter identifier to the Morse code identifier broadcasted by the VOR. Morse code is a method of communication which uses "dots" and "dashes" to transmit letters. A dot is a quick sound and a dash is a long sound. The table below shows how to map Morse code to the alphabet.

Morse Code

Letter	Morse Code	Letter	Morse Code
A	0 –	N	– 0
B	– 0 0 0	O	– – –
C	– 0 – 0	P	0 – – 0
D	– 0 0	Q	– – 0 –
E	0	R	0 – 0
F	0 0 – 0	S	0 0 0
G	– – 0	T	–
H	0 0 0 0	U	0 0 0
I	0 0	V	0 0 –
J	0 – – –	W	0 – –
K	– 0 –	X	– 0 0 –
L	0 – 0 0	Y	– 0 – –
M	– –	Z	– – 0 0

(0 = quick dot, – = long dash)

You need to determine the three-letter code of the VOR you're using. This information is contained in the Airport Facility Directory. Select World from the main menu and choose Airport/Facility Directory. Once you get to the correct area, activate the NavAids option.

If you have already entered the frequency in the VOR receiver, you can select Aircraft from the main menu and choose Navigation. Go into the Navigation Radios tab to see what VOR Flight Simulator has matched against the frequency.

Ctrl + 1 and Ctrl + 2 will allow you to listen to NAV1 and NAV2, respectively. Compare the audio code to the three-letter code listed in the airport facility directory. Once you have positively matched them, you don't need to continuously listen to the broadcast. The VOR will stop displaying the TO/FROM flag whenever it loses the signal. There's no reason to check it again.

VOR Errors

In addition to limitations in reception, VORs are subject to other types of errors. For example, let's say your aircraft is getting close to the point where

A dual VOR check determines if the VORs are working okay.

the TO/FROM flag will change from a TO flag to a FROM flag or vice versa. The VOR receiver gets confused and cannot determine what side of the VOR it's on. This is called the "zone of ambiguity." The "No Signal Received" flag will appear and the CDI needle will show a fullscale deflection. The farther you are from the VOR, the greater the size or diameter of the zone of ambiguity.

A similar problem is encountered right over a VOR. Because the radials are so close together, the VOR cannot distinguish the radials from one another. The "No Signal Received" flag will appear until you pass over the other side of the VOR. This is called the "cone of confusion." The size of the cone increases the higher you are in altitude.

Before venturing into IFR conditions, pilots are taught to check the VOR to make sure it's giving an accurate reading. In Flight Simulator, a failed VOR receiver will not lose accuracy. Instead, it will simply not receive a signal. You can purposely make the VOR receivers fail by going into the Aircraft Settings located on the Aircraft menu. Choose the Instrument display tab and deactivate the Nav option. You will notice that both VOR receivers will fail.

However, to realistically mimic an instrument flight, you should perform a dual VOR check in the aircraft with two VORs. Tune NAV1 and NAV2 to the same VOR. Rotate both OBS knobs until the CDIs center with the same TO/FROM Flag. The OBS settings on the VORs should be within four degrees of each other.

The VOR display lets you know you are east of the station.

Determining your Current Position

Now that you are sure you're receiving the correct broadcast, you can start to navigate using the VOR. The first thing you can do is determine your current position. To determine the VOR radial you are currently located on, change the OBS setting until the needle centers. The flag window will display either a TO or a FROM indication. If the VOR centers with a FROM flag, you are on the same side as the radial defined in the OBS. Fly the heading shown on the OBS, and you will fly

away from the VOR. Fly the direct opposite heading, and you will fly towards the VOR. For example, if you set the OBS to 090 and you get a FROM flag, you are due east of the station. Fly 090 and you will distance yourself from the VOR.

Suppose you were using the Miami map shown in your Pilot's Guide on page 35. If you received the indications shown in our figure at right while tuned to the Virginia Key VOR, you would be located over the Atlantic Ocean.

According to this display, the aircraft is west of Virginia Key.

If the flag centers with a TO, you are on the opposite side of the radial. Choose a heading to match the one shown on the OBS, and you'll fly toward the VOR. If you turn the OBS dial to the reverse course, the needle will center again but this time with the opposite flag indicator. For example, if you set the OBS to R-090 and get a TO flag, you are due west of the VOR. Fly a heading of 090, and you will proceed towards the VOR. If the Virginia Key VOR was used in this example, the aircraft would be located towards Miami International Airport. Notice that the VOR is not heading-sensitive. Make a circle with a centered CDI, and it will remain centered the entire time.

Since you have two VORs in the cockpit, you can further define your position. You can set each receiver to a different VOR and determine which two radials you are on. Where these two radials cross can give you a ball park estimate of your position on a map. On IFR flights, there are intersections defined by the crossing of two radials that determine when you need to make a heading change. You would set the OBS to the radials defining the intersection and wait for both needles to center. When they center, you know you have arrived at the intersection point.

Intercepting a Course

Before you can intercept an inbound course, you need to determine your current position. This will help you to determine how large an intercept angle you will need to make to get on course. Find the OBS selection that centers the CDI with a TO indication. If you find a setting that centers it with a FROM indication first, the direct opposite value will center it with a TO indication. The VOR displays the top and bottom half of the OBS display so you can easily calculate the reverse heading without needing to subtract 180 degrees in your head. Suppose you wanted to track the 180-degree radial to the VOR. Basically,

The VOR tells you where you are and where you need to go.

The course the OBS is set to is to the left.

you want to travel due north to the station. Let's say the CDI centered when you set the OBS at 150. Visually, think of where the 150 radial lies in relation to R-180. It is located east of 180.

Now you want to set the OBS to the course you want to track. To fly this radial, you will be heading north around 360 degrees, depending on the wind conditions. If you set the OBS to a value of 180, you will run into reverse sensing problems. You should always set the OBS to the heading you intend to fly. Therefore, set the OBS to 360 and turn to a heading of 360. Notice that, as shown here, the CDI deflected to the left. Thus, you will need to turn to the left to intercept the course. We had already visually determined this but it's nice to get the backup verification.

In general, 30 degrees is a good intercept angle to use. However, if you are very close to your course you may want less of an angle so that you don't blow right past it. On the other hand, if you're way off, you may want to increase the angle so that it doesn't take all day to get on track.

Since we are off course by 30 degrees, the difference between 180 and 150, we will use a 30-degree angle. Thus, visually subtract 30 degrees from the directional gyro and determine you need to fly a heading of 330. Continue flying this heading until the needle centers. Once it does, turn back to a heading of 360 and you are traveling inbound on R-180. The only thing left to tackle is the wind.

Tracking a Course and Correcting for Wind Drift

You will begin to notice that the CDI begins to drift right or left of center. If the 360 radial TO the station is being tracked inbound and the wind is blowing from the east, the aircraft will drift west of the radial and the needle will drift to the right, indicating the desired course is to the right. You should turn to the right approximately 20 degrees (which is a compass heading of 020 degrees). The needle should begin to recenter. Once it's centers, turn back half the

distance. Therefore, you are flying a heading of 010. Hopefully, leaving a ten-degree correction will compensate for the wind and the aircraft will not drift off the radial again.

However, if you continue to drift west, the wind is a bit stronger than we figured. Turn right again, this time five degrees to a compass heading of 015. When the needle centers, turn back half the distance to a heading of 012 degrees. By compromising and returning half the distance, you will eventually hit the proper crab correction. If after making a correction, the aircraft needle drifts to the left, too much correction has been added and you need to apply less of a crab angle.

To intercept an outbound course (follow a radial away from the VOR), you first need to determine your current location. Rotate the OBS dial until the needle centers with a FROM indication. Next, picture where the radial you want to fly is compared to the radial you are currently on. For example, if you are currently on the 200 radial FROM the station and want to fly outbound on the 150 radial FROM the station, you need to start heading east.

Since we are far out from the station, we'll use a 45-degree angle to intercept our VOR radial so that it doesn't take forever to get there. Therefore, subtract 45 from our heading of 150 to get an intercept heading of 105. Fly a heading of 105 and set the OBS to 150, which is the same heading we will fly once we get established on R-150. We won't need to worry about reverse sensing. If the needle is very slow to center, you may want to increase the intercept angle. On the other hand, if you are almost on the radial you want, you may want to decrease the intercept angle so that you do not fly right by it. Once the needle recenters, we are on R-150. Turn to a heading of 150 and wait and see what the wind does.

VOR Tracking Practice Exercise

Let's practice one of the VOR tracking exercises in Flight Simulator 98. Go to Flights on the main menu and select Lessons. Choose the VOR Intercept and tracking: Skylane 182S option. Once the lesson begins, pause it by pressing P. Go into World on the main menu and select Weather. Go to the Visibility tab and set the Visibility option to one mile. This will allow you to practice attitude instrument flying as well. Press P to resume the lesson.

The lesson begins with you about five miles south of the Honolulu VOR. The instructor asks you to fly inbound on the 180 radial. The 180 radial begins

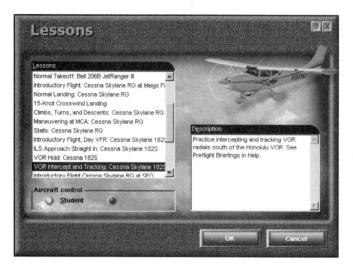

The Flight Simulator VOR tracking lessons can help you fine-tune your navigational skills.

at the VOR and extends due south. To fly inbound on this radial, you will fly a heading of 360. You will notice the CDI begin to drift to the left as you track inbound. The winds are blowing from the east at 15 knots. Since your OBS is set to 360, the same setting as your heading, you do not need to worry about reverse sensing. Apply a 20-degree wind-correction angle to the right to recenter the CDI. Once it centers, turn back ten degrees to a heading of 010 to keep it centered.

When you pass over the VOR, you will notice the TO flag change to the OFF flag. You are now in the cone of confusion. Once you finish passing over the VOR, the FROM flag will appear. You will keep the OBS set to 360 since this is the heading you are flying. The instructor will ask you to continue tracking outbound on R-360.

This lesson will then have you practice intercepting a course. You will intercept the 270 radial and fly inbound on it. To get set up for an intercept, the instructor will first ask you to fly northwest of the VOR on a heading of 315. You will be asked to fly headings of 180 and 135 to intercept the R-270. When you are on your final intercept heading of 135, you should turn to a heading of 090 as soon as the CDI starts to move.

Time and Distance to Station

You can calculate how far away you are from the VOR using the formula [minutes to station = (seconds between radial/degrees between radials)]. To do this exercise, you first need to get the needle centered and start tracking a course. The quickest way to do this is to go to Flights on the main menu and select

Lessons. Choose the VOR intercept and tracking: Cessna Skylane 182S lesson.

It's best to keep the math simple so let's calculate how long it takes to change a radial by ten degrees. Turn 80 degrees in either direction and rotate the OBS in the opposite direction. For example, turn to the right to a heading of 080 and turn the OBS left to 350. Wait for the needle to center but don't begin to time yet. Since the aircraft has been turning, you won't have accurate data. After the needle centers,

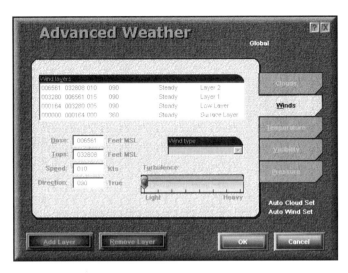

Wind is a factor in determining ground speed.

begin timing and rotate the OBS another ten degrees to the left. In this case, rotate it to a heading of 340. When the needle again recenters, note the time.

Let's say 25 seconds passed before the needle finally centered. Therefore, the aircraft is 2.5 minutes from the VOR (25/10). If you know how long it will take to get there, you can calculate how far away you are in terms of distance. Multiply your ground speed by the time to station. If you don't know your ground speed, change Flight Simulator to display True Airspeed rather than indicated airspeed. Go into Options on the main menu and Select Preferences. Go to the Instrument tab and turn off the Display indicated airspeed option.

True airspeed in this lesson is about 125 knots. To calculate the aircraft's ground speed, the wind needs to be accounted for. Go to World and select Weather from the submenu. Click on the Winds tab and you will see that a 15 knot wind blowing from 090 exists at an attitude of 4000 feet.

Use the rule of thumb presented in Chapter Three and subtract a quarter of the wind speed from true airspeed to calculate ground speed. In this case, ground speed is estimated at 121 knots (125-15/4). The distance to station in this example would be five nautical miles (121 X 2.5/60).

The aircraft is off course four degrees. The distance this relates to depends on how far the aircraft is from theVOR.

Determining How Far Off Course

When the CDI is centered, you know you're right were you want to be. But when the needle begins to drift, you want to know just how far off the mark you are. You can use the markings on the VOR display to determine this.

Notice that the VOR display has a series of five dots on either side of the center position. Each of these dots represents being off course by two degrees. The last dot represents a ten-degrees off-course deviation. This is the maximum deviation the VOR will display. As you can see here, the farther you are from the VOR, the farther you will be off course for each degree of deviation.

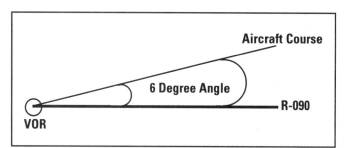

The farther away you are from the VOR, the farther you are off course for each dot of CDI deflection.

Each dot off course represents a horizontal deviation of 100 feet per nautical mile. For example, the diagram in the center of this page shows an aircraft with the OBS set to 090. Since the needle is not centered, this pilot is off course and is flying north of the radial. The needle is deflected to the right two dots. Since each dot represents two degrees, the aircraft is off course by four degrees. Each of these dots represents a 100-foot horizontal displacement for each mile of distance. Therefore, two dots represents a 200-feet off-course deviation for each mile the aircraft is out from the VOR. If the pilot is only one mile out, the aircraft is off course by 100 feet. However, if the pilot is 20 miles from the VOR, the pilot would be off by 2000 feet—nearly one-half mile.

The DME receiver.

DME

Rather than figure out the time and distance equations, a device called DME (Distance Measuring Equipment) can do it for you. The DME is used in conjunction with a VOR. As its

name suggests, the DME tells you how far away you are from a VOR. All the IFR-equipped aircraft in Flight Simulator 98 come outfitted with DME.

A DME in an aircraft sends out a signal which is received by ground equipment. This ground transmitter sends back a responding pulse. It's like a radar, but only for time-lapsed (or distance) calculations. The DME in the aircraft measures how long it took for this cycle to happen and can then calculate the distance as well as ground speed and time to station. If you have two VORs in the cockpit, you will need to switch the DME to

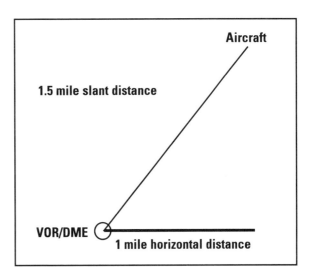

Slant distance is greater than horizontal distance.

the VOR you wish to track. A toggle switch on the DME display allows you to switch between NAV1 and NAV2. Place your cursor on this toggle to push it back and forth.

The distance determined is actually the slant distance. That is, the distance if you were to draw a line from the nose of the aircraft to the VOR on the ground. Thus, the distance is slightly greater than if measured from two points on the ground. Because of this, DME accuracy diminishes the closer you are to the VOR.

For example, if you were directly over the VOR at just under 6000 feet, the DME would register 1 NM. Slant rage becomes negligible when you are far out from the DME and at a low altitude. This error is insignificant if you are out one mile or more for each 1000 feet above ground station elevation. The DME is automatically selected when you turn in the corresponding VOR. Check if the DME is working by clicking Ctrl-3 for DME1 and Ctrl-4 for DME2, since the DME may be malfunctioning even if the VOR is working

VOR Airways

In the United States, the FAA has developed a network of routes for the efficient flow of traffic from one area to another. VOR radials define these

Even the best landmarks are useless when flying through IFR skies.

routes much like highways define routes for automobiles. Procedural instrument flying requires that aircraft fly above specific altitudes when using these airways as we discussed under FARs. This ensures that the aircraft won't hit obstacles during IFR skies and will be able to pick up the VOR used to define the route.

There are actually two separate airway systems called the Victor airway system and the Jet route system. Victor airways are for use by aircraft flying at low altitudes. These victor routes exist from 1200 feet above the ground to 17,999 feet. The Jet route systems is designed for high flying aircraft. These "J" routes exist between 18,000 and 45,000 feet.

Airway Charts

You may have seen Victor airways printed on VFR aeronautical charts. Charts with additional procedural instrument-flying detail are published for IFR flights. They get rid of all the visual matter such as roads, lakes, etc., and clarify the airway routes. These charts also provide information on ILS frequencies which can be used to help navigate.

There are two types of IFR en-route charts in the United States (US). The first is the IFR Enroute Low Altitude chart. This chart illustrates the Victor airways. The Jet route system is illustrated in IFR Enroute High Altitude charts.

These maps are published by NOS (National Ocean Service)—a division of the U.S. government. As shown in the figure to the left, 28 maps cover the entire continental U.S. To order NOS charts, call 1-800 638-8972 or visit their Internet site at www.nos.noaa.gov/aaa/welcome.html. Private companies such as Jeppesen also publish IFR charts which can be used for procedural instrument flying. Although NOS charts are cheaper, private companies tend to

produce charts that are easier to read. Jeppesen charts can be ordered by calling 1-800-621-5377.

Airway Components

We've pictured many of the components placed on NOS low altitude charts. The key consideration to procedure instrument flying is not hitting obstacles and receiving a VOR signal. The minimum en-route altitude (MEA) is the lowest published attitude on that route that guarantees this.

The minimum obstruction clearance altitude (MOCA) also guarantees obstacle clearance on the route. However, MOCA only guarantees obstacle clearance within 22 miles of the VOR. The charts also list the minimum reception altitude (MRA), which is the minimum altitude you can pick up an intersection point on a route. Also listed is the change-over point which specifies when to switch from one VOR to another. If no change-over point is listed, you would switch VORs half-way between VORs.

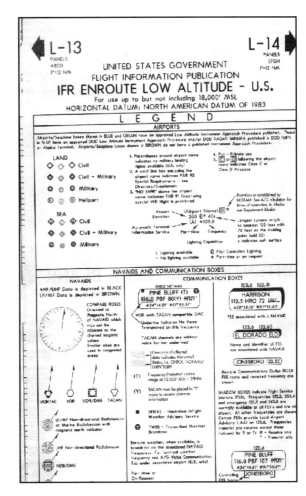

The cover of a NOS Enroute Low Altitude Chart.

VOR Navigation in Flight Simulator 98

Even if you don't purchase IFR charts, you can still use VORs to navigate in Flight Simulator 98. Your Pilot's Guide contains maps for some popular aviation areas. VORs are illustrated on these maps. If you want to travel on a

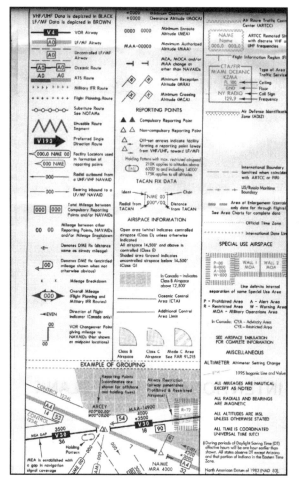

A guide to the information provided in NOS charts.

VOR route, draw a line from the VOR to the point where you want to go. For example, page ten shows the Charlotte, N.C. area. If, for example, you wanted to travel from Charlotte/Douglas International to Lincoln Co. using a VOR route, you would draw a line from the Charlotte VOR to Lincoln Co. This line passes through Charlotte's R-330. After departing Charlotte/Douglas International, you would intercept the R-330 and track it to Lincoln.

Flight Simulator Challenges

The "Lost in the USA" series of challenges in Flight Simulator 98 is a good way to test your navigation skills. Go to Flights on the main menu and select Challenges. Choose the Lost in the USA (Basic) challenge.

While it boots up, take a look at the New York area map on page 39 of your Pilot's Guide. Your goal is to get to Martha's Vineyard airport which is located in the Cape Cod area. Conveniently, there is a VOR located at the airport. The challenge tells you that your aircraft will be located near Providence at the beginning. When the challenge begins to run, you will find yourself in the C-182S.

The first thing you should do is tune the Providence VOR (115.6) in NAV1 and identify it using the Morse code broadcast. Once you know you have it tuned it in okay, rotate the OBS until the needle centers. You will find the OBS centers with a TO flag at a setting of 210. Therefore, you are northeast of

Providence. If you take a look at your DME, you will find that you are six miles from the VOR.

Martha's Vineyard is at the edge of your reception range at this time. It's an H class VOR, but you are about 60 miles away at a very low attitude. You should probably start tracking the Providence VOR to Martha's Vineyard while you gain about 1000 feet of altitude. Turn the Martha's Vineyard VOR (114.5) in NAV2 and wait for it to come in.

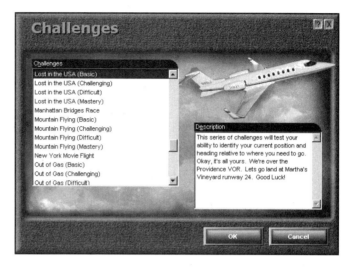

Flight Simulator Challenges can test your navigational skills.

To track the Providence VOR, draw a line from Providence to Martha's Vineyard. You will see that this line passes through the 140 mark of the Providence VOR. Turn this heading into your VOR. Once you start receiving the Martha's Vineyard VOR, track it directly to the airport.

Flight Simulator Cross Country

Flight Simulator also has a series of cross country flights to test your VOR navigational skills. Go to Flights and select Challenges. Choose the Cross Country (Challenging) option. You'll also need to take a look at the Seattle map on page 45 of your Pilot's Guide.

This lesson begins with you in the C-182S at Paine Field. For the first leg of the journey, you are to travel to the Tatoosh VOR. To simulate procedural instrument flying, you should use the Paine VOR for the first half of the journey and then switch to the Tatoosh VOR. Use the DME to identify when you are half-way between the two stations. The upper right-hand corner of the map contains a distance scale. From this, you can calculate that Tatoosh and Paine are approximately 80 miles apart. Therefore, you would switch from Paine to Tatoosh at 40 DME. These VORs are H-class and the frequencies are above 112.0, so you should not have any problems with reception.

You will find that Flight Simulator 98 has already tuned in the Paine VOR into NAV1. You should dial the Tatoosh frequency (112.2) into NAV2 so you know when you are in range of it. You need to determine what radial to track out of Paine. Draw a line from Paine to Tatoosh. You will see that the line passes through the 250 radial. Therefore, set the OBS to 250 and intercept this radial after takeoff. When you switch to the Tatoosh VOR, you should set Tatoosh into NAV1. By habit, you will find yourself using NAV1 as the primary navigation instrument.

After Tatoosh, you are headed for Hoquiam. Draw a line from Tatoosh to Hoquaim and you will determine you need to track the 150 radial out of Tatoosh. Set the OBS of NAV1 to 150 and tune in the Hoquaim VOR (117.7) on Nav 2. Center NAV1 with a FROM indication and change VORs around a DME indication of 40.

The lesson continues onto Astoria. Astoria is located on the 150 radial off Hoquaim. Astoria to Olympia will find you on the R-020 off of Astoria. Finally, to get back home, you will follow the R-020 off of Olympia all the way to Paine Airport.

The NDB Explained

Before VORS, the non-directional radio beacon (NDB) was the primary navigational tool. The term "non-directional" in the title refers to the fact that a ground-based NDB emits radio waves in all directions. These frequencies are located between 190-535 kHz.

Basic Radio Navigation

Since AM radio stations broadcast in the 540-1650 kHz range, these stations can also be tuned in on the ADF. Because the receiver can pick up commercial broadcasts, these public broadcasts were once used as part of the navigation system. To ensure they were following the signals from the correct station, a flight crew would call an airline representative on the ground who would then in turn call the radio station. The DJ would then greet the flight with a statement similar to "Pan Am flight 100, welcome to KAAF!"

The ADF (automatic direction finder) installed in your cockpit picks up these frequencies just like a radio receiver. The ADF can actually receive frequencies anywhere between 200 and 1600 kHz. Since NDBs are in the L/F and M/F

bands, reception range won't change regardless of the altitude at which you're flying.

NDB routes have essentially disappeared and been replaced by the VOR en-route navigation system. However, NDBs are far from being extinct. They are still found at numerous airports because they are very cheap compared to other types of navigation aids. They allow small general aviation airports to install their very own instrument landing systems. There are a number of these systems in use throughout the mid-western United States.

How the ADF Works

The three main components of the ADF are the receiver, antenna system, and instrument display. The ADF receiver display is the equipment installed in the instrument panel. It allows you to tune in the NDB frequency you want to track.

Antenna System

The antenna system consists of the loop and sense antennas. They are installed on the outside of the aircraft, usually on the belly. The loop antenna, which is shaped like a loop, rotates in a circle. When it is bombarded by the NDB wave, the current created in the loop varies depending on the position of the loop.

If the loop is parallel to the wave, so that a point of the wave hits one side of the loop before arriving at the other side, the voltage on each side of the loop is different, forming a current in the loop. However, if the loop is perpendicular to the wave, both sides of the loop get hit by a particular portion of the wave at exactly same time. Thus, no current is created in the loop. This is called the *null position*. When the loop is in the null position, you know that the wave is essentially passing directly through the loop.

There's one problem—the receiver can't tell if the wave is coming from a point directly in front of the loop or from directly behind it. The signal received by the sense antenna provides the missing data so that the ADF can determine exactly where the radio wave originated.

The Automatic Direction Finder (ADF) picks up all sorts of signals, including AM radio broadcasts.

Receiver/Instrument Display

The ADF cockpit display is simply a needle pointing in the direction of the NDB. If the station is directly in front of the aircraft nose, the needle points straight up. If the NDB is directly behind the nose of the aircraft, the needle will appear straight down. This is a pretty straight-forward concept but for some reason pilots have a hard time using the instrument.

Much of this could be due to the complicated literature that describes the ADF. For some reason, the RB + MH = MB formula is used again and again to describe ADF use. This is fine for academics, but it's not very practical to use in flight. You don't want to be doing math in your head when you're trying to attitude instrument fly. This chapter will go over how you should really use the ADF, as we describe the three types of ADF displays.

Fixed-Card ADF

The first type of display is called the fixed-card ADF. It is also known as the relative bearing indicator (RBI). The RBI looks a lot like a heading indicator but with north always located at the top. Because the directional background remains stationery (i.e., north is always at the top), it gets its name "fixed-card" ADF.

Let's say the aircraft is northeast of an NDB and is on a heading of 250. You tune in the ADF and the needle points thirty degrees to the left at a heading of 330. The 330 degrees is called *relative bearing*.

To determine your bearing to the station, which is the course you would need to fly to get to the NDB, someone like your old Algebra teacher would have you plug values into the formula Relative Bearing + Magnetic Heading = Magnetic Bearing. In this case 330 + 250 = 580. To convert this to a compass heading, you would need to subtract 360 from the 580 to arrive at a value of 220. Thus, your direct course to the NDB is a heading of 220. That's in a situation without any wind. To calculate the bearing *from* the station, you will need to subtract 180 degrees from the 220.

Needless to say, that was quite a bit of work for a relatively routine task in the cockpit. Let's ditch the math. Instead, you can visually superimpose the ADF onto the heading indicator. Easing this task is the fact that the two displays are calibrated in the same increments. When you mentally place that 30-degree deflection on top of the directional gyro—*surprise!*—the needle

points right at 220, the very same heading you worked so hard at calculating earlier. To get your bearing from the station, simply look at the tail of the superimposed needle. As you can see, the visualization method greatly reduces workload in the cockpit. It also takes a lot of the mystery out of NDB navigation.

Use the heading indicator in conjunction with the ADF to determine your position accurately.

The RMI

The RMI (Radio Magnetic Indicator) is another type of ADF display. The needle on the display moves the same way as on the RBI. However, you no longer need to mentally move the needle onto the heading indicator. Instead, the background directional card of the RMI rotates like the directional gyro. Therefore, the ADF needle will always point to your magnetic bearing to the NDB. You get the same information as you would from the fixed-card ADF, but you no longer need to relate it to the directional gyro. It does this for you by automatically aligning itself with your magnetic heading. The 737 and Lear 45 come equipped with an RMI.

The Rotatable-Card ADF

The rotatable-card ADF is a mix of the RBI and RMI. The card can rotate so that north doesn't always find itself stuck at the top. However, it does not rotate automatically according to your heading. Instead you must manually adjust the card. Thus, the instrument is sometimes called the "poor man's RMI." Some pilots do not utilize this functionality because they feel manually rotating the card produces more work than it eliminates. This is especially true during instrument landings where you may make several minor heading adjustments, causing you to constantly fine-tune the ADF. However, when you first intercept a course, the rotatable card can be quite handy. Once you start tracking that course, you might want to just leave it set to north.

The general aviation panels in Flight Simulator 98 come standard with the rotatable-card ADF display. To rotate the card, click on the knob on the lower left-hand side of the display. If you click on the right side of the knob, a plus sign will appear and the card will move counter-clockwise. If you click on the left side, a minus sign will appear and the card will move clockwise.

Identifying the NDB

The ADF does not flag when it has lost a signal or has otherwise malfunctioned. It just keeps on pointing in a particular direction—it "sticks." Therefore, whenever you are using an NDB for navigation, you should continuously monitor its ID over the radio. The ID is essentially the code for the NDB broadcast in Morse code.

You should translate the Morse code to determine if it matches the identifier of the NDB you are tracking. Go into the Airport/Facility directory located on the World menu to get the NDB identifier. Once you are in the area of the Airport/Facility directory the NavAid is located in, activate the NavAids option.

Press Ctrl + 5 to listen to the ID of the NDB you have tuned in and compare the Morse code to the NDB identifier listed in your airport facility guide. Once you know you have the correct station tuned in, you should leave the ID broadcast on. It can get annoying after a while, so you might want to turn the volume down of the Navigation slider that's located on the Sound tab of the Preferences selection under Options, but you shouldn't turn it off. You want to turn down the volume rather than turn off the sound completely, because it's the only way to determine if you are still receiving a signal. Otherwise, you may follow a faulty signal.

Tracking a Course

The hardest part about tracking a course is first getting established on it. Let's say you're east of an NDB and wanted to track the 270-degree inbound *bearing to* an NDB. If you were established on the 270 bearing to the station, you would be on a compass heading of about 90 degrees depending on the wind conditions. Your outbound *bearing from* the station would be 90 degrees.

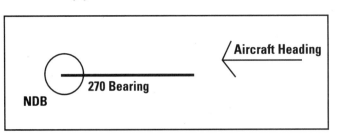

Tracking the 270 bearing to the station.

Determining Course Deviation and Intercept Angle

To determine how far off course you are, a sure-fire technique is to turn the aircraft to the same heading as your desired bearing to the station. Using the example above, you would turn to a heading of 270 degrees and observe where the needle is pointing. It will tell you right off what direction you need to turn to get to your course without you needing to perform an analysis—it points right to it!

It also gives you an idea of how big an intercept angle you should choose. If the needle has deflected to one side more than 45 degrees, you may want to intercept your course at a 45-degree angle. If it moved between five and 45 degrees, you may want to make a 30-degree intercept. For anything less than five degrees, you are pretty much already on your course. You should probably make a ten-degree "cut."

The ADF needle points to the NDB.

Suppose the needle was deflected 30 degrees to the left and was pointing at 330. Let's say you decide you don't want to be bothered using the rotatable-card feature of your ADF. Going back to the example, you can see that you are north of your desired bearing of 270 so you need to head south. This was determined by visualizing compass headings in your mind. If you didn't realize that, relax, the ADF is pointing left (which is south).

Since you are currently on the 240 radial to the station, you need to subtract thirty degrees from your current bearing. Since 240 - 30 = 210, you should make a left hand turn to 210. Alternatively, you could look at your DG and visually determine what heading is 30 degrees less than your current bearing. You are now on an intercept course for the 270 bearing to the NDB.

Determining When You're on Course

Notice that your ADF needle has now turned in the opposite direction. Continue on this heading until the needle "falls" to a deflection equal to our intercept angle. The total intercept angle is 60 degrees (270-210). Thus, when the needle is deflected 60 degrees, pointing at 060 on the ADF, you are located on the 270 bearing to the station. In your mind superimpose a needle pointed at

Intercepting the 270 bearing to the NDB.

Course interception is marked by the needle pointing to the correct bearing to the station.

Now you're back on track.

060 onto the DG. It would point right at a heading of 270.

If you were to then turn to a heading of 270, the needle should appear straight up. The aircraft is back on its inbound course.

If you were to go through the course, the needle would continue to fall past the 060 position. Overshooting the course in this example is shown on the next page.

Determining Course Interception with the Rotatable Card

Alternatively, you could have used the rotatable card option to more easily recognize when you are on course. After turning to a heading of 210, you could have also rotated the ADF card to 210. With the ADF card and heading indicator aligned, you know you're on your desired course when the ADF needle points to it.

In this case, the needle would point right at 270 when you were on the 270 bearing to the station.

As you can see, the rotatable card definitely has advantages. It would have been even easier using the RMI in the 737. You would have turned to 210 and just waited until the ADF pointer hit 270. Obviously, during intercepts, the rotatable card and RMI reduce workload. Reduced workload while navigating will allow you to concentrate on attitude instrument flying.

Wind Correction—Tracking Vs. Homing

Now that you're established on your track doesn't mean you can relax. The wind will most likely blow you off this course. You could just turn the aircraft nose to wherever the ADF needle is pointed and you would always be heading to the station. This is called "homing" and is a poor technique in either VFR or IFR flying. You will eventually get to the station, but not by following a predetermined track over the ground. In IFR flying, you are putting yourself at risk because you have no idea what you will hit when you fly off course.

The way to prevent this is to "crab" into the wind. By heading into the wind, you will compensate for the wind and will be able to stay on your bearing to the station. For example, if you're tracking the 270 bearing to the station and the wind is blowing from the south, you will be blown to the north and your ADF needle will turn to the left.

You are not sure how powerful the wind is, so it takes a bit of experimenting to find the proper crab correction. A good rule of thumb is to multiply the ADF deflection angle by two and turn by that many degrees into the wind. You should hold this intercept heading until the needle "falls" to your intercept angle.

Suppose the ADF deflected by ten degrees to the left while you were tracking inbound on the 270 bearing to the station. Therefore, you turned to a heading of 250 to intercept the 270. You waited until the needle "fell" to a value of 020 or until the superimposed needle pointed to a value of 270. You are now back on track. However, turning back to your original heading of 270 will only result in you being blown back off course to the north. Therefore, you should turn back *half* the distance and see what happens. In this case, you should turn to a heading of 260.

Since the aircraft nose is not pointed straight at the NDB, the ADF needle will show a ten-degree deflection to the right and point at a value of 010. If it stays there, the ten-degree crab correction is working. If you get blown off course again

Overshooting your desired course.

The rotatatble card feature of the ADF can help identify course interception.

The wind can blow you off course quickly.

Use a wind correction angle to stay on course when wind conditions exist.

to the north, you need to repeat the procedure, but this time with less of a crab. Since the 20-degree intercept brought you back to your course, you know that the heading you're looking for lies somewhere between a ten- and 20-degree angle. This time turn five more degrees into the wind. When your course comes in, turn back two and one-half degrees.

There's also a chance the ADF may "fall" below the ten-degree mark. In this case, your crab correction is too much. You repeat this procedure until you find a heading that will hold you on your desired inbound bearing. This technique is called *bracketing*. If you get confused during this process, simply turn back to your desired course (270) and start over.

Tracking an Outbound Course

To track an outbound course from an NDB, you apply the same principles. Since the NDB is behind you, the needle will point to a position behind you. Suppose you wanted to fly outbound on the 270-degree bearing to the station. You would be flying on a heading of 90 degrees.

Turn the aircraft to a heading of 090 to find out where you are in relation to your heading. If the needle points to the right, you are north of this bearing and need to turn to the right. If the deflection is around 30 degrees, you would intercept using a 30-degree intercept angle. Looking at your directional gyro, you can determine that a 30-degree intercept is a heading of 120 degrees. Make a right-hand turn to this heading. You make a right-hand turn simply because it is closer to the heading you want than a left-hand turn.

If you are using a rotatable-card ADF, rotate the card to a heading of 120 degrees. When the needle points to a heading of 270, you are on your desired radial. Turn the aircraft right to your outbound heading and the needle should be pointed straight down. Now you need to wait and see how the wind effects your track. You should also turn the ADF back to a northward heading. Now that you are tracking a course you don't want to have to be resetting the card to your compass

direction. You will now use the ADF as a fixed-card ADF.

Let's say the wind is from the south and pushes you back toward the north. Your ADF will show that you are drifting north by deflecting to the right. Basically, the ADF is saying "Hey—your course is *that* way!" You will now practice your bracketing procedures on an outbound course.

Turn back to your course using an angle equal to two times the needle deflection. Let's say this turns out to be 20 degrees. Fly a heading of 110. Notice that the ADF needle rises 20 degrees. Wait for the needle to "fall" until it shows a deflection of only 20 degrees. If it never reaches this value, you need to increase your crab angle. If it "falls" below this value, you went right through your desired course. You need to reduce your intercept angle. Once it is deflected to a value of 20 degrees, turn back half the distance. In this case, you would fly a heading of 110. Wait and see if this crab angle holds you on your outbound course. If it doesn't, you need to repeat the bracketing procedures until you capture the correct angle.

NDB Errors

There are several factors that reduce the accuracy of the ADF display. First of all, you must correlate the ADF display to your heading. Therefore, you must check that your directional gyro is still calibrated to the compass when using fixed-card or rotatable-card ADFs. You should reset your directional using "D" on the keyboard every 15 minutes unless you have your "gyro drift" flight setting turned off.

In addition, xit is vital that you maintain your desired heading without deviation. If you drift off your heading, you will have to repeat your intercept procedures to get back on your desired course. Practice your attitude instrument flying procedures until you can hold heading within three degrees.

NDB Practice Exercise

Go to Flights on the main menu and select Challenges. Choose the Cross Country (Difficult) challenge. You will need to look at page 61 of your Pilot's Guide as well.

The lesson begins with you tracking the 051 radial to Le Bourget (108.8). Once you pass over the VOR, you are to track to the ORLY NDB. If you draw a line from Le Bourget to ORLY, you will see that ORLY is located on R-175.

You will also notice when you pass over the VOR, the ADF needle when superimposed on the heading indicator points to 175. Turn to a heading of 175 and use the NDB as your primary method of navigation. The winds are calm so you should have too much trouble tracking the NDB course. You know you are at ORLY when the ADF needle reverses direction.

Chapter Six

An Overview of Charts

The radio navigation methods discussed in the last chapter allow you to fly from one location to another during periods of low visibility. Once you get to your final destination, these methods do not provide the ability to descend to the airport safely. Instrument approaches bridge the gap between en-route navigation and the aircraft wheels touching down on the ground.

Using radio navigation aids, instrument approaches provide both horizontal and vertical guidance to an airport. The aim of an approach is to get an aircraft as close and as low as possible to an airport so that the pilot will be able to identify the runway and land. Most approaches guide the aircraft to a point within 200 to 800 feet above an airport. Some will even guide the aircraft all the way down to the runway itself.

Approach procedures for specific airport runways are published on charts. This chapter will teach you how to read an instrument approach chart and how to fly basic approaches in Microsoft Flight Simulator 98.

Instrument Approaches

As mentioned above, an instrument approach allows you to descend from a cruising altitude to the airport below during periods of low visibility.

Approaches are not meant for en-route navigation. The approach begins with the aircraft already at a point near the airport. The approach can then provide a route the aircraft can follow to the airport.

An approach guides the aircraft to the runway.

Non-precision Approaches

Non-precision approaches provide horizontal and vertical guidance oriented to the runway or airport environment. Horizontal guidance ensures that the aircraft stays centered on an approach path to the airport. That is, the aircraft won't drift right or left of the published course. Vertical guidance is also provided in the form of altitude restrictions. The pilot must remain above altitudes specified in the approach procedure. Most non-precision approaches will allow the pilot to descend to 800 feet above ground level.

When a pilot descends to a lower altitude on a non-precision approach, there are recommended descent rates the pilot can follow. Refer to the IFR Approach Descent (non-precision) configurations presented in Chapter Three to determine what rate of descent you should use on non-precision approaches.

An airport may not have any instrument approaches due to the cost of installing an approach system. Others may have both precision and non-precision approaches. Most general aviation airports have non-precision approaches which rely on VOR and NDB navigation. These methods are less costly to install than precision approaches. Other types of non-precision approaches will be discussed in Chapter Seven.

Advanced Instrument Landing Systems

A category II ILS will usually allow an aircraft to descend to 100 feet above the ground, while category III ILS permits a plane to descend all the way to the ground. Both require special equipment and tend to be utilized only at very large airports. The list of equipment that FARs state must be installed in the aircraft can take a while to read through. Basically, the aircraft is full of dual instruments, including radar altimeters. Although some small general aviation aircraft have been approved by the FAA as meeting category II requirements, it's very unusual. It would seriously restrict the useful load available for a C-182 to take off with all that hardware onboard. In addition, the pilot must receive an endorsement from the FAA to fly these types of approaches.

Precision Approaches

Precision approaches are usually found at larger airports. Like non-precision approaches, they also provide horizontal and vertical guidance to the runway. However, the ground equipment used to guide the aircraft is more sophisticated than the equipment used in non-precision approaches. Therefore, an aircraft on

a precision approach can safely descend closer to the airport than one on a non-precision approach.

The horizontal guidance provided always leads the aircraft straight to a specific runway. In addition, the vertical guidance is constantly provided along the entire approach procedure. As a result, the pilot is also at the proper height and location.

The ground equipment used for these types of approaches can be very expensive. The most common precision approach is the ILS (Instrument Landing System). When the term ILS is used, the speaker is most likely referring to a category I ILS approach which usually allows an aircraft to descend to 200 feet above the ground, predicated on at least 1/2 mile visibility upon arrival at that point.

Circle-to-Land

A non-precision approach procedure may not lead the aircraft straight to a runway. The approach procedure has done its part in getting you as close as it could to the airport. Now it's up to you and your VFR skills to transition from instrument to visual skills and onto the ground, without flying back into IFR conditions.

Even if the approach is runway specific, a pilot may choose to circle-to-land on another runway. The pilot may do this if the winds favor landing on a different runway. It's better to land into the wind since it will help slow your ground speed. A pilot may also want to land on a longer runway or one closer to the parking area. Circle-to-land procedures will be described in detail in Chapter Seven.

Charts

Regardless of the type of approach, all are published in approximately the same format called *charts* (although they're also often referred to as *approach plates*). These charts provide you with all the details you need to know to properly execute a particular IFR approach. The two sources of approach charts are the United States NOS (National Ocean Service) Department and a private company called Jeppesen Sanderson. In addition, your Pilot's Handbook includes several approach charts.

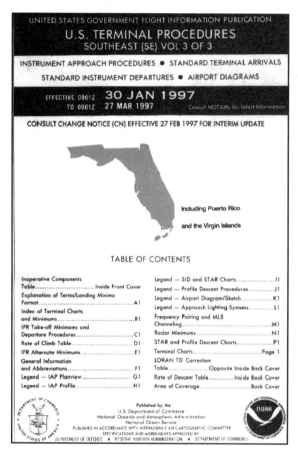

UNITED STATES GOVERNMENT FLIGHT INFORMATION PUBLICATION

U.S. TERMINAL PROCEDURES
SOUTHEAST (SE) VOL 3 OF 3

INSTRUMENT APPROACH PROCEDURES ● STANDARD TERMINAL ARRIVALS

STANDARD INSTRUMENT DEPARTURES ● AIRPORT DIAGRAMS

EFFECTIVE 0901Z **30 JAN 1997**
TO 0901Z **27 MAR 1997**   Consult NOTAMs for latest information

CONSULT CHANGE NOTICE (CN) EFFECTIVE 27 FEB 1997 FOR INTERIM UPDATE

Including Puerto Rico

and the Virgin Islands

TABLE OF CONTENTS

Published by the
U.S. Department of Commerce
National Oceanic and Atmospheric Administration
National Ocean Service
PUBLISHED IN ACCORDANCE WITH INTERAGENCY AIR CARTOGRAPHIC COMMITTEE
SPECIFICATIONS AND AGREEMENTS APPROVED BY
DEPARTMENT OF DEFENSE ● FEDERAL AVIATION ADMINISTRATION ● DEPARTMENT OF COMMERCE

The cover of a set of NOS charts.

NOS, Jeppesen, and your Pilot's Handbook charts provide the same information. Many commercial pilots tend to buy subscriptions to Jeppesen because they feel the charts present the information in a format that is easier to read. NOS charts, on the other hand, are cheaper. The symbols used on each type of chart differ slightly. You can reference the legend included in the chart package of the set you choose to determine what every detail means. The legend for the Pilot's Handbook charts is on page seven.

NOS Charts

NOS charts, officially called U.S. Terminal Procedures, can be purchased at your local FBO (Fixed Based Operator). These are the folks at your general aviation airport that sell fuel, rent small airplanes, and hanger aircraft.

NOS reprints charts every 56 days and pilots are required to have the most current editions when making an IFR approach. You never know when a new radio tower or building has been constructed on the approach path. Since you won't have this problem with Flight Simulator 98, you may want to find out when the latest batch of approach charts expires and head to the FBO at that time and try to get some old and expired ones for free. They will probably rip the front cover off and give them to you. Seventeen volumes of U.S. Terminal Procedures cover all the IFR approaches in the entire continental U.S. Each of these volumes costs around $4.00.

Less fun than an outing to the FBO is ordering charts directly from the government, either by calling (800) 638-8972 or contacting NOS via the Internet at www.nos.noaa.gov /aaa/welcome.html.

U.S. Terminal Procedures contain much more information than just the approach charts (NOS refers to these as terminal charts). Several pages of the Terminal Procedures are

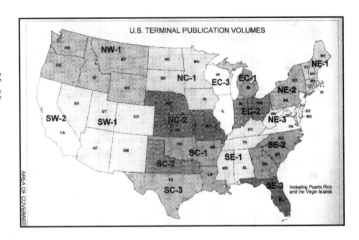

NOS charts are published by area.

dedicated to a legend. Several symbols may appear on a chart and it is unlikely you will always remember them all. When you first buy charts you should take some time and review all the symbols before moving on to the approach charts.

Also included in the front of the NOS booklet is the inoperative components table. How low you can descend on an approach depends often on what approach lighting is available at the airport and how runway visibility is measured. However, if one of these components is malfunctioning, the approach can still be completed if a higher minimum visibility is used. The inoperative components table is used to determine how much the visibility requirement needs to be increased to legally complete the approach. Various other pieces of general information are also presented in the Terminal Procedures booklet.

Jeppesen Charts

A Jeppesen subscription can supply all your chart needs. Jeppesen is also a convenient one-stop source to get international charts. The charts are hole-punched so they can be placed in a binder. After receiving an initial edition, Jeppesen will send you updates of only those charts which have been changed. The old chart must be removed from your edition and replaced with the latest updated chart.

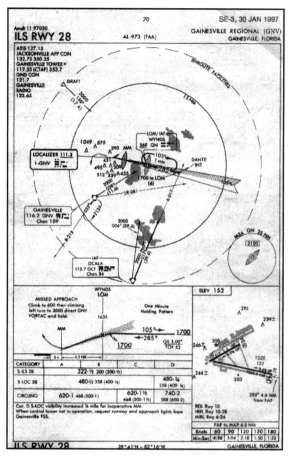

An approach chart for runway 28 at GNV.

Some pilots like this while others find it a hassle. Jeppesen has recently launched a new program where charts for your local area can be purchased at your local FBO like NOS charts. Instead of replacing individual charts, you simply throw out the old charts and put the new charts in your binder. To compete with Jeppesen, NOS charts can now be purchased hole-punched so that they can be organized in a binder. To order Jeppesen charts, call (800) 621-5377.

Jeppesen charts also contain additional information such as a legend and inoperative components information. Jeppesen prints *descents minima* on individual charts (how low the aircraft can descend if a component is inoperable) so that the pilot does not have to mentally calculate it.

In addition, you can order NOS and Jepp plates through supply catalogs. One popular source is Sporty's Pilot shop. You can order a catalog by dialing 1-800-LIFT-OFF. Sporty's has all sorts or aviation paraphernalia from charts to jackets and offers several videos on instrument flight. A software package called Final Approach can also be used to reproduce charts.

Pilot's Handbook Charts

Your Pilot's Handbook contains several charts. The following table specifies what approaches are included.

Airport	Approach	Page
Hartsfield Atlanta International	ILS Rwy 8L	9
Charlotte/Douglas International	ILS Rwy 36L	11
University of Illinois-Willard	ILS Rwy 32	13
Cleveland-Hopkins International	ILS Rwy 28	16
Dallas-Fort Worth	ILS Rwy 18R	18
Denver International	ILS Rwy 35L	20
Detroit Metro Wayne County	ILS Rwy 3L	22
Hilo International	ILS Rwy 26	25
Honolulu International	ILS Rwy 4R	26
Kahului	NDB Rwy 20	26
Houston Intercontinental	ILS Rwy 26	29
Los Angeles International	ILS Rwy 24R	32
Van Nuys	ILS Rwy 16R	33
Miami International	ILS Rwy 9L	35
Martha's Vineyard	ILS Rwy 24	39
San Diego International	ILS Rwy 9	42
Snohomish County	ILS Rwy 16R	46

An Overview of Approaches

All IFR approaches are composed of the following elements:

- Feeder Route (Arrival Segment)
- Initial Approach Segment
- Intermediate Approach segment
- Final Approach Segment
- Missed Approach Segment

Feeder Route (Arrival Segment)

When travelling an airway, you need a way to transition from your current heading to a point on the approach. Specifically, you want to get to the initial approach fix (IAF) which is the starting point of any approach. The feeder route (also known as the arrival segment) provides you with this ability.

The feeder route is usually a course flown from a VOR or NDB located on your en-route airway. The approach chart will specify the NavAid to use, the minimum altitude to fly, the course to fly, and the distance from the NavAid to the IAF. A chart may have several feeder routes to the IAF or conversely, no feeder routes at all. If no feeder route is shown, it means that your en-route navigation airway will provide a method to get to the IAF. On the other hand, there may be multiple feeder routes to the IAF.

An approach may have more than one IAF, each with its own feeder route. You would choose the most convenient one. On the feeder route, you should get into your approach-level configuration. Refer to Chapter Three for the configuration which applies to the aircraft you are flying.

Initial Approach Segment

Once the aircraft is at the IAF, it may not be lined up on the approach path to the airport. For example, you might arrive at the IAF for an approach into the due-north runway and you are currently heading due-south. In addition, the IAF may not be located on the final approach segment.

The initial approach segment provides a method to turn the aircraft to the correct heading for the approach path with assured obstacle clearance. This segment will also give you some distance to lose altitude that you were required to keep on the feeder route, if the approach allows you to descend to a lower altitude.

The procedure turn is the most commonly used method to turn around. Basically, you fly an outbound course for one minute and then turn back towards the IAF on an intercept course for the inbound path. Normally, the pilot can use his own discretion to determine at what angle to make the procedure turn. The requirement is that the pilot must turn in the same direction as the approach chart indicates. This turn is usually made at 90 or 45 degrees in relation to the outbound course. NOS approach charts illustrate the procedure turn using a 45-degree angle and this is what most pilots use.

For example, if the approach outbound course is 174 degrees, a right-hand procedure turn would be made to 219. Other initial approach segment techniques such as holding patterns will be described in detail in Chapters Seven and Eight. When you first pass over the IAF, you usually fly an outbound heading for approximately two minutes. You would then execute your outbound procedure turn for one minute. You can shorten these times if you like, but

make sure you leave yourself enough time to stabilize the aircraft for the approach and give yourself a chance to catch your breath since many things happen in rapid succession during the approach. If you like, you can also lengthen these times to give yourself more time to stabilize the aircraft. You should be using your approach level IFR attitude/power configuration during this phase. Just remember that you should stay within a ten-mile radius of the main navigational aid used in the approach.

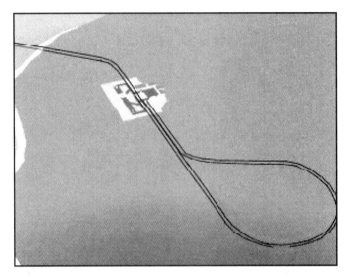

A procedure turn will turn an aircraft around during an approach.

Intermediate Approach Segment

The intermediate approach segment begins when the aircraft has finished the initial approach segment and is aligned with the inbound course to the airport. It transitions the initial and final approach segments.

Occasionally, radar vectors will be given by ATC so that the aircraft flies directly to the final approach segment, bypassing the need for the initial and intermediate segments. This is called performing a *vectored approach*. Many of the lessons and challenges in Flight Simulator 98 will allow you to perform vectored approaches.

Approaches that use all the initial and intermediate approach segments are termed *full approaches*. Radar-vectored approaches are easy after mastering full approach techniques. Most ILS approaches are performed at airports with ATC control. Therefore, very few full approach ILSs are actually performed.

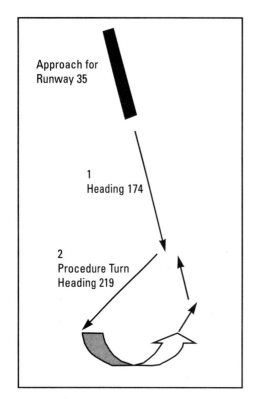

Approach for
Runway 35

1
Heading 174

2
Procedure Turn
Heading 219

A right hand procedure turn.

Final Approach Segment (Non-precision Approach)

The final approach segment is the point when the aircraft begins its final descent for landing. On a non-precision approach, the final approach segment begins at the final approach (FAF) fix. The FAF may be the same NavAid used as the IAF. The less NavAids used on the approach, the easier it is to tune in frequencies and execute the approach procedure.

The final approach segment ends at the MAP (Missed Approach Point) rather than at a specific altitude. When you reach the MAP depends on where the NavAid you are tracking to the airport is located. If the NavAid you are tracking is located right on the airport, the MAP is the point when you pass over the NavAid.

If you are using an off-airport NavAid, you determine when you are at the MAP by measuring time. The distance from the FAF to MAP is on the approach plate, as are many time schedules (at the bottom) based upon various ground speeds You would start timing as soon as you passed over the NavAid. Based on this time and your ground speed, you will be able to determine your expected arrival at the MAP.

Because the MAP is not based on altitude, many pilots like to descend as quickly as possible on non-precision approaches. This allows them to get out of IFR conditions quicker and spot the airport sooner.

Final Approach Segment (Precision Approach)

On a precision approach, the final approach segment begins with a glide slope intercept, even if before the final approach point (FAF). This is the point located somewhere between 4 to 7 NM from the runway threshold. On the final

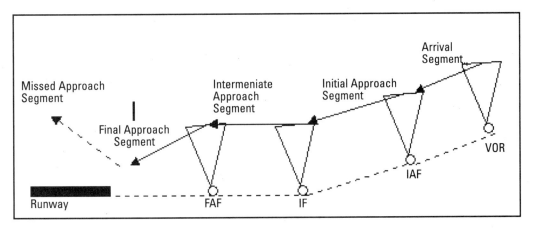

An approach begins with the arrival segment and ends with the final approach segment.

approach segment, you should use the approach descent configuration for your aircraft to efficiently get on the proper descent rate and airspeed.

Because the pilot descends on a clearly defined vertical glide path to the airport during a precision approach, the MAP is always encountered at a specified altitude. This altitude is called *decision height* (DH) and you must execute the missed approach procedure as soon as you arrived at that attitude—unless, of course, you have visual contact with the runway.

Missed Approach Segment

Hopefully, you will see the runway at the end of the final approach segment and make a landing. If not, you will need to go ahead and execute the missed approach procedures.

Usually, the aircraft climbs to a specific fix and flies in a holding pattern oval around it until the pilot is ready to attempt another approach or move on to a different airport to attempt a landing there. You should review this procedure before you get to the MAP or DH because when you need to do it, it must be mandatory and precise. You should execute the missed approach any time you get significantly off your approach path. For example, if you get a full-scale CDI deflection, you should just start climbing at your cruise climb configuration .

If the missed approach procedure specifies a turn and you are executing it early, you should climb first in the direction of the approach course. You do not want to make a turn earlier than the approach chart specifies.

Reading a Chart

It's a shock the first time you look at a chart. Don't panic. It's like the first time you looked at the cockpit of the 737. It's intimidating at first, but with some time and effort, it's soon easily understood. You will soon find charts fun to read and perform. They all have the same basic elements. These are the identification margin, the plan view, the profile view, missed approach procedure, approach minimums, and runway chart. Let's take a closer look at what each of these are.

Identification Margin

The top margin shows the type of approach (NDB, VOR, ILS, etc.) and the runway designated. Runways are named according to compass heading alignment with the last digit dropped. For example, the southwest runway heading in a compass direction of 230 degrees is called 23 ("Two three"). The north northeast runway heading in a compass direction of 100 degrees is called 10 ("One zero"). The north northeast runway heading in a compass direction of 090 is called nine ("Nine"). You may find an R, L, or C listed after the runway number. Some airports may have two or three runways all heading in the same compass direction. The R stands for the runway on the right as you are approaching for landing. Likewise, the L stands for the runway on left while C represents the runway in the center.

Some approach plates have an A or B listed instead of a runway number. This is because the approach doesn't line up with a specific runway. Instead, it takes the aircraft to the airport where you must then fend for yourself in getting lined up with a runway. The letter 'A' identifies the first approach leading to the airport, the letter 'B' identifies the second approach leading to the airport, etc.

	70	SE-3, 30 JAN 1997
Amdt 11 97030		GAINESVILLE REGIONAL (GNV)
ILS RWY 28	AL-973 (FAA)	GAINESVILLE, FLORIDA

The identification margin.

An approach is designated with a letter rather than a runway number when the approach path is at an angle greater than 30

degrees from a runway centerline. Thirty degrees is a lot considering you will most likely be in low visibility. When you break out, you should not look for the runway straight ahead of you but at a point 30 degrees to the side. The runway chart will aid you in determining where to look for the runway.

A pilot may perform a "side-step" maneuver. This is done when an approach is made for one runway and the pilot maneuvers to land on a parallel runway after entering visual conditions. This side-step maneuver can be executed only when the parallel runway is not more than 1200 feet away. A pilot may do this wanting a longer runway—or perhaps a shorter taxi time to the airport lounge.

The right side of the top margin shows the airport name and three-letter airport identifier. It also shows the city where the airport is located.

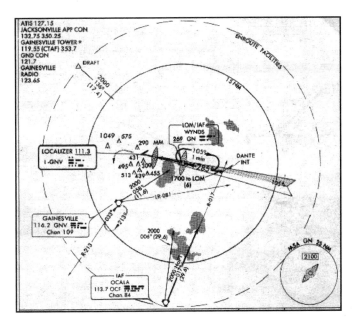

The plan view.

Plan View

The next part of the approach plate is the plan view. It's a picture of the approach as if you were looking down on it. This is why it is sometimes called the "bird's eye view." Basically, it shows the track of the approach over the ground.

The upper right corner of the plan view lists important radio frequencies. Notice that two sets of frequencies are given. The high bands are used by the military. Civilian aircraft, like those featured in Flight Simulator 98, should use the lower bands.

```
ATIS 127.15
JACKSONVILLE APP CON
132.75 350.25
GAINESVILLE TOWER *
119.55 (CTAF) 353.7
GND CON
121.7                    DR.A
GAINESVILLE      △
RADIO
123.65
```

Frequencies used during the approach.

The ATIS frequency broadcasts a continuous recording of airport information which includes current weather, ceiling (clouds), visibility, temperature, dew point (a temperature/humidity index), magnetic wind direction and velocity, altimeter setting, runway use, and cautionary advisories that are updated hourly. Each update has a code word using the phonetic alphabet (Alpha, Beta , Charlie, etc.). To verify the pilot has the most current information, he or she tells ATC the code word of the information. To get ATIS information in Flight Simulator, choose Aircraft from the Main Menu and select Communications. Activate the option Replay ATIS information.

The next frequency given is approach control. Approach will keep the aircraft clear of other traffic and will eventually tell the pilot to contact the airport tower when the aircraft is established on the approach procedure. One ATC agency passing an aircraft to another ATC agency is known as a "hand-off." After landing on the ground, the tower will hand the pilot off to ground control. The clearance delivery frequency is used before takeoff to receive an IFR clearance.

In Flight Simulator 98, adventures such as "Dallas to Denver: Boeing 737-400," can simulate ATC components. Otherwise, only the ATIS and tower frequencies can be simulated on flights.

MSA

You will find a large circle around the main navigation aid used in the approach in the plan view. This circle has a radius of 10 NM on NOS and 5 NM on Jepp charts. Any tall obstacles are illustrated within this ring. The pilot can use these as a visual reference when he breaks into VFR conditions.

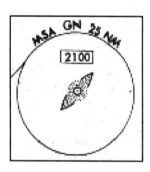

Stay above the MSA and you won't hit any obstacles in the area.

This circle also serves to remind the pilot the importance of staying on the approach path. If a pilot chooses a circle-to-land approach, he may want to consider where these obstacles are located before going ahead and maneuvering around the airport area.

In the plan view you will find a circle titled MSA (Minimum Safe Altitude). If you stay within a 25-mile radius of the object identified in the middle of the circle at the altitude specified, you are guaranteed not to hit anything. In fact, you will be at least 1000 feet above any obstacle in that range.

However, this altitude will not guarantee that you will pick up any navigation radio signals. How important this is in Flight Simulator 98 depends on whether the tall obstacles are located in your scenery file and your Scenery Density setting.

MSA is sometimes referred to as *emergency minimum altitude*. Sometimes the circle may be segmented into several regions, each with its own MSA. The object in the middle of the circle is usually an NDB or VOR.

Other Items

If a feeder route is used, it will be illustrated on the chart along with the initial, intermediate, final and missed approach paths. Some approach plates say "RADAR REQUIRED." Usually, this means that the IAF cannot be found using the instruments in the pilot's cockpit and ATC must guide the pilot to it. Occasionally, the phrase "NO PT" will be printed on the approach chart. This means that a procedure turn is not allowed under any conditions. This is usually done because of an obstruction of some sort making a procedure turn dangerous. The chart will provide an alternative method of heading back to the airport. Notice that the plan view did not specify any altitudes It simply gives heading information. Altitude information is found in the profile view.

Profile View

The profile view is found below the plan view. The profile view shows the approach procedure as if looking at it from the side rather than from the top. Therefore, the pilot can determine what altitude the aircraft must be above at during each phase of the approach.

The FAF for non-precision approaches is shown on the profile view as a Maltese cross. For ILS approaches, the Maltese cross represents the altitude at which you can confirm you are correctly tracking the glide slope. Above the Maltese cross is an altitude

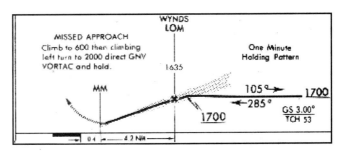

The profile view.

without any bold font. This represents the altitude you should maintain if you are on the glide slope over the outer marker. Also shown is the glide slow descent angle (which is usually around 3.00 degrees), the TCH (Threshold Crossing Height), and useful horizontal distance information in nautical miles.

If the altitude is underlined it means you cannot go below that altitude. If it also has a line above it, you can not go above that altitude. If it has no lines, it is only a recommended altitude. The altitudes shown are in MSL.

Missed Approach Procedure

Within the profile view area is a text description of the missed approach procedure. It describes clearly what altitude to climb to, what heading to follow, and what direction to turn. It complements the visual description drawn on the plan view.

Approach Minimums

The bottom center of the chart is the list of the "minimums." Minimum altitudes are set according to the performance category of the aircraft making the approach.

Performance category speed is calculated by multiplying 1.3 by the stall speed of the aircraft in a landing configuration at maximum gross landing weight. You then look at the performance category table to determine which category range the speed lies in. This speed should also be the speed at which the approach is performed. You will be making approaches at about 90 knots in the C-182S and should use category A minimums. Refer back to the IFR configurations table in Chapter Three to determine the approach speed for other aircraft in Flight Simulator 98.

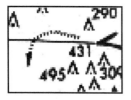

The missed approach procedure is your contingency plan during an approach.

Performance Categories

Category	Speed (knots)
A	0-90
B	91-120
C	121-141
D	141-165
E	Above 165

On non-precision approach charts, the HAA (Height Above Airport) is shown. This is the height above the highest point on the airport that the aircraft will ready at the end of the approach. Next to the minimum is the reported runway visibility required to

CATEGORY	A	B	C	D
S-ILS 28	322-½ 200 (200-½)			
S-LOC 28	480-½ 358 (400 ½)			480-¾ 358 (400-¾)
CIRCLING	620-1 468 (500-1)		620-1½ 468 (500-1½)	740-2 588 (600-2)

Cat. D S-LOC visibility increased ¼ mile for inoperative MM.
When control tower not in operation, request runway and approach lights from Gainesville FSS.

You cannot descend below these minimums if the runway is not in view.

make the approach. If a transmissometer (a visual measurement device) is located on the runway, the visibility will be listed as RVR (Runway Visual Range). The required RVR is listed on the approach plate in hundreds of feet. If no transmissometer is at the airport, visibility minimums will be listed as statute miles.

On precision approach charts, the HAT (Height Above [runway] Threshold) is displayed. This is the height above the runway threshold the aircraft will ready at the end of the approach. Notice that following each minimum is a second set of minimums in parenthesis. These minimums are for use by the military only. In addition, several sets of minimums may be shown. An approach procedure may be made for a certain runway but if you

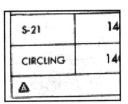

S-21	14
CIRCLING	14(
⚠	

This airport has special requirements if it is to be used as an alternative airport.

decide to circle to land for another runway, you must use different minimums. A circle-to-land maneuver requires additional altitude to be achieved safely. Therefore, one set of numbers will be listed for the circle-to-land maneuver (indicated by the word *circling*) and one for the straight in approach (indicated by an 'S').

Sometimes increased minimums will be listed if a distant ATC facility provides the current altimeter pressure setting. An ILS can be completed as an ILS or a LOC (Localizer) approach. A Localizer approach uses alignment but not glide slope, and is therefore a non-precision approach. If the LOC is performed, as described in Chapter Seven, it will have its own minimum requirements listed in the table.

If an airport does not report the runway visual range you can convert the minimums to statute miles. In Flight Simulator 98, you can always determine visibility. However, to mimic actual IFR flight, you many want to increase minimums at certain times using the following table:

Increased Visibility Minimums

RVR (feet)	Visibility (statute miles)
1600	1/4
2000	3/8
2400	1/2
3200	5/8
4000	3/4
4500	7/8
5000	1
6000	1 and 1/4

Approach charts also contain information not specific to the approach. For example, you may also see a triangle with an 'A' or 'T' inside it. The 'T' means that special IFR takeoff procedures apply for this airport. Before takeoff, you should check out the takeoff minimums section of the NOS booklet to determine what special requirements exist. If the 'A' appears, special rules exist if the airport is to be used as the alternate airport filed on the IFR flight plan. This may be due to tall obstacles near the airport.

Runway Chart

At the far right of the chart is an illustration of the airport. It shows the HAA and HAT along with other information such as obstacles close to the airport. This is especially important to know if you plan to make a circle-to-land maneuver. Also shown is the tract of the approach path to the airport. This is important because the path can be off by the runway centerline by as much as 30 degrees. When breaking out of the clouds near minimums, you need to know where to look for the runway. This can be particularly confusing when you have a crab angle set up to counteract the wind.

At the lower right-hand section of the chart is a matrix of times. To determine when some non-precision approaches are over, you must watch how much time has elapsed since passing over the FAF. The duration for which you are waiting is listed in this chart. The time varies with the ground speed of the aircraft. For the practice approaches you do in the C-182S, you will most likely make the approaches at 90 knots. You can use a speed not listed in the table but you will need to extrapolate the time value. To simplify matters in the cockpit, you should try to use one of the ground speeds provided in the table.

Be careful using these values since they change depending on the wind conditions. If you have a tailwind or headwind, you need to calculate your actual ground speed using the techniques presented in Chapter Three. Then use the matrix which applies to this speed.

Advanced Chart Reading

Occasionally, a DME arc is used as the initial segment of the approach. Basically, you complete an arc around a VOR at a fixed DME distance. You continue this arc until you intercept the inbound approach path. The arc is drawn on the approach chart with the attitude you should fly it, the VOR's three-letter identifier, direction of the arc, and the DME distance you want to keep from the VOR.

The DME arc begins with you following a feeder route towards the VOR. When the DME display shows you to be on the DME arc, you are at the IAF and should turn in the direction illustrated on the chart. You should keep making turns so that you are always a fixed distance away from the VOR. Eventually, you will find yourself on the inbound course designated on the approach chart. You should turn to that inbound course and execute the approach as normal. Chapter Seven will illustrate flying a DME arc.

Another type of initial approach segment is the holding pattern. When you cross the fix, you enter a race track pattern around the fix. When you are on the inbound leg, you will follow normal approach procedures. Holding pattern entries include the direct, parallel, and teardrop maneuvers. These will be described in further detail in Chapter Eight.

A handy symbol on approach charts is the *leading radial*. It acts as a reference radial. It is represented on NOS charts as an arrow designated by the two-letter code "LR" followed by the radial it uses. Basically, it is

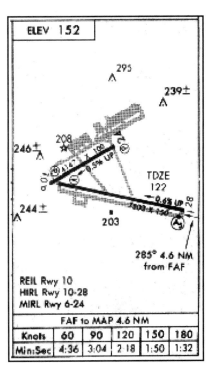

The runway chart.

FAF to MAP 4.6 NM					
Knots	60	90	120	150	180
Min:Sec	4:36	3:04	2:18	1:50	1:32

FAF Time Matrix.

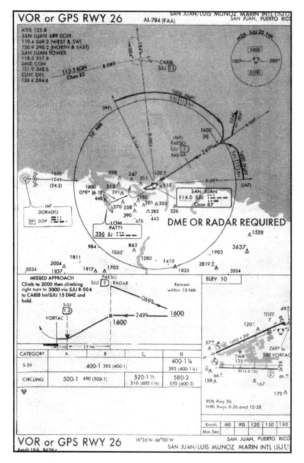

A DME arc is used on the San Juan approach.

used to help you intercept the approach inbound course. Often a feeder route will intersect the approach course at a difficult angle that's hard to track. Instead of using a procedure turn to get lined up with the inbound course, you can turn toward your inbound heading early when a leading radial is in place. When you intersect the leading radial, you can start to turn toward the inbound course. The GNV ILS chart uses a leading radial.

You will notice on the profile view of some approaches that you can descend to a certain point, but then must stop until you reach another fix. The Detroit Metro Wayne ILS Runway 3L on page 22 of your Pilot's Handbook is a good example of this. Once you are past that fix you can begin to descend again. This may occur several times on the approach. This is called a *multiple step-down approach*.

These fixes are usually DME indications or radial intersections. If you do not have the navigation equipment to pick up these step-down fixes, you cannot go to the next set of minimum altitudes. You should have the equipment loaded in your aircraft to identify these fixes on any approach you choose to do—unless some are inoperative. Unfortunately, if this happens, ATC cannot point them out to you as they would during actual flight.

EFIS

The Electronic Flight Instrument System in Flight Simulator 98 visually presents the approach path you should fly to the airport. It creates a series of graphics you can follow down to the airport. You can also lock the EFIS to the ILS you are following.

To turn EFIS on, select Aircraft from the main menu and select Navigation. Click on the EFIS/CDPD tab and activate the EFIS master switch. However, to realistically simulate IFR flight, you should keep EFIS turned off.

Picking out Charts and Setting Up for Approaches

With Flight Simulator 98, you have a distinct advantage over pilots engaged in actual IFR flight training. By merely clicking "Go To Airport," you gain access to over 3000 airports! Most of these airports have several approaches into them. Just because you go to a particular airport and are set up on Runway 9 doesn't mean you can only make the approaches for 9. The NavAids around the airport allow you to use any approach into the airport.

This is an IFR pilot's dream. When they practice approaches, they are limited to the same old approaches they have made during every previous flight. There may not even be certain types of approaches in that area. My advice is to take full advantage of this opportunity—practice as many different types of approaches as possible.

Several adventures are already set up in Flight Simulator 98 for ILS-vectored approaches like the Space Center Executive ILS 36 in the C-182. Although it is not set up in actual IFR conditions, it's a realistic radar-vectored approach to try. In addition, with the program setting up the radios, you can concentrate on fine-tuning the IFR configurations needed to fly the aircraft according to your exact performance requirements.

Flight Simulator 98 has lessons for full approaches as well. You should get some additional training on the ILS with procedure turn into MacArthur Field or the VOR with procedure turn into Flying Cloud. Once you master the lessons, you can perform full approaches into any airport for which you have a chart. You might want to try some simple ones first like the NDB 7 into Marathon Key. The complexity of an approach can usually be gauged by the amount of "stuff" on the chart. Basically, take off and fly outbound so that you get established on the feeder route.

To simulate your own vectored approach, fly outbound for about ten minutes in a direction downwind of the inbound approach course. Again, use slew to speed the process. Then turn to intercept the approach course, using an angle of about 30 degrees.

Before takeoff, get your navigation equipment set up with the right frequencies and set the weather dialog to approach minimums. The next chapter will give some helpful hints on handling approaches.

VOR Lesson 1

Let's make the VOR practice approach in Flight Simulator 98. Select Flights from the main menu and choose Lessons. Select the VOR Approach with procedure turn for the Cessna Skylane RG.

This lesson takes place in visual meteorological conditions (VMC). When you are first learning the procedure, leave the weather conditions alone so you can benefit from the flight instructor's suggestions (provided by the lesson). Once you feel you don't need the instructor's prompting, change the weather so that you can practice the approach under actual IFR skies. To do this, press P to pause the lesson. Select World from the main menu and choose Weather. Click on the Clouds tab and set the Cloud type to Cumulus and Coverage to Overcast. Set the Cloud base to 1500 feet MSL and the Cloud top to 5000 feet MSL. This will keep you in IFR conditions until you are at the end of the approach procedure. Click on the Visibility tab and set visibility to two

Try the VOR approach Flight Simulator lesson to perform an approach.

miles. Press P again to resume the lesson.

The lesson asks you to perform the full VOR approach to Runway 9 at Flying Cloud airport in Minneapolis. The lesson refers you to an approach chart in your Pilot's Handbook. However, you will find that this is an error and the approach chart is *not* included in the handbook.

When the lesson begins, you will find yourself at an altitude of 4000 feet MSL in the Cessna 182RG. NAV1 will be set to the Flying Cloud VOR and you will be tracking inbound on R-080, on a westerly heading.

While you are tracking to the VOR, get into your IFR approach level configuration, as presented in Chapter Four. Use the same settings for the C-182RG that were presented for the C-182S. You'll want to get your airspeed down to 90 knots. The final descent to the

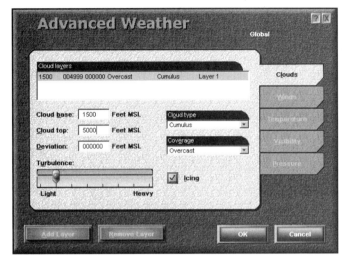

Set the visibility to two miles and a low cloud ceiling to increase the difficulty of the lesson.

Tracking R-080 to Flying Cloud.

airport will be made at 90 knots. The sooner you get the aircraft slowed to this speed, the less you will need to do later on.

Continue tracking the R-080 until you pass over the VOR. Since the OBS is set to 260, the receiver flag will display the TO indication (triangle pointing up). As you approach the VOR, you will enter the cone of confusion and the TO indication will change to the "No Signal Received" indication (a red and

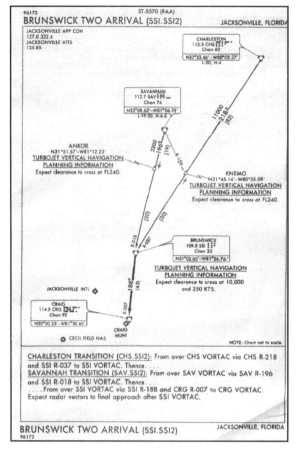

96172
ST-5570 (FAA)

BRUNSWICK TWO ARRIVAL (SSI.SSI2)
JACKSONVILLE, FLORIDA

JACKSONVILLE APP CON
127.0 322.4
JACKSONVILLE ATIS
125.85

CHARLESTON
113.5 CHS
Chan 82
N32°53.66'-W80°02.27'
L-20, H-4

SAVANNAH
112.7 SAV
Chan 74
N32°09.63'-W81°06.75'
L-19-20, H-4-5

ANKOR
N31°51.57'-W81°12.23'
TURBOJET VERTICAL NAVIGATION
PLANNING INFORMATION
Expect clearance to cross at FL240.

11000
2182
(92)

2200
1982
(19)

R-150

KNEMO
N31°45.14'-W80°55.08'
TURBOJET VERTICAL NAVIGATION
PLANNING INFORMATION
Expect clearance to cross at FL240.

R-018
R-037

BRUNSWICK
109.8 SSI
Chan 35
N31°03.03'-W81°26.76'

TURBOJET VERTICAL NAVIGATION
PLANNING INFORMATION
Expect clearance to cross at 10,000
and 250 KTS.

JACKSONVILLE INTL

188°
(43)

CRAIG
114.5 CRG
Chan 92
N30°20.33'-W81°30.60'

R-007

CRAIG
MUNI

CECIL FIELD NAS

NOTE: Chart not to scale.

CHARLESTON TRANSITION (CHS.SSI2): From over CHS VORTAC via CHS R-218
and SSI R-037 to SSI VORTAC. Thence . . . .
SAVANNAH TRANSITION (SAV.SSI2): From over SAV VORTAC via SAV R-196
and SSI R-018 to SSI VORTAC. Thence . . . .
. . . . From over SSI VORTAC via SSI R-188 and CRG R-007 to CRG VORTAC.
Expect radar vectors to final approach after SSI VORTAC.

BRUNSWICK TWO ARRIVAL (SSI.SSI2)
JACKSONVILLE, FLORIDA
96172

Sample approach procedure chart.

white striped box). Continue tracking your last heading until you pass to the other side of the cone of confusion. At this point, the receiver flag will change to the FROM indication (triangle pointing down).

Now that you have passed over the Flying Cloud VOR, you want to get established on the inbound approach course of 096. To do this, you will first need to track outbound on this course. The outbound course is 276. Turn to a heading of 276 and set the NAV1 OBS to 276. Track this radial until the DME for NAV1 reads 5.4. At this point, you can start to make your procedure turn. You will want to turn the OBS to your inbound heading of 096 at this point. You want the OBS to match the inbound course so you won't have to worry about reverse sensing on your final descent to the airport. It would be procedurally illegal to do so. The earlier you set the OBS, the less you will have to worry about later.

From here you want to return to the inbound course. The approach specifies a left-hand procedure turn. To help you out, the approach tells you what is the heading for a 45-degree left-hand procedure. In this case, it's a heading of 231. After turning to this heading, use the clock on the upper left-hand side of the control panel to time one minute. When this minute is up you can turn back to the inbound course. The approach also specifies you can begin to descend to 2600 feet MSL.

After one minute is up, make a right-hand turn to re-intercept the inbound course. The lesson recommends a 30-degree turn. A standard-rate turn (18-

degree bank in the C-182RG) is easier to control in IFR weather. Keep turning until you are on a heading of 051.

As soon as the CDI begins to move, you know you are getting close to the inbound course. Begin a standard-rate turn to your inbound heading of 096. After you roll out on 096, make any corrections needed to get the needle centered. Once the needle is centered, you can begin the final approach segment. Using the IFR approach descent (non-precision) configuration presented in Chapter Four, decrease power to achieve a 90-knot descent at 700 feet-per-minute.

According to the approach procedure, you are allowed to descend to 1280 feet MSL. Continue descending until you reach this MDA or pass over the VOR. You know you're over the VOR when you enter the cone of confusion and the receiver flag changes from a TO to a FROM. If you get to the MDA before passing over the VOR, level out at 1280 feet until you see the airport or pass over the VOR.

At 5.4 DME, you're ready to begin the procedure turn.

Fly outbound on the procedure turn for one minute.

The procedure turn outbound puts you on an intercept course for the inbound approach course.

Instrument Flight Techniques

For Microsoft **Flight Simulator 98**

You can begin your descent to the MDA once you are established inbound.

The runway is in sight at the end of the approach.

VOR Lesson 2

Let's review another sample approach. Below is the approach procedure chart for the VOR at Sheboygan County Memorial airport (SBM) on Runway 21.

To begin the approach, we need to get to the IAF. Looking at the plan view, we see that the IAF is the Falls VOR located at the airport. To get to Falls, we can use one of two feeder routes. If you used the OSH route, you would track R-111 and fly at an altitude of 3000 feet MSL. The total distance between OSH and the Falls VOR is 33.4 NM. On this route you would want to use your approach level IFR configuration.

Let's use this feeder route to start this exercise. To find out the exact location of the OSH VOR, select World from the main menu and select the Airport/Facility directory. Choose Wisconsin off the global map and click on the NavAids option. Find OSH on the list and you will see that OSH is located at a latitude of N43 degrees 59.40 and a longitude of W88 degrees 33.40.

Now select World from the main menu and choose Go To off the submenu. Pick the Exact Location option. You will get a dialog box. Set in the proper latitude and longitude values. Also set Altitude to 3000 feet MSL and airspeed to 120 knots.

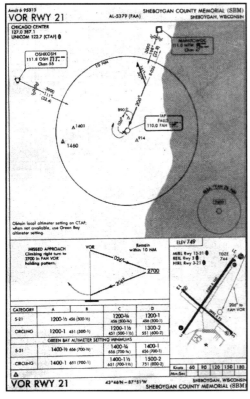

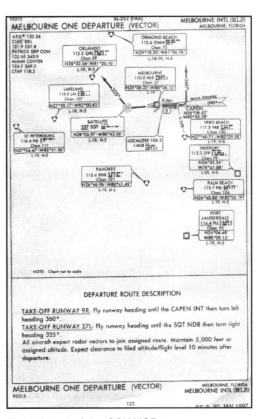

The approach procedure for Sheboygan County VOR runway 21.

Track R-111 of the OSH VOR to get established approach.

When you come back into the exercise you may find your airspeed low, so be prepared to hit F3 to avoid losing altitude or stalling. Next, you need to set your navigation radios. Select Aircraft from the main menu and choose Navigation. Go to the Navigation radios tab and set

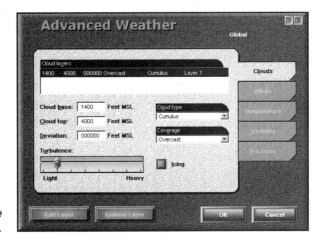

Set IFR conditions to practice attitude instrument flying.

Instrument Flight Techniques
For Microsoft Flight Simulator 98

Go To Exact Location

To return to a place after you have saved it as a flight, click Select Flight. To place your aircraft in a particular place or set tower position fill in the information in the fields below.

Existing flights

Select an existing flight

[Select Flight...]

Aircraft position

Latitude: N43° 59.40'

Longitude: W88° 33.40'

Altitude(MSL): 3000   Heading: 111   Airspeed: 120

Tower position

Latitude: N43° 46.07'

Longitude: W87° 50.71'   Altitude(MSL): +848

[Set Tower from Aircraft]

[Airport/Facility Directory...]   [OK]   [Cancel]

In Flight Simulator, you can go to an exact point on the approach procedure.

Navigation

NAV 1

Frequency: 111.8   Ident: OSH
OBS Course: 111   Name: OSHKOSH
Lat.: N43° 59.40'
Long.: W88° 33.40'

Navigation Radios

Transponder / ADF

EFIS / CFPD

NAV 2

Frequency: 110.0   Ident: FAH
OBS Course: 026   Name: FALLS
Lat.: N43° 46.10'
Long.: W87° 50.90'

[OK]   [Cancel]

Set NAV1 to the radial you will be tracking.

NAV1 to OSH. Set the frequency to 111.8 and the OBS to 111. Set NAV2 to Falls. The Frequency is 110.00 and the OBS is 026.

To make this exercise more of a challenge, set IFR conditions. Select World from the main menu and choose Weather. Set the Cloud type to Cumulus and the Coverage to Overcast. The Cloud Top should be set to 4000 feet MSL and the Base to 1400 feet MSL. This will ensure that you stay in the clouds until the end of the approach. Click on the Visibility tab and set Visibility to two miles.

Turn to a heading of 111 degrees and see what the CDI on NAV1 does. Use the course-tracking procedures presented in Chapter Five to track R-111 outbound. Press CTRL + 1 and CTRL + 3 to audibly identify the VOR and DME.

Because the OSH VOR symbol on the plate has bold edges, you can receive DME from it. Notice that Falls VOR does not have bold edges, so it does not have DME capability. To know

how close you are to Falls, you must use the OSH DME. Toggle the switch on the DME indicator to NAV1. According to the approach chart, Falls is 33.4 DME from OSH. To speed up the process, you can change the simulation rate. This functionality causes events to happen at a faster or slower rate than normal. Choose Options from the main menu and select Simulation Rate. Click on the 4xSpeed option. Remember to return it to normal when you get around 30 DME.

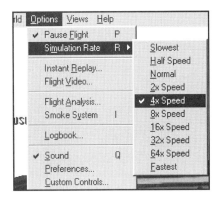

You can get to SBM quicker by speeding up Flight Simulator's simulation rate.

Take a look at the MSA diagram on the bottom right-hand side of the plan view. This tells us that if you remain above an MSL altitude of 2600 feet and are within 25 NM of the Falls VOR, you will not hit any obstacles. Therefore, you will be safe flying at 3000 feet MSL.

When NAV2 begins to center, you are on the proper Falls radial. When the flag changes from TO to FROM, you have just passed over the Falls VOR. You now will start the initial segment and fly outbound on the approach path. The plan view indicates the approach paths inbound heading is 206 degrees. The exact opposite of 206 degrees is 026 degrees and is calculated for you on the plan view. Make a left hand-turn to 026 degrees at standard rate. In addition, turn the OBS to 026 degrees. Once you complete your turn, start timing (using your watch or the cockpit clock) and adjust your heading to re-center the VOR needle.

After two minutes has elapsed, it's time to make the procedure turn. If you want to give yourself some extra time to prepare for what is happening, you may want to take three minutes instead. The plan view indicates you need to make a left-hand turn to a heading of

Once you get to SBM, track the outbound approach course.

Fly outbound on the procedure turn for one minute.

341 degrees. Remember to make the turn at standard rate. Once the turn is complete, start your stopwatch again.

After one minute has elapsed, the plan view indicates you need to make a right-hand turn to 161 degrees. After completing the turn, switch the OBS dial back to the inbound course of 206 degrees. Follow a heading of 161 until the needle re-centers.

The intermediate segment is not needed in this type of approach since no FAF is used.

When the VOR needle re-centers, turn to an inbound heading of 206 degrees. Vary this course to keep the VOR needle centered. You are now on the final approach course and can begin your descent. Set up your IFR configuration for approach descent (non-precision). You should be descending at a rate of about 700 feet-per-minute.

The bottom of the chart indicates what minimum altitude you can descend to and the required runway visibility range. If you plan to land on Runway 21, you can descend to 1200 feet MSL. To begin this approach, the reported runway visibility for the airport must be at least one half-mile. If you plan to

Turn to 161 to reintercept the inbound approach course.

circle-to-land on another runway, you can still descend to 1200 feet but the reported runway visibility must be at least one mile. If you don't have SBM's current altimeter setting and used Green Bay's instead, you could descend only to 1400 feet MSL.

The airport illustration at the bottom right hand-side of the chart shows that the touchdown zone of Runway 21 is at an altitude of 744 feet above mean

sea level. Therefore, at 1200 feet, you are actually 456 feet above the ground at the end of the approach. This number is calculated for you and is also shown in the minimums box. This same number is calculated for the circle-to-land minimums using the airport elevation at its highest point, rather than the height of the touchdown zone.

The airport will come into sight as you track the approach course inbound.

Once you reach 1200 feet, you must stay at or above this altitude until the end of the approach. Raise the nose to level flight and add approach level power until the end of the final approach segment.

The approach is over when you see the runway and make a landing or when you pass over the VOR. You know you have passed over the VOR when the TO flag changes to FROM. At this point, you are at the MAP and must make the missed approach procedure. In this case, make a climbing right run to 2700 feet and hold at the Falls VOR.

NDB Lesson

Page 26 of your Pilot's Handbook shows the NDB approach procedure for Runway 20 at Kahului. Go to Kahului airport by selecting World from the main menu and choosing the Airport option. Change the State/Province option to

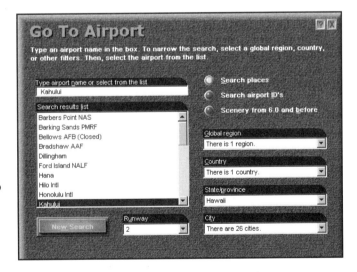

Go to Kahului airport to try an NDB approach.

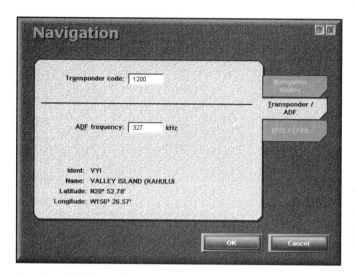

Set the ADF frequency to 327 to tune in Valley Island NDB.

Hawaii. Then select Kahului off the Search results list.

To set IFR weather, select World from the main menu and choose Weather. Set an overcast layer of Cumulus clouds, then set the base to 800 feet and the ceiling to 5100 feet to keep you in IFR conditions during the entire approach. Then click on the Visibility tab and set Visibility to two miles.

The Valley Island NDB is the radio aid used in this approach. Select Aircraft from the main menu and choose Navigation. Click on the Transponder/ADF tab and set Frequency to 327 KHz. When you tab out of the box, Flight Simulator 98 should fill in the Valley Island details. You can also audibly identify the station by pressing CRTL + 5.

You will find yourself lined up on Runway 2 at Kahului. This is the opposite direction of the approach inbound course of 204. After takeoff, fly outbound on the inbound course. Fly a heading of 024 after takeoff and climb to 5000 feet. The approach specifies an altitude of 5000 feet MSL until established in the procedure turn. Keep the needle on the 204 bearing to the station while you climb.

Once you get to 5000 feet, you should turn around. The approach specifies a left-hand procedure turn to a heading of 330. Make this turn at standard rate. Once

Track the NDB outbound after take off.

you are heading outbound on the procedure turn, you can begin to descend to 2200 feet MSL.

After one minute, turn back to the right to a heading of 159. Fly this course until you re-intercept the inbound course. Use the rotatable feature of the ADF to help identify course interception. Rotate the ADF to the course you are flying, which is 159. When the arrow points to 204, you know you are on your inbound course and can turn to your inbound heading of 204.

Track the 204 bearing to the station and descend to 700 feet MSL. Notice that the airport is not easy to identify when you get to 700 feet MSL. Level off at 700 feet MSL and fly until you see the airport and make a landing or until passing over the NDB. The ADF needle will flip when you pass over the NDB. If this happens, you will need to execute the missed approach procedure. According to the chart, you will climb to 3,000 feet and hold on the 186 bearing to the station.

The procedure turn outbound should be flown for one minute.

The rotatable ADF feature can help you identify course interception.

After descending to the MDA, the airport may be difficult to identify.

Chapter Seven

Advanced Navigation

The previous chapter explained the basic components of an instrument approach, such as the initial- and final-approach segments. This chapter will delve into the more complex procedures you might encounter on certain approaches, such as DME arcs and circle-to-land techniques. Precision approaches, which use more sophisticated technology than non-precision approaches, will also be explained in detail. A guide to flying the unique Hong Kong "Checkerboard" approach will be provided along with general tips to help you fly efficient precision and non-precision approaches in Microsoft Flight Simulator 98.

The ILS and LOC Approach

The ILS (Instrument Landing System) category I approach is the most commonly used precision approach procedure in the United States. The ILS consists of four elements: localizer (LOC), glide slope (GS), marker beacons, and approach lights.

The Localizer

Like a VOR, the localizer sends out a signal you can track in an aircraft. Specifically, it creates an airway lined up with the centerline of the runway. You can then determine if you lined up with the runway properly or if you are to the

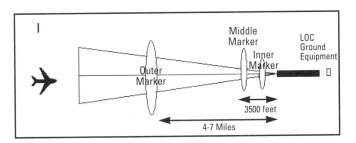

The localizer helps you make approaches that are smooth and steady.

right or left of it. Marker beacons, which will be discussed later in this chapter, mark distances along the localizer path.

The localizer ground-based equipment consists of a radio antenna aligned with the centerline of the runway. It's usually located about 1000 feet away from the far end of the runway. Therefore, if you were performing the LOC for Runway 9, the localizer antenna would be located closer to the threshold of Runway 27.

This localizer antenna radiates signals directly forward, toward the actual runway and along the extended runway behind it. These are called the *front course* and *back course*, respectively. Actually, two signals are broadcast in both directions. One signal is broadcast to the right of the runway and the other to the left of the runway. The intersection of these two signals forms the path to the runway. This path becomes increasingly narrow as you approach the runway.

The localizer transmits its signal on VHF frequencies between 108.10 and 111.95 MHz. Thus, you can pick up the signal on your cockpit NAV receiver like you would a VOR signal. Keep in mind that the localizer signal is narrower than a VOR transmission. Therefore, the CDI needle will react much more sensitively to heading changes when using a localizer signal. The LOC is calibrated so that the NAV display will show a full-right or full-left CDI deflection when you are not within a 700-feet area around the centerline, at a point above the runway threshold.

Unlike the VOR, the localizer transmission is single-directional. When you set the OBS to a specific radial when receiving a VOR signal, the CDI will rotate depending on where you are in relation to the selected radial. When using a localizer signal, the CDI reflects your position in relation to the single radial transmitted by the localizer. Rotating the OBS does not affect this calculation. Therefore, it is not critical that you set the OBS during an ILS or LOC approach. However, setting it can act as a quick reminder of what inbound course is used during the approach.

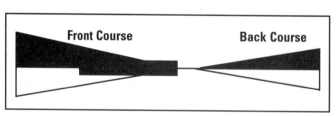

Front Course   **Back Course**

The localizer forms both a front course and a back course to a runway.

Tuning in a Localizer Signal

To determine an LOC frequency at a particular airport, go to World on the main menu and select Airport/Facility Directory. Click on the area of the world the airport is located in and verify that the Airport option is activated. If a particular runway at an airport has a localizer, its frequency will be listed under ILS/LOC frequency. The ILS/LOC heading is

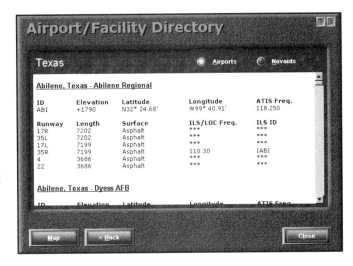

It's easy to locate an LOC frequency by using the Airport/Facility Directory.

given because tuning in the LOC will also tune in its associated glide slope, if it has one.

Notice that the identifier is four characters long. When you press CTRL + 1 to identify the LOC tuned in NAV1, be prepared to interpret four Morse codes rather than the three used by VORs and NDBs. The first will always be an 'I.'

Flying the LOC

Although an LOC is part of an ILS approach, it can also be used on its own as a non-precision approach. This is called an LOC approach. In addition, most ILS approaches have a contingency LOC approach procedure listed on the chart in case other components of the ILS are malfunctioning. At some airports, the back-course signal can also be used for an approach into the opposite runway. For example, an airport with an ILS or LOC 9 may have an LOC BC for Runway 27.

A full scale CDI deflection will occur when the aircraft is off the LOC approach path by more than 2.5 degrees. In VOR navigation, a full-scale CDI deflection represents that you're off course by more than ten degrees. Thus, the localizer is four times more sensitive then the VOR!

Because the LOC is so sensitive, you need to constantly check your heading. The best way to do this is to make sure your scan includes the AI. You want to be sure the miniature wings stay parallel with the horizon bar when tracking the LOC unless you are making a turn. The DG will verify whether or not you are maintaining straight flight.

Tracking the LOC

As you first approach the localizer, you will have a full-scale deflection unless you are already lined up with the landing runway. As you approach the inbound course, the CDI will begin to center. As soon as it starts to move, you should turn immediately to your inbound course using a standard-rate turn. Otherwise, you may fly through it because it is so narrowly defined.

You do not have to worry about reverse sensing on an ILS or front-course LOC. Therefore, if the needle drifts left you should turn to the left to re-intercept it. If it drifts right, you should again fly towards the needle. Because the LOC path is so narrow, you should correct CDI deviations immediately. Letting the CDI go uncorrected can lead to large CDI deviations quickly. To get back on course, aircraft heading changes should be made at or below five degrees before passing over the final-approach fix and around two degrees after passing over the final-approach fix. Otherwise, you may fly through the inbound course and deviate on the reverse side.

When you fly a back-course localizer approach, the NAV receiver will be subject to reverse sensing. Instead of flying towards the deflected needle, you would fly *away* from it to get back on course. If you perform an LOC using the HSI on the 737 rather than a standard NAV display, you are in luck. Like VOR tracking, the HSI eliminates any problems that result from reverse sensing.

LOC Final Approach Segment

The final-approach fix on an LOC-only approach is usually determined when you pass over the beacon used as the outer marker. At this point, you would start timing your descent and descend toward the airport to a specified altitude. You would abandon the approach when the time reached a certain point. This time value is based on your ground speed and is listed on the approach chart.

Many of the ILS charts in the Pilot's Handbook do not list the time to use when performing an LOC-only approach. To estimate this value, multiply the distance from the outer marker to the runway threshold by 60 and divide this

value by your ground speed. For example, look at the profile view of the approach chart for Paine Field on page 46. The distance from the outer marker to the runway threshold is (7.3 + .5) = 7.8 nautical miles. Therefore, the approximate time needed to fly the final-approach segment when doing the LOC-only approach in the Lear 45 is 3.34 minutes (7.8 X 60)/140.

The Glide Slope

The glide slope provides vertical guidance to the runway threshold. At each location on the LOC path, a specific altitude is set by the glide path. The angle this glide slope forms with the horizontal is usually somewhere between 2.5 and 3.0 degrees. It passes over the middle marker at 200 feet and over the outer marker at 1400 feet.

The technology behind the glide slope is very similar to the LOC. The ground-based equipment directs two signals towards the approach path. The area where these two signals meet defines the vertical course to the ground. Unlike the LOC, these signals are only broadcast to the front course. Therefore, you will not receive a glide-slope signal when approaching the opposite runway.

When you tune in the LOC, you automatically tune in its glide slope. The NAV receivers that are found in the aircraft in Microsoft Flight Simulator 98 all have a second CDI needle known as the glide-slope needle. The glide-slope needles in the Cessna Skylanes are attached to the VOR so that it can move up and down rather than to the left or right. In the Lear 45 and Boeing 737-400 (B-737), the glide-slope indicator appears beside the HSI and an indicator moves up and down along the display.

Once the needle is active, you track it similarly to the way you would track a course. If the needle is above the center point, you are above the glide path and should lose some altitude by reducing power and/or

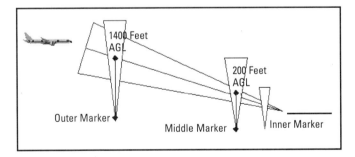

By providing vertical guidance, the Glide Slope keeps everything steady during your descent down to the runway threshold.

The glide-slope indicator and the LOC share much of the same signal-transmission technology.

If safety means anything to you, you'll trust that it's better to fly above the glide path than below it.

lowering the nose depending on your descent rate and approach speed. If the needle sinks below the center mark, you are low and need to level out until you re-intercept the glide slope. When no signal is received by the NAV radios in the Cessna Skylanes, both needles will lay idle and the "No Signal Received" flag will appear, just like in VOR navigation. In the Lear 45 and B-737, a red 'X' will appear on the display and the CDI arrow will not display.

It is better to be flying above the glide path than below it, to ensure that you won't hit anything. The glide slope is three times as sensitive as the localizer. A full-scale deflection means that the aircraft is .7 degrees above or below the glide path. On a typical approach, this translates to a 350-foot vertical deviation at five NM from the transmitter and a 70-foot deviation at one NM from the transmitter.

If the needle in the glide-slope indicator in the Boeing 737 is above the center point, you'll need to lose some altitude before you set that big bird down.

Flying the Glide Slope

The goal of an ILS approach is to get the LOC and glide-slope needles centered. Holding the glide slope can be tricky since it is 12 times as sensitive as the VOR. To hold a specific glide slope, a specific rate-of-descent is required. The descent table published with approach charts shown in the table below can help determine what rate of descent you should use to stay on the glide slope.

For example, if you were on a glide slope with a 3.0-degree descent angle to the runway threshold and had a ground speed of 90 knots, you would need to descend at approximately 480 feet-per-minute. Unfortunately, the Pilot's Handbook does not list the descent angle of a particular glide slope. You can calculate the descent rate either by using an estimated descent angle of three degrees and making corrections during the approach, or by consulting the actual NOS or Jeppesen Chart. The descent angle is prefixed with a "GS" on charts.

If you don't want to reference the descent table before making an approach, you can also use a rule-of-thumb to determine what descent rate you should use. Multiply five by your ground speed to determine this rate. In the above example, you would multiply five by the ground speed of 90 knots to obtain a descent rate of 450 feet-per-minute.

Descent Table—Feet-per-Minute

Ground Speed

Angle of Descent (degrees and tenths)	30	45	60	75	90	105	120	135	150	165	180
2.0	105	160	210	265	320	370	425	475	530	585	635
2.5	130	200	265	330	395	465	530	595	665	730	795
3.0	160	240	320	395	480	555	635	715	795	875	955
3.5	185	280	370	465	555	650	740	835	925	1020	1110
4.0	210	315	425	530	635	740	845	955	1060	1065	1270
4.5	240	355	475	595	715	835	955	1075	1190	1310	1430
5.0	265	395	530	660	795	925	1060	1190	1325	1455	1590

Aircraft Control During an ILS

You should scan the AI often to maintain the proper nose-down attitude and set your power to the precision-approach decent configuration given in Chapter Four. Use the NAV display as a performance instrument to determine how well you're staying on the glide path. If you fall slightly below or rise slightly above the path, make pitch changes to return to course. Calibration marks are placed above and below the center point to gauge how far you have deviated from the glide slope. If you go more than two bars below the glide slope, you may want to add climb power to help get back onto the glide slope.

If you are off your target airspeed by more than five knots, use power to get it back in line. If you are high and slow, when you lower the nose you will raise airspeed at the same time due to the aerodynamics of flight. If you are low and fast, trade airspeed for height. Raise the nose to get back on the glide path and you will notice the airspeed bleed off. If you find yourself with a full-scale deflection during the final-approach segment, you should abandon the approach by executing the missed-approach procedure and then try again.

ILS Final Approach Segment

The final-approach point is the point where you are flying inbound on the localizer and the glide slope centers. You can then begin your descent down to decision height. The final-approach point begins close to the outer marker.

If you're doing an ILS, you should also start a timer as soon as you reach the final-approach point. If the glide slope suddenly breaks down, you can continue on with the LOC if you have started timing over the outer marker. If you didn't note the time, you would have no idea when the LOC missed-approach was due. You would then have to abandon the entire approach and start from scratch.

Marker Beacons

Marker beacons are used so that you can determine your position along the ILS. These beacons transmit a signal straight up in a fan-shaped pattern so that an aircraft receiver will receive it only when it is overhead. Beacons transmit on a frequency of 75 MHz. The aircraft automatically tunes in this frequency so that you do not need to worry about it.

The outer, middle, and inner markers help determine where you are during an approach.

Two markers exist on the ILS called the outer marker and the middle marker. The outer marker is located between four and seven NM from the runway threshold and the middle marker about .6 NM from the runway threshold. Sometimes inner markers are used as well. They are located between the middle marker and the runway threshold. An airplane over the outer marker and on glide slope is approximately 1400 HAT. At the middle marker the aircraft is

approximately 200 HAT. This means that the missed-approach point is close by when you pass over the middle marker.

Market Beacon Identification

Beacon	Color	Morse Code Ident
Outer	Blue	2 dashes per second
Middle	Amber	Alternating dots and dashes at 6 per second
Inner	White	6 dots per second

When you pass a marker beacon, your marker beacon detection equipment will visually and audibly inform you of this progress. The marker-beacon display contains three lights. This panel is located on the upper center control panel in the Cessna Skylanes and on the far-left panel in the B-737. The blue light flashes when you are over the outer marker (the indicator light on the far left displays the letter 'O'). The amber light activates when you're over the middle marker (center indicator light displays the letter 'M'). Finally, the white light turns on when you're over the inner marker (the indicator on the far right displays the letter 'I'). In addition, each beacon emits a distinct broadcast. If the noise bothers you, you will have to either turn down you computer volume, adjust the Navigation Sound level under Options: Preferences, or wait a few seconds to pass over it.

Approach Lighting

The approach lighting system (ALS) helps direct the pilot to the runway. Although this is certainly useful under VMC, it's especially helpful when visibility is low. There are several ALS configurations that are illustrated in the beginning of NOS Terminal Procedures. The runway chart on an approach chart lists which configuration is used on a particular runway. Flight Simulator 98 models a few standard configurations such as the MALSR and ALSF-2.

An ALS is usually T-shaped, designed with red and white lights, which extend from the centerline. Precision-approach lighting systems are 2400-3400 feet long. Non-precision systems extend for 1400-1500 feet.

Marker beacons use a color-coded system of display lights to keep you informed of your progress.

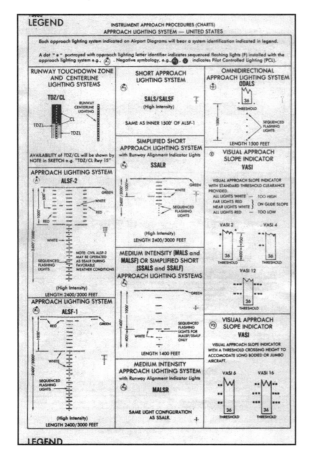

ALS configurations are illustrated in the beginning of NOS Terminal Procedures.

An Approach Lighting System (ALS) uses red and white lights to keep runways clearly and sufficiently illuminated.

Some approach lighting systems use Runway Alignment Indicator Lights (RAIL), which appear as bursts of high-speed lights traveling toward the runway. These flashing lights, along with Sequenced Flashing Lights (SFL), are dubbed the "rabbit" by pilots. This refers to the mechanical "rabbit" used to lead greyhounds at dog races. An aviation "rabbit" is used to help guide a pilot to a runway during low visibility, at the end of an approach. An aviation rabbit isn't powerful enough to guide the aircraft from a high altitude down to the runway.

Runway lights are also helpful when you near the ground and visibility hasn't improved all that much. Runway edge lights border the runway edges. On runways with an approach, the edge lights are white except on the last 2000-foot stretch of the runway. In this area, they shine amber. If the runway is shorter than 4000 feet, the last half of the runway lights are amber. This helps the pilot determine how much runway room is left for landing.

Tips on Flying Approaches

This section will present some tips to help you keep your bearings during an approach. Remember that you can always press P to pause Flight Simulator and sort out what your next maneuver will be.

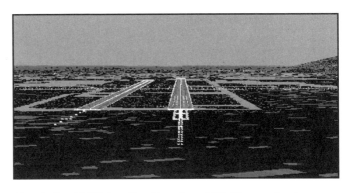

Here's the ALSF-2 at San Francisco 28R. You can't miss the runway at the end of the beautiful Bay Area approach challenge.

Situational Awareness

Whenever you perform an approach, you should always know exactly where you are. This is especially true if you are receiving a vectored approach during one of the lessons in Flight Simulator 98. You should not become complacent about knowing

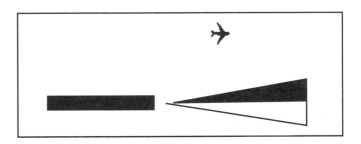

The LOC needle will deflect to the left side when flying on the black side of the LOC beam.

your current location. If you have a sudden engine failure, you want to know exactly were the closest airport is.

To aid in visualizing your position on an ILS/LOC, you can use the color-coding shown on the approach path on the chart. One half is black and the other is white. The left side of your NAV display represents the black half of the course and the right side represents the white side of the course. The memory aid is "black and white" to help remember which is which. If the needle is pointed to the left (black) side of the NAV display, you are on the side of the chart on which the black course line is drawn and vice versa. This works no matter where you are on your approach.

Heading Reminders

Keeping a specific heading is key during an approach. Therefore, you should reset your DG by pressing D right before the approach if you have the Gyro Drift option turned on. In addition, you should use the heading bug on the DG. It acts as a reminder of what your current heading should be. This is especially useful when making corrections for the wind. You can also quickly see when you have drifted off that heading. Adjust the heading bug using the lower-right knob on the DG. Use your mouse to rotate the bug either clockwise or counter-clockwise.

Even though the OBS on the NAV receiver is not course-sensitive when tuned into a LOC, you should turn it toward your inbound course as a reference. You will be viewing the NAV often during your scan to see how you're doing holding the approach path. While you're scanning, you can check the inbound course to remind yourself of what it is. This is especially helpful if you have made a lot of heading changes during the approach.

Highlighting Reference Information

You should keep the approach plate someplace where it can be easily referenced when you are making an approach. You should highlight important information, such as the MDA and the inbound course. Otherwise, it will be difficult to find these individual elements during the actual approach. You should set your radios to the proper frequencies during the arrival segment. If you're just going up to for a few practice approaches, you should set your radios before takeoff or press P to pause the simulation.

Keeping Track of Time

Many approaches require you to time the duration of the final-approach segment. You can use wristwatch or the clock on the instrument panels of the aircraft in Flight Simulator 98. However, this is a cumbersome process. You need to calculate when the necessary number of minutes and seconds has elapsed. Mental workload should be reduced as much as possible during an approach.

A stopwatch that can count down as well as up would aid in this. Then you could set the approach time on the watch and start the timer at the appropriate point. When you get to zero, you would therefore know when time was up. Even better: get a stopwatch that beeps when the time is up, so that you do not have to scan the timer as often.

Breaking Below Clouds Quickly

On non-precision approaches, try to descend at a rate that's a couple of hundred feet-per-minute greater than you would use for a precision approach. This will allow you to get below a layer of clouds sooner and you'll have more time to try to spot the airport. Be careful when you see the airport and proceed using VFR skills. You could still have a long haul to the airport and the cloud layer may be quite variable. Keep an eye on your instruments so that you are prepared to get back on the instruments if need be.

Stabilizing the Aircraft

Get your aircraft into the approach-level configuration on the arrival or initial segment. Consult your IFR configurations in Chapter Four for the proper settings. You will find approaches much easier if your aircraft is stabilized before you start making your descent to the airport. Remember to correct for deviations from your desired aircraft performance as soon as possible.

The Five Ts

A process known as "The Five Ts" can help an approach go much smoother, especially since so much is happening in a relatively short amount of time. You're making turns, timing segments, descending to specific altitudes, and tracking very sensitive courses. It's easy to forget something. For example, it's common during IFR flight training for a pilot to pass the FAF, start their timer, and continue to track the inbound course...but then forget to initiate their descent to the MAP.

The Five Ts prevents these types of errors from occurring. The order of the Five Ts is *Turn, Time, Twist, Throttle,* and *Talk*. Whenever you make a turn during the approach, just *turn*. Don't try changing the OBS or descending at this point. Concentrate on maintaining level flight and rolling out on the proper heading. Once the turn is completed, ask yourself if you should start to *time* the segment. Once decided whether or not to start your timer, *twist* your OBS to a new radial and change the frequency if required. Next, determine if you need to use the *throttle* to either slow down to your approach level speed or to begin a descent.

Talk refers to communicating with ATC. It's last on the list becomes it is the least important. (Remember, your main goal is always first and foremost to fly the airplane.) For example, if you need to request a landing clearance, you would do so after getting the aircraft settled from your last maneuver. The Five Ts can be helpful in all areas of IFR flight including holding patterns and en-route navigation. You might want to say each of the five tasks aloud as you perform it, as an easy way of remembering all of them.

Alternate Procedure Turns

The 45-degree procedure turn is illustrated on most NOS procedure plates. However, you have other options you can use or that you may find outlined on a chart.

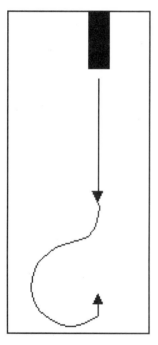

The 80/260 procedure turn can save you time, and reduce your cockpit workload as well.

80-260 Procedure Turn

A lesser-known type of procedure turn is called the 80-260, and it can reduce your workload in the cockpit. It's a maneuver that not only cuts down the total duration of the procedure time, but also negates the need to time the procedure turn. When you are flying outbound on the approach course, you should make a standard-rate turn 80 degrees in the direction of the procedure turn. To determine what heading is 80 degrees away from your heading, simply refer to your DG and visually obtain the value.

For instance, let's say you are flying outbound on a course of 180 and need to make a right-hand procedure turn. You would take a look at your DG and see that the heading 80 degrees to the right of 180 is 260. You would then make a right-hand standard-rate turn to 260. When you reach a heading of 260, immediately turn back to the left at standard rate until you get to your inbound heading. You have just made a pretty snazzy procedure turn without needing to use the stopwatch. You've reduced your workload and made an efficient turn. The 80-260 is usually used only on ILS and VOR approaches because it loses its ease-of-use when used in other types of approaches.

Teardrop Procedure Turn

The Teardrop procedure turn is another option. Take a look at the Denver International approach on page 20 of the Pilot's Handbook. After passing over the airport, the aircraft does not fly the outbound on the inbound approach path. Instead, the aircraft flies 40 degrees east of the inbound course. At DME 21.4, the aircraft begins a standard-rate turn back to the inbound approach course. The resulting track is a teardrop-shaped pattern.

ILS Lesson

Flight Simulator has several ILS lessons and challenges to choose from in different aircraft. The weather is more difficult to handle in some of the challenges than others. This section will concentrate on a basic ILS approach in the Lear 45.

Select Flights from the main menu and select Challenges. Click on the IFR Paine Learjet (Basic) challenge. Although it has the word "basic" in the title, this flight from Boeing Field/King County to Paine Field takes you through a heavy cloud layer with a low ceiling. Look in the Pilot's Handbook on page 45.

The journey departs Boeing Field King Co International and will follow R-160 to Snohomish County (Paine Field).

You will climb to 4000 feet. Take a peek at the weather by choosing World from the main menu and selecting Weather. Click on the Clouds tab and you will see that a layer of stratus clouds extends along your route with a base at 1000 feet and a top at 3000 feet. You will climb above it but will need to descend below it to find Paine airport.

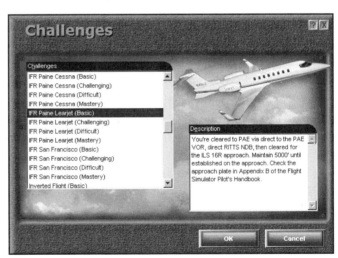

IFR Paine Learjet (Basic) Challenge sends you into skies that have a heavy cloud layer and low ceiling.

On the ground at Boeing Field, where you should check the approach plate for ILS Runway 16R.

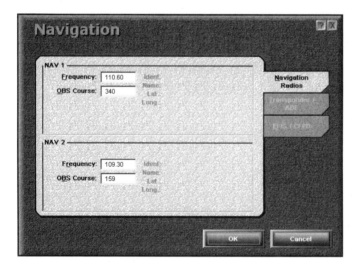

Reset the radios for easier en-route navigation.

Once on the ground at Boeing Field, take a look at the approach plate for ILS Runway 16R on page 46 of your Pilot's Handbook. After you pass over the PAE VOR, you will track to the Ritts NDB. When you pass over the NDB, continue to track outbound for two minutes. After two minutes, you will make a right-hand procedure turn and re-intercept the ILS and track it inbound.

The profile view shows that you must be at least 3000 MSL until tracking inbound on the LOC. No decision height is given in this chart. The airport diagram below the chart lists the airport elevation as 606 feet. Since most ILS procedures end 200 feet above the runway, let's say you can descend to 806 feet MSL.

Go into Aircraft on the main menu and select navigation. Click on the Navigation Radios tab. NAV1 is set to the Paine LOC on 109.3 and NAV2 to the VOR on 110.6. You may want to set the VOR in NAV1 while you track to Paine since it will be your primary guide during the first leg of the trip. You should reset the OBS of the LOC in NAV2 to 159, the inbound LOC course.

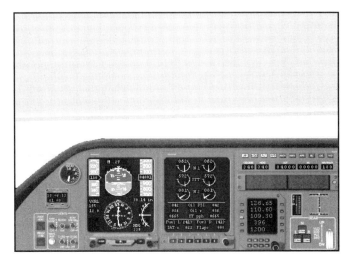

On course on R-160, headed for Paine Field in IFR weather.

Track R-160 inbound to Paine Field. It's a short hop in the Lear 45, so you should get into your approach level configuration right away. Set 45-percent power and strive for 180 knots. Press F7 to lower eight degrees of flap. Go to Communication on the Aircraft submenu and set Comm 1 frequency to ATIS on 128.65. Paine Fields ATIS information Mike will display that the reported ceiling at Paine is 900 feet MSL. Therefore, expect to be in IFR weather for almost the entire approach.

You have the option of displaying the CDI for both NAVs and the ADF needle on the HSI or displaying just one of the CDIs. The NAV1 needle will be displayed more prominently than the others. The NAV2 display will appear as a light gray arrow. The ADF needle will be displayed as a thin, bright blue arrow. To display the second NAV needle, click on the VOR 2 toggle on the lower left-hand side of the HSI. Click on it again to remove NAV2 from the display.

Use the toggles to choose which radio signals to display on the HSI.

The ADF toggle is located on the lower right-hand display. Click on it to display and remove the ADF needle. The LOC course tuned in NAV2 shows that the LOC course is located to the left.

After passing over the Ritts NDB, continue tracking outbound on the 339 bearing from the NDB. Start timing and wait for two minutes to elapse.

After two minutes has passed, you can begin the procedure turn. The chart specifically illustrates a left procedure turn. Turn left 45 degrees to a heading of

Fly outbound for two minutes after passing over the outer marker.

294 using a standard-rate turn. After rolling out on 294, start timing. When one minute passes, you can turn right to a heading of 114 to intercept the inbound course. You are allowed to descend to 3000 feet MSL on the approach, so begin your descent to 3000.

After flying outbound on the procedure turn for one minute, you can turn right to a heading of 114. During this segment, you will find that the LOC needle displays a red 'X', which means the LOC signal is not being received. You need to start executing the missed approach procedure, which begins by flying to the Ritts NDB. Instead of flying directly to the NDB, though, continue to fly at 114. When the needle diverts 45 degrees to the right, track to the NDB. This is the same course as the LOC. Since the LOC failure is only temporary in this lesson, you will still be set up for the ILS.

Once the LOC comes back in, continue tracking it inbound. When the glide-slope needle centers, you can begin to descend to 806 feet. Lower the gear by pressing G and lower the remaining flaps by pressing F7. In the Lear 45, you should try to hold 140 knots airspeed during the final descent.

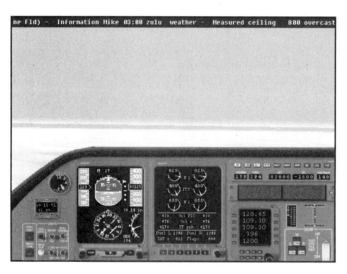

Timing is practically everything when making outbound procedure turns.

Continue tracking the ILS and plan to execute the missed approach procedure at 806 feet MSL if you still don't see the runway. You will find that you will break out of the clouds at 1000 feet MSL with the runway straight ahead of the aircraft's nose.

Modifying the Lesson for LOC-only Approach

Let's say that the LOC failure that occurred on the procedure turn inbound ended with the LOC coming back in but with the glide slope remaining inactive. You can still execute the approach by making an LOC-only approach. You would continue on the inbound procedure turn to intercept the LOC.

After intercepting the inbound course, ignore the glide-slope display. Instead, wait to pass over the Ritts NDB. You know you are over the Ritts when the ADF needle turns 180 degrees. At this point, start timing. Although not listed on the Flight Simulator chart, the NOS approach plate indicates an aircraft with a ground speed of 120 should time for three minutes 54 seconds and one travelling at 150 knots should time for three minutes and seven seconds. You must extrapolate the data to figure out how long you should time when using a ground speed of 140 knots. The difference between 150 and 120

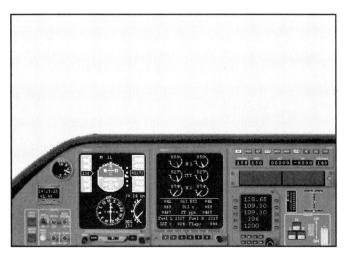

In the clouds, tracking the ILS to Runway 16R...and prepping for the final descent.

Breaking out of the clouds at 1000 feet MSL with the runway straight ahead.

is 30 knots. The difference in time is 47 seconds. Therefore, you should add about 1.5 seconds (47/30) to three minutes seven seconds for every knot below 150 knots. Therefore, you should time for three minutes 22 seconds (10 X 1.5 plus three minutes seven seconds).

FAF to MAP 7.8 NM on NOS chart

Knots	60	90	120	150	180
Min: Sec	7:48	5:12	3:54	3:07	2:36

You would descend to the missed-approach point and level off. Use a missed-approach point of 975 MSL in this example. When three minutes 22 seconds was up, you would execute the missed-approach procedure if the runway was not in sight.

Hong Kong Checkerboard Approach

The Hong Kong "Checkerboard" approach gets its name from the large checkerboard patterns on the hill the aircraft flies toward during the final-approach segment. The aircraft follows the IGS (Instrument Guidance System), which provides both horizontal and vertical guidance using radio signals. Because HKG is surrounded by hills, this path does not lead straight toward a runway. Instead, it leads the aircraft toward the large checkerboards. The aircraft then makes a steep right-hand turn to make a landing into Runway 13.

The large checkerboard patterns on the mountain by the runway threshold distinguishes the Hong Kong approach from other approach procedures.

Let's take a look at how the Checkerboard Approach is used in a Flight Simulator 98 Adventure. After taking off in the Checkerboard Approach: Boeing 737-400

While awaiting takeoff at Hong Kong, take a moment to check your radios.

After takeoff, the Boeing 737-400 will circle to the south to set up for the approach.

Adventure, the B-737 will fly a pattern which sets it up for the approach. First, runway heading will be flown until the 23 DME point and the aircraft will ascend to 6000 feet. Then, the aircraft will turn left to a heading of 330 to intercept the 090 radial off of the Cheung Chau VOR. After passing over Cheung Chau, you will continue to fly the R-270 for an additional seven miles.

At this point, ATC will clear you to turn to a heading of 045 and to descend to 4500 feet. On this heading,

At 23 DME you can begin your turn to intercept the Cheung Chau VOR.

you are on course to intercept the 088 course towards the KL IGS. After intercepting the IGS, turn to a heading of 088 and track it toward the checkerboards. When you get to about 1.2 DME, Runway 13 will be toward

Flying R-090 to Cheung Chau, as the Adventure continues.

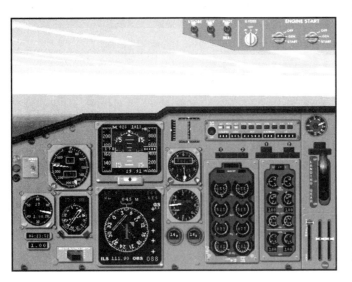

On an intercept path for the IGS, which Flight Simulator conveniently tunes for you.

your right. Make a steep right-hand turn and land on Runway 13.

To start this Adventure, choose Flights from the main menu and select Adventures. Click on the Checkerboard Approach: Boeing 737-400 option. You will find NAV1 set to the HK ILS on 109.9 and the OBS set to 315. You can then track the LOC part of the ILS to be sure you are staying on runway heading. Climb to 6000 feet MSL.

When the DME in the upper left-hand corner of the HSI reads 22 NM, you should begin a left-hand turn to 330. Flight Simulator will set the Cheung Chau VOR to a frequency of 112.30 and the OBS to 270. The midsection of the arrow will deflect toward the top of the display, indicating that you are flying toward the selected radial of 090. Get into your approach-level configuration of 180 knots and 55 percent power (Press F2) with ten degrees of flap (Press F7).

As you are tracking toward the VOR, ATC will

tell you to expect further clearance within the next five miles. The centered CDI arrow lets you know you are on course for the Cheung Chau VOR.

ATC will clear you to intercept the IGS and will ask you to fly at heading 045 and descend to 4500 feet. The IGS will be tuned in automatically by Flight Simulator on a frequency of 111.9 and the OBS will be set to 088, which is the inbound heading on the IGS. Be prepared for system failures on this leg. You are approximately 18 miles from the airport at this point.

When you intercept the IGS, the CDI arrow center will align itself with the arrow's head. Turn to a heading of 088 and track the IGS to the checkerboards. Begin your descent using your IFR configuration. Lower the remaining flaps by pressing F7 and lower the gear by pressing G. Descend at an airspeed of 140 knots.

Toward the end of the IGS, you can see how the lighting systems curve

Tracking the IGS to the checkerboards. You're almost home-free.

The unique lighting system at Hong Kong guides the aircraft from the IGS to the runway threshold.

toward the runway. Around 1.2 DME, make a sharp right-hand turn to land on Runway 13.

A Guide to ILS Approaches in Flight Simulator has a great variety of preset ILS approaches from which to choose. In addition to the ones listed below, several of the cross-country adventures end in an ILS approach. To get to Flight Simulator 98's Select Flights, Lessons, and Challenges, choose Flights on the main menu.

Pre-set ILS Approaches in Flight Simulator 98

Title	Runway	Aircraft
Select Flights		
San Francisco 28L ILS	28L San Francisco	B-737
Stormy Approach at Champaign	32L Champaign	Lear 45
Stormy Approach at Oakland	11 Oakland	B-737
Lessons		
ILS with Procedure Turn: Boeing 737	6 MacArthur Field	B-737
ILS Approach Straight in: Boeing 737	36 Space Center Exec	B-737
ILS Approach Straight in: Cessna Skylane 182S	36 Space Center Exec	C-182S
ILS with Procedure Turn: Cessna Skylane 182S	6 MacArthur Field	C-182S
ILS with Procedure Turn: Lear Jet 45	6 MacArthur Field	Lear 45
Challenges		
Beautiful Bay Area at Night	28R San Francisco	B-737
Bumpy Ride into Boston	4R Boston	B-737
IFR Cessna (Basic)	32L Chicago	C-182S
IFR Cessna (Challenging)	32L Chicago	C-182S
IFR Cessna (Difficult)	32L Chicago	C-182S
IFR Cessna (Mastery)	32L Chicago	C-182S
IFR Lear Jet (Basic)	32L Chicago	Lear 45
IFR Lear Jet (Challenging)	32L Chicago	Lear 45
IFR Lear Jet (Difficult)	32L Chicago	Lear 45
IFR Lear Jet (Mastery)	32L Chicago	Lear 45
IFR Paine Cessna (Basic)	16R Paine	C-182S
IFR Paine Cessna (Challenging)	16R Paine	C-182S
IFR Paine Cessna (Difficult)	16R Paine	C-182S
IFR Paine Cessna (Mastery)	16R Paine	C-182S
IFR Paine Lear Jet (Basic)	16R Paine	Lear 45

Pre-set ILS Approaches in Flight Simulator 98, continued

Title	Runway	Aircraft
IFR Paine Lear Jet (Challenging)	16R Paine	Lear 45
IFR Paine Lear Jet (Difficult)	16R Paine	Lear 45
IFR Paine Lear Jet (Mastery)	16R Paine	Lear 45
IFR San Francisco (Basic)	28R San Francisco	Lear 45
IFR San Francisco (Challenging)	28R San Francisco	Lear 45
IFR San Francisco (Difficult)	28R San Francisco	Lear 45
IFR San Francisco (Mastery)	28R San Francisco	Lear 45
Landing Blind at Heathrow	9R Heathrow	B-737

Adventures

Cessna Skylane RG ILS at Van Nuys, CA	16R Van Nuys	C-182RG
Checkerboard Approach: Boeing 737	13 Hong Kong	B-737

Other Types of Precision Approaches

Other types of precision approaches exist, although they are not modeled in Flight Simulator 98. Most of these approaches are infrequently used in aviation. The following section provides an overview of these types of approaches.

MLS

MLS (Microwave Landing System) was meant to be the "next generation" ILS. It broadcasts on the SHF (microwave band) at frequencies between 5031-5091 MHz. It incorporates a special type of DME called "DME/P" and can be received using standard aircraft ILS equipment. The advantage of MLS over ILS is that it can track a curved path in addition to a standard straight ILS path.

However, the FAA got way behind in MLS implementation plans. In fact, the program has lingered for so long that MLS technology has been superseded by GPS.

PAR/ASR

The PAR (Precision Approach Radar) and ASR (Airport Surveillance Radar) are very similar, although a PAR is defined as a precision approach and the ASR as a non-precision approach. They are both used at only a few civil terminals, although PAR is found on most military bases. The Navy calls it *Ground Controlled Approach* (GCA).

On both types of approach, the controller verbally vectors the pilot onto the approach. The pilot strives to descend on a glide slope of three degrees. If the pilot loses communication with ATC, the missed-approach procedure is executed.

LDA

LDA (Localizer-type Direction Aid) is very similar to the localizer approach. However, the course does not lay right on the extended centerline of the runway. If the LDA is for a specific runway, the approach ends with the aircraft somewhere between the runway centerline and the LDA course. If the LDA is for the airport only, the LDA will end with you needing to circle to get lined-up on a runway.

SDF

SDF (Simplified Directional Facility) is sometimes called the "poor man's localizer." It works just like a localizer but the antenna isn't quite as impressive, making it much less costly to install. However, the course is not as narrowly defined as the localizer approach. In addition, it may not be aligned with the centerline.

Visual and Contact Approaches

Although IFR approaches are fun, they take time to complete. The pilot must first get to the IAF and then execute the initial, intermediate and final segments. Some pilots just want to get on the ground as soon as possible. Visual and contact approaches allow the pilot to fly directly to the airport and enter the traffic pattern.

Visual Approach

If a pilot is in VFR conditions and can remain in them all the way to the airport, the pilot may request that ATC issue a visual approach. In addition, ATC might want to expedite traffic and request that the pilot perform the visual approach.

It is the pilot's right to refuse such a request. This may be done if the pilot is unfamiliar with an area or just wants to keep IFR currency up. ATC may vector the aircraft during a visual approach if the cloud ceiling is 500 feet above the controller's minimum vectoring altitude. The visual clearance does

not cancel the pilot's IFR clearance so that the advantages of an ATC clearance (such as traffic advisories) are still provided.

Contact Approach

A pilot can request a *contact approach* even when the weather conditions offer less-than-VFR skies. The pilot feels that enough visibility exists to fly to the runway. There must by at least one mile of visibility and the aircraft must be able to stay clear of clouds.

ATC cannot request that a pilot execute a contact approach. The pilot must initiate the request. ATC will continue to separate the pilot from other traffic, but the pilot must negotiate obstacles himself. If the weather goes below one mile and clear of clouds, the pilot must inform ATC and return to IFR flight procedures.

Flying the DME Arc

The concept behind the DME arc is easy to grasp. Flying the arc, however, is another story. How does one fly a continuous curved path with a constant radius? The answer is, one *doesn't*. Instead, you fly a series of tangents. A *tangent* is a line that touches a circle at one and only one point. In practice, most pilots tend to fly a tangent line that cuts through ten degrees of the arc.

For example, a pilot would fly one heading from the 090 radial to the 100 radial and then change heading. A 360-degree arc would then require 36 heading changes. Of course, a perfectly distanced arc will not be flown but it's a good-enough approximation. The length of each of these 36 segments varies with the size of the arc. The FAA designs arcs with radii between seven and 30 miles.

Take a look at the DME arc at the University of Illinois-Willard on page 13 of the Pilot's Handbook. There is an arc north of the airport that runs clockwise to intercept the ILS course 316. There is also an arc south of the airport, which runs counter-clockwise toward the ILS. Both arcs use a DME value of 12 NM on the CMI VOR.

To begin this lesson, set the aircraft above the CMI VOR located at the airport. If you go to World on the main menu and select the Airport/Facility Directory, you will find exact coordinates of the CMI VOR in the NavAids listing for Illinois. Select Go To from the main menu and choose Exact location. Set Latitude to N40 degrees 2.10 feet and Longitude to W88 degree

Setting your exact location over the CMI VOR.

Setting the NAV radios for the DME arc.

16.60 feet. The altitude should be set to 2600 feet MSL, which is the minimum altitude shown on the chart. The course from CMI to the beginning of the arc is 006. Therefore, put in a Heading of 006 and an airspeed of 120.

When you come back to the game you may need to add power quickly by pressing F3. Press P to pause the game and select Aircraft from the main menu. Go into Navigation and select the Navigation Radios tab. Set NAV1 to the primary aid you will be using during the arc—the CMI VOR. Set the Frequency to 110.0 and the OBS to 006 since you will track the arc, which is north of the airport. Set NAV2 to the ILS. The Frequency is 109.10 while the OBS is set to 316.

Press P to resume the game and track R-006. Get the aircraft into the approach-level configuration described in Chapter Four. When you get close to DME 12.0, you will start the DME procedure. Usually, within .5 miles is a good place to start the procedure. Therefore, wait until you are at the 11.5 DME indication.

When you get to the 11.5 DME, turn in the direction of the arc. In this case, you will be making right turns. Your heading should be tangential to the arc, or 90 degrees from the radial you are on. You are currently on the 006 radial. (You can round this to 005 to simplify the math.) The heading 90 degrees to the right of this is 095. Turn at standard rate to 095. After you roll out, turn the OBS in the same direction by 10 degrees. In this case, rotate it to a heading of 015. The CDI will deflect all the way to the right, which represents being off-course by ten degrees.

Continue flying 095 until the needle centers. You'll notice that the DME reads 12.2 DME. Because the aircraft is a bit outside the DME arc, the aircraft heading may need to point back toward the arc to make up for the deviation. When the needle centers, it is time to "turn and twist ten" again.

Flying 006 until you reach the 11.5 DME indication.

While flying 095, you'll need to twist the OBS to 015.

When the CDI centers, it's time to "turn and twist ten."

Steady as you go, continuing on the 12.0 DME arc.

The aircraft should turn ten more degrees to the right, in this case to a heading of 105 and the OBS rotated ten degrees to 025. The CDI will again deflect all the way to the right and you will wait until the needle re-centers before repeating the procedure. Because the DME indication shows the aircraft on the 12.4 DME arc, the heading should be increased form 105 to 115 to get back onto the arc.

You will continue with these procedures until it's time to rotate the OBS to 125 and fly a heading of 215. There is a leading radial off of R-123. The leading radial signifies a point where you can begin to make an intercept angle for the inbound-approach course. Set the OBS to 123 instead of 125. When the needle centers, you can turn to a heading of 286 which is an intercept angle of 30 degrees.

A leading radial can help intercept the ILS.

The CDI in NAV1 will begin to drift while the LOC in NAV2 will begin to center. When the CDI on NAV2 begins to move, turn right to a heading of 315 and track it to the runway. You need to press P to pause the simulation and turn in the ILS on NAV1 so that your primary navigation tool is set in NAV1. Additionally, the NAV2 in the Cessna Skylane 182S does not have a glide-slope indicator.

Fly a heading of 286 until you intercept the localizer.

Instrument Takeoff

The trick in an instrument takeoff is transitioning from VFR flight to IFR flight. Make sure you begin scanning the instruments before you enter IFR conditions. To help with the transition, get into to IFR-climb configuration as soon as possible to stabilize the aircraft's performance.

Takeoff Minimums

To take off in IFR conditions, standard takeoff weather minimums, described in NOS and Jeppesen approach charts, are applied. The standard takeoff visibility must be at least one statute mile for aircraft with one or two engines. This minimum applies to commercial flights only. So, if you're flying the 737, you may want to use it. However, general aviation pilots do not need to adhere to these standards. You can take off in zero visibility in the C-182S despite having less equipment on board than a commercial airliner. Some airports have non-standard take-off minimums.

Checking your Instruments

If the weather conditions make a takeoff feasible, you should check the aircraft's instrument before departing. You may want to make a few turns on the runway to check that your heading indicator and turn coordinator are working okay. Pilots sometimes do a "BELT" before taking off. The 'B' stands

for *seat belts* and is not something you need to worry about in Flight Simulator. So, in fact, you really only need to make an "ELT" check.

The 'E' stands for *electrical*. You should verify that your radios are turned on, your ammeter is showing the proper discharge, and that your transponder is turned on. The 'L' stands for *lights*. Make sure any lights are functional (such as your instrument panel lights) by flipping the instrument-light toggle switch.

The final 'T' stands for *time*. You should use the cockpit clock to note the time you are taking off and also use it to determine flight data such as estimated time of arrival at your destination. When going into visible moisture, as most IFR weather is, it's also a good idea to turn the pitot heat on (even if the temperature's above-freezing) by flipping the pitot toggle switch. If you make a habit of checking the pitot heat, you won't forget it when it really counts. You should calibrate the DG to your compass and make sure it also reflects the heading of the runway you are on. Check that the altimeter is set to the right pressure setting. Select Aircraft from the main menu and choose Aircraft Settings. Click on the Realism tab and compare what your altimeter calibration to the actual pressure.

On the ground, set all your radios to the frequencies you will be using and dial in the correct OBS settings. Have your flight plan handy so you know where to go after take-off. In addition, you should have the approach plate handy for the airport you are taking off from. This is in case you have an engine problem and need to get back down in a hurry. During rollout, apply the power slowly and maintain your heading using rudder. Check that your airspeed indicator is active and that your suction gauge is in the green range.

Climb Rate

If you are using the standard minimums, you must be able to maintain a particular climb rate. This rate is 200 feet-per-nautical mile. This is not the same climb rate shown on the VSI. The VSI measures feet-per-minute. Feet-per-nautical mile can be converted to feet-per-minute using a calculation based on ground speed. NOS Terminal Procedures provide a table to do this conversion. If you have a 90-knot ground speed, you must climb at 300 feet-per-minute to also climb at 200 feet-per-nautical mile. This will guarantee that you won't hit any obstacles on takeoff. You should maintain runway heading until you are at least 400 feet above the ground so that you will be sure not to hit any obstacles.

Occasionally, on an NOS approach chart, you will see a triangle with a 'T' in it. This means that the takeoff minimums for the runway are not standard. You will need to reference the front of the booklet to see what special minimums apply. Usually, the special minimum will require that you climb more than 200 feet-per-nautical mile or turn to a specific heading. At other times, it might specify a particular cloud ceiling and visibility so that you will be responsible for navigating around any obstacles near the airport.

IFR Rate-of-Climb Table

Required Climb Rate (Ft/NM)	Ground Speed 90	120	140
200	300	400	467
250	375	500	583
300	450	600	700
350	525	700	816
400	600	800	933

Instrument Landing

When you are performing the approach, your attention will be focused on the instruments. However, you need to look out every once and a while and see if the runway is in sight. Diverting your attention between the gauges and the outside view can be tricky during single-pilot operations.

The view at the MAP on the NDB Runway 3 at Peter O Knight in a "No Wind" situation.

Finding the Runway

Finding the runway in low visibility is often difficult. Complicating matters is the fact that the approach path may be set off from the runway centerline by as much as 30 degrees. Factor in the wind correction and

the runway might be directly off the wing tip!

Therefore, you must study the runway chart and visualize your wind correction so you know where to look. Once you see the lights and runway environment, you can't go completely off the gauges unless you are confident you won't re-enter zero visibility conditions during the rest of the approach. On the ground, use lighting references to help keep direction on rollout and while taxing.

Circle-to-Land

You may choose to perform a circle-to-land approach if you follow the circle-to-land minimums published on the approach chart. This is usually done on approaches that lead to the airport only, and not to a specific runway. It's also used to get lined-up on a runway that favors the prevailing wind conditions. When you circle to land, you should stay at or above the MDA specified for the approach. You should not wander too far from the airport (to avoid any obstacles around the airport). The amount of airspace safe for an aircraft to circle in is defined by its category, as described in Chapter Six. This circling area has a radius of approximately 1.3 NM for category A aircraft.

A circling maneuver may be as simple as diverting to a parallel runway. A pilot may perform this "side step" maneuver to land on a longer runway or one that is closer to the hanger.

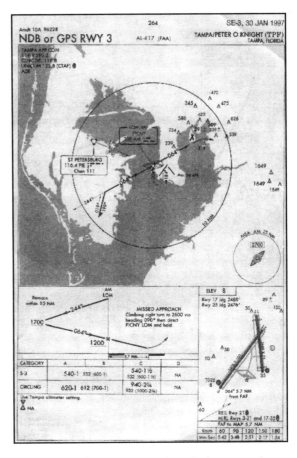

Note the 30-degree approach path drawn on the runway chart for the NDB Runway three at Peter O Knight.

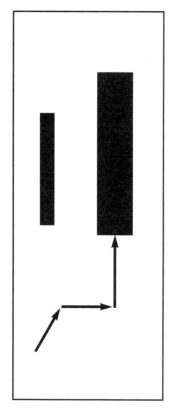

"Side-stepping" onto a parallel runway.

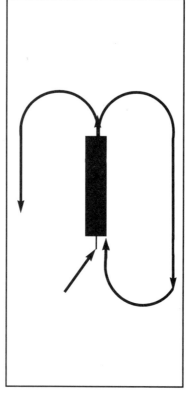

Coming back around to a runway, ready to make another approach.

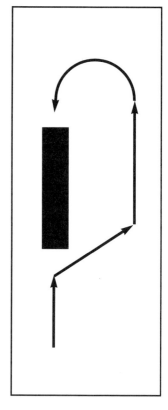

Pilots can land on the direct-opposite runway from the one they originally intended, provided wind conditions warrant making the switch.

A pilot may also perform an approach for the runway on which he intends to land, after he's seen the airport too late to enable a safe landing. In this case, the pilot should fly directly over the runway and then make a downwind turn to enter the traffic pattern.

In some cases, the pilot may want to land on the direct-opposite runway. This may be done if the winds favor landing in a different direction. The pilot will enter the downwind segment of the traffic pattern.

The FAA determines the MDA for a specific approach by looking at the highest obstacle in the circling area. It adds 300 feet to this height to determine the MDA. Depending on how good your attitude control skills, you may find this a small cushion to circle in. If no obstacle is in the circling area, the FAA will still assume the largest obstacle is 100 feet high. This buffer accounts for fast growing trees. Thus, the MDA would be 400 feet. The approach chart will show where obstacles are located. You may want to circle in a direction away from them.

Martha's Vineyard Runway 06 is150 feet wide, which is about the average width for runways.

Landing Illusions

When landing, you may encounter several visual illusions. If you are landing on a runway that's narrower than a standard runway, you may feel higher than you actually are. Most runways have a width between 150 and 200 feet. Runway 06 at Martha's Vineyard is 150 feet wide.

Considerably skinnier is Martha's Vineyard Runway 15, only 50 feet wide (one-third the width of Runway 16).

The airport chart on page 39 of the Pilot's Handbook shows that Runway 15 at Martha's Vineyard is only *50* feet wide. Therefore, you must avoid the

Runway 18 at Chicago's Meigs Field...and the weather's fine.

Runway 18...during visibility of one-half mile.

temptation to fly a lower-than-normal approach when landing on this runway. On the other hand, if the runway is wider than normal or slopes down, you will feel higher than you really are and may fly a higher-than-normal approach. On a clear day, you may make a perfect approach into Chicago's Meigs Field. You may have gotten used to what it's like to land there under these conditions.

During hazy conditions, the runway will look farther away than it really is. This may also result in you flying a lower-than-normal approach.

Chapter Eight

Advanced Instrument Training

The previous chapters have discussed instrument flight basics—how to control an aircraft solely by referring to its instruments. In this chapter we'll take a look at some of the more advanced instrument flight concepts modeled in Microsoft Flight Simulator 98. Specifically, we'll talk about weather hazards, holding patterns, the Autopilot, and how to identify and cope with instrument failures. Finally, we'll discuss how to get your aircraft back under control when you suddenly find yourself in a steep bank- or pitch-angle.

Weather Hazards

Even though IFR skills allow you to fly in low visibility, they do not give you a free pass through all weather situations. Flight Simulator 98 can create weather hazards that require special techniques to safely manage. Icing, windshear, and turbulence can cause you to lose control of the aircraft, whether you're in VMC (Visual Meteorological Conditions) or IMC (Instrument Meteorological Conditions). However, you are more likely to encounter these situations when you set Flight Simulator to IFR skies. Whenever you fly in clouds, the elements exist for icing and turbulence.

Icing

When you fly in clouds of below-freezing temperatures, you run the risk of ice forming on the aircraft. This ice can cause your airspeed indicator to stop functioning correctly. Without an airspeed indicator, attitude instrument flying becomes more difficult since you have less information at your disposal.

As discussed in Chapter Four, the airspeed indicator determines how fast the aircraft is travelling by measuring how fast air molecules hit the aircraft. Specifically, it measures how fast air molecules enter a device called a pitot tube. The pitot tube is located on the outside of an aircraft.

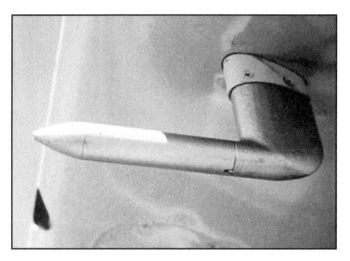

The pitot tube serves the airspeed indicator by measuring how fast air molecules are moving outside an aircraft.

Tip: *In reality, depending on the amount of ice already accumulated, applying pitot heat may not work if icing has already blocked the pitot tube. This is because there simply might not be enough heat available to melt the ice off the tube after it has already formed. Therefore, most manufacturers recommend turning on pitot heat upon entering icing conditions, rather than after noticing a problem or encountering visible icing.*

A toggle switch allows you to turn pitot heat on and off.

When the pitot tube becomes blocked (in this case by ice), the airspeed indicator does not register that any molecules are hitting the aircraft. Thus, it calculates that the aircraft is traveling at zero knots. To keep the pitot tube free of ice, most aircraft that fly in IMC have a pitot heater. Theoretically, when pitot heat is switched on, the ice in the tube will melt, allowing the airspeed indicator to properly calculate airspeed.

The pitot heat switch in the Cessna Skylane RG (C-182RG) and Cessna Skylane S (C-182S) is located in the lower left-hand corner of the control panel. To turn it on, place your cursor on the switch and move it into the Up position. In the Lear 45, the pitot heat control is located in the same area but instead of a toggle switch, a button is used to turn it on and off. Simply click your cursor on this button. You know it's on when it lights up. In the Boeing 737-400 (B-737), the pitot switch is located on the top control panel. You switch it on the same way as in the C-182S.

Icing will occur any time you are flying in clouds and the air temperature is below freezing (32 degrees Fahrenheit). This is because clouds are made up of water vapor. Use the temperature gauge to determine the outside air temperature whenever you're flying in clouds.

To display temperature in Celsius rather than Fahrenheit, go to the Options menu located on the main menu and click on Preferences. Select the International tab and change the Units of measure option to Metric (altimeter feet). The freezing level in Celsius is located at zero degrees.

A temperature gauge inside the aircraft lets you know just how cold it is outside.

There is a point when it's too cold for ice to adhere to the aircraft. If the temperature is below 15 degrees F (-10 degrees C), chances are you will not have to worry about pitot icing. Nevertheless, it's a good habit to go ahead and turn the pitot heat on anyway, just in case. In fact, if you turn it on every time you enter IMC, you will be sure not to forget it when you really need it.

Simulating Pitot Icing in Flight Simulator 98

To discover the effects of icing first hand, let's create a cold day at Chicago's Meigs Field. Go into Flights on the main menu, and choose Select Flights from the submenu. Click on Default Flight—Meigs Field.

Next, you need to be sure you have Flight Simulator 98 set up for high flight realism. Otherwise, the program will take it easy on you and not create any pitot ice. Select Aircraft on the main menu and choose Aircraft Settings. Click the Realism tab and slide the Flight Realism bar from Easy to Real.

Now you need to create a cloud layer so that there will be moisture available to freeze on the pitot tube. Choose World from the main menu and select Weather. Click on the Clouds tab and change the Cloud Type option to Nimbostratus. Nimbostratus clouds are a type of rain cloud and will be

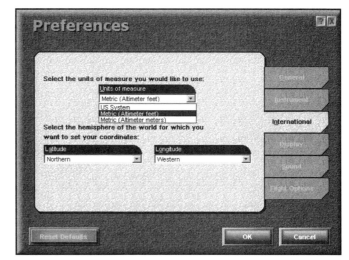

Flight Simulator 98 can be set with English or Metric units of measurement.

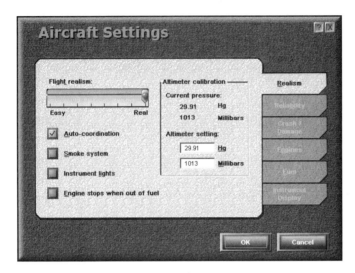

Set Flight Realism to Real if you want to experience icing conditions.

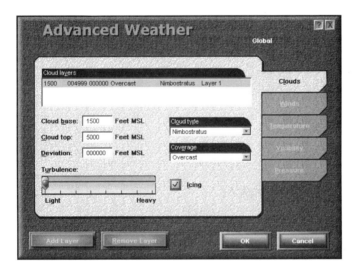

Icing conditions can be found in a Nimbostratus cloud layer.

sure to have plenty of moisture available to freeze on your aircraft. The Icing field should automatically activate when you choose this cloud type. Set the Cloud Base to 1500 feet MSL and the Cloud Top to 5000 feet MSL. This will allow you to get into the cloud soon after takeoff.

Finally, you need to create the freezing conditions. Temperature tends to decrease as altitude increases at a rate of two degrees Celsius for every 1000 feet increase in altitude. Flight Simulator 98 allows you to specifically set a temperature at various altitudes. Go back into the Weather dialog box and select the Temperature tab.

First create a Surface temperature layer. This is the outside temperature as you wait on the runway for takeoff. Click on the surface layer under the Temperature Layer box. When you look at your altimeter, you see that Meigs Field is located at an altitude of about 600 feet. Go ahead and enter 600 feet MSL into the Altitude field and 30 degrees F into the Daytime Temperature box.

Next, click on the Low layer option. Set the temperature to 25 degrees F at 2000 feet MSL. Notice that you have the option to vary the temperature at a specific altitude by using the Variation range field. You can set up to four temperature layers in Flight Simulator 98.

Back in the aircraft at Meigs Field you will notice the temperature gauge reads 30 degrees F. Take off and fly runway heading at an airspeed of 80 knots. Be sure that your pitot heat is turned off before takeoff. As you climb, you will notice that your temperature gauge shows the temperature dropping as you climb. At about 1700 feet MSL and 27 degrees F, you'll notice your airspeed indicator suddenly falls to zero. This is because ice has clogged your pitot tube. Now go ahead and flip on the pitot heat. After about 30 seconds have passed, your airspeed indicator will begin to function properly again. Leave the pitot heat on until you exit the icing conditions.

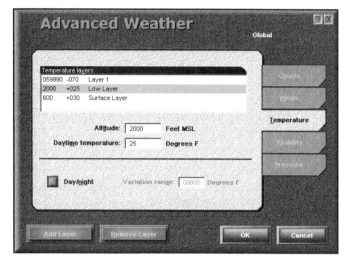

A specific temperature can be set at various altitudes.

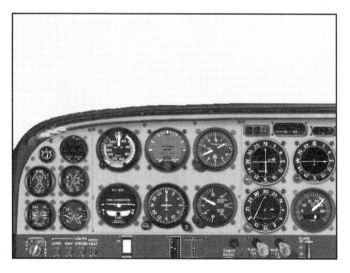

Pitot ice will cause your airspeed indicator to malfunction.

Windshear

To most people, windshear has generally been associated with thunderstorms during a landing approach because windshear has caused major airline catastrophes. However, windshear is really just a change in wind direction and/or wind speed. Windshear (under much milder levels than catastrophe-strength) usually results in two conditions called *overshoot effect* and *undershoot effect*.

Overshoot effect is when an aircraft flies above its desired approach path and/or experiences an unwanted increase in airspeed. This is encountered when the airplane suddenly flies into an increasing headwind, into a decreasing tailwind, from a tailwind into a headwind, or into an updraft. Undershoot effect is when you fly below your flight path and/or suffer from a decrease in airspeed. It is caused by flying into a decreasing headwind, into an increasing tailwind, from a headwind into a tailwind, or into a downdraft.

Simulating Windshear in Flight Simulator 98

Let's go back to Meigs Field to simulate the problems associated with windshear. Click on World and select Weather from the submenu. Click on the Winds tab to get the Weather dialog box. First, let's add a surface layer. Click on the Add Layer button and select Surface layer. In the Depth field, enter 200 feet AGL. This means the wind between field elevation (600 feet MSL) and 800 feet MSL will possess the wind characteristics you set for this layer.

Set Wind Speed to ten knots and Wind Direction to 360 degrees. Wind Direction on the surface layer is defined using magnetic headings. In this case, the wind is coming from a

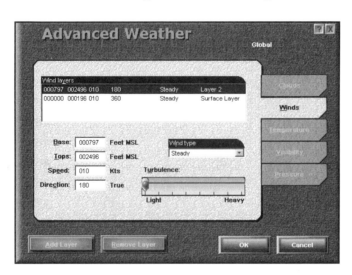

Creating windshear with the Advanced Weather option.

direction of magnetic north and is blowing toward magnetic south. Since you are departing from Runway 36, the wind is blowing right on you. The Wind Type setting should be left at Steady. If you choose a Wind Type of Gusty, the wind speed will vary rather than remain constant at ten knots.

Let's add a second layer right above the surface layer. Click on the Add Layer button and define a layer with a Base at 800 feet MSL and a Top at 2500 feet MSL. Set the wind speed to ten knots again. However, set Wind Direction to 180 degrees. Wind directions on the upper layers are measured against true north rather than magnetic north. Magnetic North is where your compass registers magnetic north. True north is measured in relation to where north is located on a map. At 800 feet MSL, the wind will radically change direction, leaving you to deal with windshear.

Back at Meigs Field you are ready to take off. You have a direct steady wind so

Go ahead and perform your climb-out before encountering windshear conditions.

Windshear is exposing this aircraft to the undershoot effect.

You never know when, or how often, you'll find your aircraft in windshear conditions.

Windshear can cause your aircraft to encounter undershoot effect on landing, right when you need it least.

you begin your ground roll and climb-out worry-free. It's business as usual as you fly through the first 200 feet of altitude.

However, as soon as you get to 800 feet MSL, your headwind ceases and you find yourself dealing with a tailwind. You will now be in undershoot effect. Your airspeed will decrease rapidly and you will lose altitude. You need to get your airspeed up as quickly as possible by making sure you have full power on. You will need to raise the nose of the aircraft to begin climbing again.

Go back into the Weather and Select the Winds tab. Reverse the direction of the Surface layer from 360 degrees to 180 degrees and the direction of the Lower layer from 180 degrees to 360 degrees. Let's say you're returning to Meigs Field after a long journey and have noticed the wind blowing from the north. You assume the wind at the surface must be the same and decide to land on Runway 360. As you approach for

landing, everything is going smoothly.

As you get within 200 feet of the runway threshold, you encounter the windshear conditions and suffer from the undershoot effect. On landing, the nose of the aircraft will rise and your airspeed will bleed off. You need to quickly add power to avoid stalling.

Thunderstorms and Turbulence

Thunderstorms are a hazard because of the severe turbulence they produce. When you fly in a thunderstorm, you will have a hard time controlling the aircraft by the instruments because your aircraft will be tossed around so much. If you do find yourself in a severe storm, don't fight the controls to try to maintain altitude. Just strive to keep the wings level. Slow down to the aircraft's published maneuvering speed. This is 101 knots in the C-182S, at a weight of 2600 pounds. Luckily in Flight Simulator

Real World Weather Avoidance

In Flight Simulator 98, you always know where weather hazards exist. Either you have personally set them or, in the case of Lessons and Adventures, you can take a peek at the Weather settings to see what the Flight Simulator programmers have in store for you. In real aviation, it's not nearly as cut and dry.

ATC can help pilots steer clear of inclement weather by vectoring them around severe weather they register with radar systems. Unfortunately, ATC can not predict or report all weather. They are often too busy with their primary mission, IFR separation, to give the latest weather reports. At other times, their equipment isn't sophisticated enough to know exactly what it's like to fly in a certain area of airspace.

Many aircraft have their own airborne weather radar systems to help circumvent storms. This radar can detect water droplets. It works by sending a signal and receiving a return signal back. A display in the cockpit paints the "returns" on a screen. The returns are color-coded depending on the intensity of the shower picked up. This device works on the assumption that the intensity of a shower is related to the intensity of downdrafts and turbulence.

Another cockpit weather detection device is called Storm Scope. This device registers lightning strikes. It paints a picture of where the concentrations of lighting strikes are occurring. Obviously, the pilot would be wise to avoid these areas.

Pilot reports are also used as a way to avoid trouble areas. When using a pilot report, pilots must remember that a C-182 may not be able to negotiate what a B-737 was able to handle with ease. In addition, weather changes rapidly. What one pilot might have gotten through a few moments ago in the C-182 might have been a tame storm. But a Lear 45 pilot venturing in the same area a few minutes later might find the storm has suddenly become violent.

Thunderstorm conditions contain severe turbulence, and can be created by choosing Cumulonimbus clouds within the Weather options.

98, you fly through thunderstorms quickly.

Severe turbulence is not only found in thunderstorms. You can purposely set severe turbulence using the Advanced Weather dialog box. The severity of turbulence can be set on both the Clouds tab and the Winds tab.

Simulating Thunderstorms

In VMC, you can see thunderclouds coming. To create these dangerous conditions, go into Weather on the World submenu. Choose a Cloud Type of Cumulonimbus and set Coverage to Dense. The Icing option should automatically activate.

The problem in IMC is that you can't see when you're heading straight for a thundercloud. When thunderstorms are hidden within other cloud layers, they are referred to as *embedded* thunderstorms. Let's say you were to create a layer of dense thunderstorms from 3000 feet to 8000 feet MSL. You could create a second layer of cumulus clouds located between 3000 feet and 4000 feet MSL. If you were cruising at an altitude of 3500 feet MSL, you wouldn't have any warning before entering a thunderstorm cloud.

Holding Patterns

Holding patterns are often found on IFR-approach procedures as procedure turns or missed-approach procedures. But boiled down to its essence, a holding pattern is simply a *race track* pattern flown in a specific area of airspace. You may encounter a holding pattern instead of a procedure turn on the initial approach segment of an approach procedure. This technique allows the aircraft

to get turned to the proper inbound course. After completing one lap around the track, the aircraft will be lined up on an inbound heading.

You'll also notice most missed-approach segments specify a holding pattern. While holding, you'll have time to get set up for another approach. You can reset your navigation instruments, set your stopwatch, and get the aircraft back into an IFR approach-level configuration. You could also take this time to plan your route to another airport.

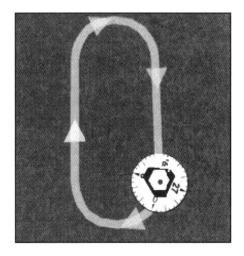

The holding pattern should look familiar to you, especially if you're a racing fan.

Elements of a Hold

If you are going to execute a holding pattern, the first thing you need to do is determine *where* you are going to hold. Usually, the holding fix is a VOR or NDB. However, sometimes the holding fix is a bit trickier to identify. For instance, the holding fix could also be an intersection of two VORs, or a particular DME location on a VOR radial.

Once you know what the fix is, you have to decide what radial or bearing from the fix you will travel on during your inbound leg. For instance, let's say the fix you choose to hold around is the PGE VOR. You then might choose to hold on the 180-degree radial from this fix. At this point, you need to decide if you will make your loop on the east or west side of the 180-degree radial. Usually, all turns in the holding pattern are made to the right. Therefore, you would hold on the eastern side of the radial.

Now you know where to hold—the next question is how big you should make your laps. The length of the

Getting Put On Hold

Another reason for a pilot entering a "hold" is simply because ATC requests it. They will do this when they need to slow down traffic to safely flow everyone through a particular piece of airspace. For example, when several aircraft are trying to land at a busy airport, they may have to hold and wait their turn for a landing "slot." In this case, there will probably be several aircraft waiting in the same landing queue. They will all circle around the same location but at different altitudes. Some pilots may also hold hoping the weather will clear below before attempting their approach.

pattern is a factor of how long you fly each leg. If you are flying below 14,000 feet MSL, a standard leg is one minute. If you're flying above 14,000 feet you should make each leg 1.5 minutes. Once in a while you may come across a hold that specifies the leg be a certain distance rather than a specific length of time. This location is usually a DME fix.

Maximum Speeds

The maximum speed for a propeller-driven aircraft in a hold is 175 knots. You should not have a problem meeting this requirement in the C-182S. The reason for the speed limit is to ensure that you won't leave protected airspace when you are making your one-minute legs. However, if you're flying the Lear or B-737, your maximum speed limit jumps to 265 KIAS if you're above 14,000 feet and 230 KIAS if you're flying below 14,000 feet.

Entering a Hold

Typically, the most common problem students have with holding patterns is simply how to get into one. There are three standard entries, called the *direct*, *teardrop* and *parallel* entries. They are designed to allow you to easily transition from your current location to the holding pattern. To determine which one you should use, you should visualize your location in relation to the holding pattern. Mentally draw a line from your current position to the holding fix and determine what entry method will be most efficient.

The direct entry is used when you already are on a course close to the inbound heading. Simply fly toward the fix until you pass over it.

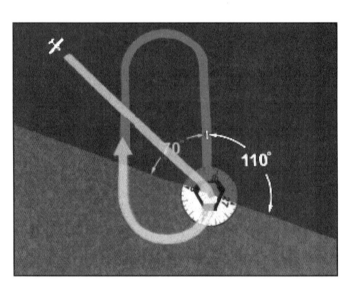

A direct entry into a holding pattern.

Then you're ready to begin the standard holding pattern techniques.

The parallel entry is used if you are flying a course almost directly opposite the inbound course of the holding. You would again fly right to the fix. However, when you fly over the fix you would not turn inbound on the inbound course. Instead, you would pass over the fix and fly *outbound* on the inbound course for one minute. After one minute was up, you would make a 280-degree turn toward the inside of the holding pattern. You would stay on this course until you re-intercepted the inbound course. You would then turn inbound on the inbound course and follow your holding pattern procedures.

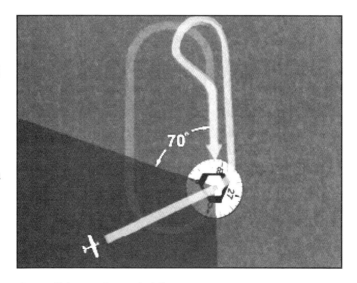

A parallel entry into a holding pattern.

The teardrop maneuver is used for when you are approaching the holding pattern from an area located on the same side of the holding pattern as the inbound course, between the area used for a direct entry and a parallel entry.

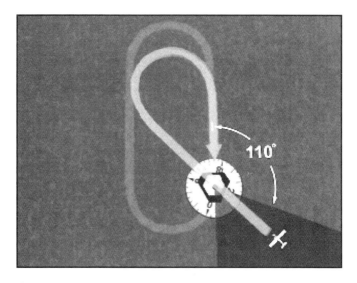

A teardrop entry into a holding pattern.

Basically, after you fly over the fix you would turn to a heading 30 degrees off the outbound course. You would fly in this direction for one minute. For example, if the hold was north of R-90, you would fly a heading of 60 degrees for one minute. After one minute, you would turn inbound to 090 degrees and begin your holding pattern procedures.

Holding In Flight Simulator 98

Let's practice a hold in Flight Simulator 98, using one of the pre-built holding lessons. Go to Flights on the main menu and select Lessons. Click on the VOR Hold: Cessna Skylane 182S lesson. After the lesson loads, you will find yourself at an altitude of 3000 feet MSL and a heading of 360 degrees. NAV1 is tuned to the Richmond VOR. You may want to pause the lesson for a moment and go into World on the main menu and select the Weather option. You can go to the Visibility tab and change the Visibility to one mile to practice your altitude-instrument flying in a hold.

This lesson prompts you to fly to the Richmond VOR and fly a holding pattern on the 180-degree radial. The lesson also specifies that you should make turns to the right. Therefore, you will be holding southeast of the Richmond VOR and your inbound leg will be a heading of 360 degrees.

Your OBS is set to 360 degrees and the needle is centered with a TO indication. Therefore, you are due south of the Richmond VOR. Since you are already on the inbound course, the best entry pattern to choose is a direct entry. Keep flying toward the VOR until you pass over it. When you are directly over the VOR, the NAV radio will not pick up a signal since it is in the cone of confusion discussed in Chapter Five.

Clearance to Leave a Hold

Pilots who fly an actual holding pattern need to receive the Expect Further Clearance time (EFC) from ATC. This is the time the pilot can expect to be able to exit the hold and continue on with his flight plan. Although it seems like a minor piece of information, it is actually quite important. Technically, if there was a communications failure with ATC, the pilot would not be able to leave the hold if the EFC had not been issued. If an EFC is issued, ATC expects to issue an additional (exit) clearance before or after that time, but with communications failure the pilot is authorized to depart the Holding Pattern athe EFC time.

Continue flying at 360 degrees until you pass over the VOR. This is the point where you exit the cone of confusion and the TO/FROM flag begins to display a FROM indication.

Once you pass over the VOR, make a standard right-hand turn to the outbound heading. As Chapter Four explained, a standard-rate turn in the Cessna 182S requires

18 degrees of bank. The outbound heading, 180 degrees, is the reverse of the inbound heading. At the completion of the turn, you are waiting for the aircraft to be positioned next to the VOR. At this point, the VOR will be located straight off the right wing tip. The aircraft is referred to as being "abeam" the VOR.

There are two ways to determine when you are abeam the VOR. First, the OBS of your NAV1 radio is still tuned to 360. When you are abeam the VOR, you will be on the 090 radial. As discussed in Chapter Five, the zone of ambiguity will effect your NAV1 radio and the TO/FROM flag will disappear. Because the C-182S comes equipped with a second NAV radio, you can use it to help identify when you are abeam the VOR. You can set the OBS to 090 and wait for the needle to center. At this point, you know you are on the 090 radial. The figure at right illustrates how your NAV radios will look when you are abeam the VOR in this lesson.

When you're "abeam" the VOR, the VOR will be located next to your aircraft.

Once you are abeam the VOR, you should start timing your outbound leg. After one minute has passed, begin a standard-rate turn back to your inbound heading of 360 degrees. During your turn, check NAV1 and determine how close your rollout will be to the inbound course. For example, if you are within 30 degrees of your inbound course and the CDI has yet to move, you should roll out of your turn early. Once the CDI begins to show some interception progress, restart your turn. On the other hand, if you overshoot the course, you may want to increase your turn rate on the next lap.

As soon as you complete this inbound turn, begin timing again. You want to determine if the length of your inbound leg will also be one minute. Hopefully, when you arrive at the holding fix, you find that exactly one minute has elapsed. If not, you need to adjust the length of your outbound course to account for the wind. You will find in this lesson that wind is not a factor. Once you pass over the holding fix, you repeat the entire procedure.

If you choose to practice holding with a wind, you would observe the following procedures. If you finished your inbound leg early, you would fly the outbound leg by an additional amount equal to one-half the deviation. If the inbound course was longer than one minute, you would decrease your outbound leg by one-half the overage to compensate for the headwind.

Modifying the Lesson for Different Entries

You can modify this lesson to practice parallel and direct entries. The instructor in this lesson will try to correct your procedures since they do not follow the lesson outline. Therefore, you may want to turn down the Adventures sound volume while you practice these maneuvers.

To practice the parallel entry, continue flying a heading of 360 degrees for one minute after you pass over the Richmond VOR. Then make a standard right-hand turn back to a heading of 180 degrees and track a direct course to the VOR. You are now set up for a parallel entry. Keep flying direct to the Richmond VOR until you pass over it. When you pass over the VOR, track outbound on the 180-degree radial for one minute. After one minute has passed, make a left-hand standard-rate turn until you are on a heading of 330 degrees. You would continue on this heading until you re-intercepted the 180-degree radial, and then you would follow the standard direct-entry procedures.

To simulate a teardrop entry, track to the Richmond VOR. When you pass over it, continue flying straight ahead for one minute like you did to simulate the parallel entry. Make a left-hand standard-rate turn to a heading of 180 degrees and fly direct to the Richmond VOR. When you pass over the VOR, turn to a heading of 150 degrees and fly this heading for one minute. Then make a standard right-hand turn back to 360 degrees and follow the direct-entry procedures.

Recognizing Instrument Failures

Just like in the real world of aviation, you cannot always count on your instruments working correctly in Microsoft Flight Simulator 98. Unfortunately, most instruments do not notify you immediately when they have failed. You must figure it out for yourself or you will be making decisions using incorrect information. Flight Simulator 98 gives you a warning that something is wrong by displaying "Aircraft system malfunction" on the top left of the screen. This warning may refer to the fuel system rather than the instruments. You need to determine if it is instrument-related and if so, fly using a technique called *partial panel*.

`Aircraft system malfunction.`

Flight Simulator 98 warns you about system malfunction.

Setting Instrument Failure

There are two ways to make instruments fail in Flight Simulator 98. You can purposely "fail" a specific instrument or have Flight Simulator 98 randomly fail instrument systems. To select a specific instrument to fail, select Aircraft Settings from the Aircraft menu. Then choose the Instrument Display tab to get to the window. Here you can set any of the primary instruments to be rendered inoperative.

You can also fail an entire system by deactivating one of the systems displayed in this tab. If you deactivate the pitot-static system, your airspeed indicator, vertical speed indicator (VSI), and altimeter will malfunction. If you turn off the vacuum system, only the C-182S, C-182RG, and E300S will be effected. The attitude indicator (AI) and heading indicator will malfunction in these aircraft. These instruments run by electric

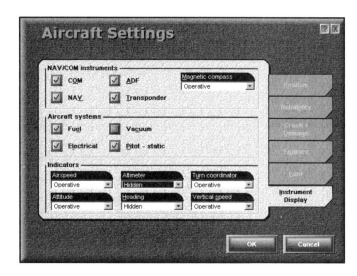

You can program several instruments or instrument systems to go inoperative.

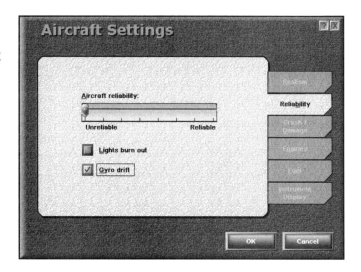

To create random instrument failure, you must make sure your aircraft is suitably unreliable.

power in the B-737 and Lear 45, and will only become inoperative due to an electrical failure. Electrical failure will also cause the navigation and communication radios to fail. The turn coordinator in the C-182S and C-182RG will malfunction due to electrical failure.

If you want Flight Simulator 98 to randomly fail instruments for you, you need to increase the simulated flight realism. Go into Aircraft Settings on the Aircraft menu. Select the Realism tab and slide the Flight Realism control from Easy to Real. If you have trouble determining which instruments have failed when you use this option, you can peek at the Instrument Display tab to see which ones have been set to inoperative.

Recognizing Vacuum Failure

The vacuum instruments, which consist of your AI and heading indicator in the Cessna Skylanes and E300S, require an adequate level of suction pressure to operate properly. You need to incorporate a glance at the suction gauge into your scan to make sure the gauge is always pointing to the green arc. If it's outside this range, you're due for some instrument failure.

The suction pressure gauge (the needle should always be pointing to the green arc).

When the vacuum instruments fail due to lack of suction, they will gradually spin down. The background of the AI will gradually fall down. If you suspect vacuum failure, the turn coordinator will not turn in the same direction as the bank indicator on the AI. The AI will not reflect the same information the airspeed indicator is showing.

For example, let's say we're flying an aircraft making a climbing right turn from a heading of 360 degrees, and we have vacuum failure. The turn coordinator (TI) is showing a right-hand turn while the AI displays a left-hand turn. The heading indicator is still displaying a heading of 360 degrees despite the fact the turn has already been initiated. The AI shows a very steep nose-high attitude while the airspeed indicator shows that the aircraft is not pitch-high enough for an 80-knot climb speed.

An inoperative AI, possibly shut down due to vacuum failure.

Recognizing Electric Failure

If your electrical power is lost, you will lose your use of the turn coordinator and radios. In the B-737 and Lear 45, you will also lose your AI and TC. Because you lose your radios, it's a pretty good sign something is wrong. You'll quickly notice you have a problem, especially if you were initiating a climbing right-hand turn. The AI would show a right-hand climb. The VSI and airspeed indicator would also reflect that a climb is happening. The turn coordinator, however, would show no turn at all.

Handling a climbing right turn with vacuum failure can be a tricky business.

Recognizing Pitot-Static Failure

The airspeed indicator, VSI, and altimeter form the pitot-static system. The airspeed indicator uses information from the pitot tube as discussed in the section on icing. These instruments also use information obtained through the static port. These instruments measure the pressure of the air coming in

Equally treacherous: a climbing right-hand turn...with electrical failure.

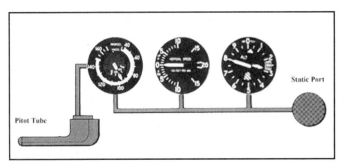

The pitot-static system is also subject to failure, especially when icing conditions are prevalent.

A climbing right-hand turn, made in a plane experiencing pitot-static failure.

from the static port. Since air pressure changes with altitude, these instruments can detect changes in altitude. When the static port becomes blocked, these instruments do not detect any change in altitude. The airspeed indicator and altimeter will remain fixed at their last indication. The VSI will show zero rate of climb.

For example, let's say you're making a climbing right-hand turn with a blocked static port. The AI would indicate that the aircraft is making a right-hand climb. The TC verifies that a turn to the right is being made. However, the VSI shows no climb and the altimeter is fixed at 700 feet MSL.

Flying Partial Panel

Partial panel flight refers to attitude-instrument flying when one or more of the six primary instruments are malfunctioning. It usually implies that the AI and heading indicator have malfunctioned. Since your scan should revolve around the AI, you have lost your major control instrument.

The first thing you must train yourself to do during partial panel is not to look at the broken instruments. This is surprisingly hard to do. In Flight

Simulator 98, you should set the failed instruments to Hidden. Use the Instrument Display tab to change the instrument status from Inoperative to Hidden.

Controlling Bank

Instead of controlling bank on the AI, you will use the TC. Concentrate on keeping the wings level with the ball centered, and you should stay on your heading. To determine how well you are doing at holding a heading, you will use the magnetic

Hide inoperative instruments so they don't wind up distracting you.

compass as a performance instrument. To get the compass into view, select Views from the main menu and choose Instrument Panel on the submenu. Click on the Compass option.

Let's say you're using the magnetic compass in the C-182S. Notice that a direction of 030 degrees is located to the left of north. On the heading indicator, 030 degrees is located to the right of north. You still need to turn right to get from a heading of 360 degrees to 030 degrees. It's just that when you use the magnetic compass, you need to think about which direction you need to turn into. You will also find that the compass is hard to read in turbulent situations because aircraft movements effect it.

Magnetic Error

Turns can either be made using the compass or by timing turns. If you make a turn using the compass, you need an understanding of magnetic errors or you will soon find yourself cursing the compass. In the northern hemisphere, the compass lags when making turns from a northerly heading. The compass will initially show a turn in the opposite direction than the one you are actually turning to.

The magnetic compass can be effected by aircraft movement, making it less-than-reliable during turbulence.

Magnetic error during a right-hand turn, resulting in two very different "stories" from the heading indicator and the compass.

If you're traveling on a southern heading and you turn, the opposite problem occurs. The compass will initially show that the aircraft has turned farther than it actually has. To remember how the compass will react in a turn, you can use the memory technique "NOSE." This stands for "North—Opposite, South—Exaggerate." NOSE errors are most significant at the pole and gradually decrease as you head towards the equator. This type of error is not a factor when making turns from an easterly or westerly heading.

A different type of magnetic error occurs when you are flying on an easterly or westerly heading, called *acceleration errors* and *deceleration errors*. For example, let's say you were flying an eastbound aircraft and had just decreased your power setting. You might notice the compass showing a turn to the south during this deceleration. If the aircraft increased speed, the compass would show a turn to the north. You can use "ANDS" ("Accelerate—North, Decelerate—South") to remember how the compass will react on east and west headings.

Compass Turns

The extent of NOSE errors correspond with the latitude at which you're flying. For example, Jacksonville, Florida is located at a latitude of 30 according to the

Magnetic error during deceleration— are you sure you know where you're heading?

Airport Facility Guide. If you were to turn from a heading of 360 degrees to 090 degrees, you would normally lead the rollout by one-half the angle of bank. At a bank angle of 18 degrees, you would lead the rollout by nine degrees, which would be a heading of 081 degrees. However, to account for the lag error, we will actually add the lag error of 30 to our calculation. On this compass turn, you would begin your rollout when the compass displayed a heading of 051 degrees.

Timed Turns

Timed turns use mathematics to make precision turns using the compass. Since a standard-rate turn results in a turn of three degrees per second, you use time to determine how many degrees you have turned. If you divide the number of degrees you need to turn by three, you know how many seconds you need to turn to get to that heading. For example, if you wanted to turn from 360 degrees to 020 degrees you will need to turn 20 degrees to the right. Therefore, you will need to make a standard right turn for approximately seven seconds (20/3).

You shouldn't begin timing the turn until your rate-of-turn equals standard rate. Don't stop the turn until you have finished timing. When you get back to straight and level flight, the compass may not immediately display your true heading until the NOSE and ANDS errors subside.

Half-standard-rate turns should be utilized any time you need to turn 15 degrees or less. A half-standard-rate turn will result in you turning 1.5 degrees per second. The TC needle will be halfway between straight and level and a standard-rate calibration mark. You may also wish to count the seconds off in your head rather than use a watch for these quick turns.

Holding Pitch

The VSI and altimeter are used to control pitch during partial panel. To climb at constant airspeed, raise the nose slightly, apply full power and keep the wings level with the TC. Hold this configuration and determine your performance on the airspeed indicator. Trim becomes increasingly important in assisting you in holding a specific attitude. Keep the altimeter in your scan and start to level off 50 feet below your desired altitude.

To descend, reduce the power to cruise descent and lower the nose. Use the airspeed indicator as a performance instrument.

Partial Panel Exercises in Flight Simulator 98

Flight Simulator 98 has several partial panel exercises pre-configured with instrument failures. Click on Flights on the main menu and select Challenges. You can pick from four partial panel exercises. All of these exercises take place

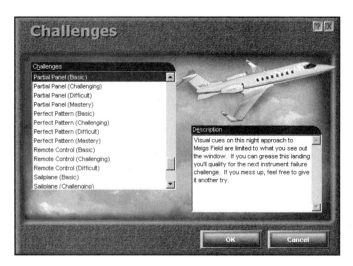

Four partial panel challenges await you in Flight Simulator 98.

in VFR skies in the C-182S. To increase the difficulty level, you can select World from the main menu and choose Weather. Click on the Visibility tab and set visibility at two miles.

In the Partial Panel (Basic) challenge, you will be asked to make a night landing at Meigs Field with all six primary instruments malfunctioning. The Partial Panel (Challenging) scenario places you at Port Angeles with the instruments malfunctioning one at a time. You will find yourself in similar circumstances in the Partial Panel (Difficult) challenge. Only this time, you are trying to land at Champaign. The Partial Panel (Mastery) flight is *extremely* difficult. You are on a night ILS into Oakland. However, your attitude indicator, heading indicator, turn coordinator, altimeter, and VSI are all inoperative. You must make the approach with only your airspeed indicator and NAV radios.

Recovering from Unusual Attitudes

An *unusual attitude* is experienced when an aircraft gets into a bank of over 30 degrees, a nose-high attitude with decreasing airspeed, or a nose-low attitude with increasing airspeed. They usually are caused when you aren't paying very close attention to Flight Simulator. Unusual attitudes occur during both IMC and VMC, but are much harder to correct during IMC.

Practicing flying at unusual attitudes can improve you reaction time when attitude-instrument flying. The key to recovering from an unusual attitude is not making movements that will overstress the aircraft. You should go into Aircraft Settings on the Aircraft menu and select the Crash/Damage tab. Activate the Aircraft Receives Damage From Stress option to accurately gauge how well you handle unusual attitudes.

The following procedures can help you tackle unusual attitudes. If the nose is low and your airspeed is rapidly increasing, you should reduce power, level the wings, and smoothly raise the nose. Don't try to level the nose before leveling the wings. Otherwise, you could quickly overstress the aircraft. After you get the aircraft under control, recover to cruise flight by adding power and climbing back to your original altitude. If you are trying this partial panel, use the TC to level the wings.

Let's say you've put the aircraft in a steep left descending turn. First press F1 to cut the power level. Next use Keyboard 5 to center the wings. Once the wings are level, use your keyboard controls or joystick to raise the nose to level flight and transition back to level flight.

Conversely, let's say the aircraft is nose-high and the airspeed is rapidly decreasing. You should add full power using F4 and lower the nose at the same time to avoid a stall. Next, level the wings using Keyboard 5 and recover back to straight and level flight.

A left-descending unusual attitude requires you cut your power level and center your wings before returning to level flight.

An unusual climbing attitude will test your mettle as a pilot.

The Autopilot

The cruise control in a car can give a driver a break from constantly regulating their speed during long journeys. The *Autopilot* is a device in the cockpit which performs a similar function. In addition to controlling speed, the Autopilot can automatically keep the aircraft on a heading or altitude. It can even follow the indications of a VOR display, and climb at a specific climb rate. The Cessna Skylanes, Boeing 737-400, and Lear 45 all come equipped with Autopilots. The features of the Autopilot vary slightly among these aircraft.

Autopilot Features

Go to Aircraft on the main menu and select Autopilot. A window for controlling the Autopilot will appear. The Autopilot can also be set directly on the aircraft console. Use your mouse to click various options on and off and to tune various frequencies. To turn the autopilot in the aircraft on, activate the Autopilot On option. The following Autopilot options are available.

LVL—Wings Leveler: Activating this option will keep the aircraft wings level with the horizon. Do not assume this will also hold a specific heading. Because of yaw, the aircraft may drift off a specific course.

HDG—Heading Hold: This option allows you to specify a certain magnetic heading to hold. It keeps the wings level and compensates for yaw, to make sure you stay on your desired heading.

ATT—Pitch-and-Bank Hold: This option will keep the aircraft in its last pitch-and-bank altitude. For example, suppose you want to make a climbing right-hand turn at ten degrees of bank. When you placed the aircraft in this configuration and selected this option, the ten degrees of bank and nose-high altitude would be held by the Autopilot.

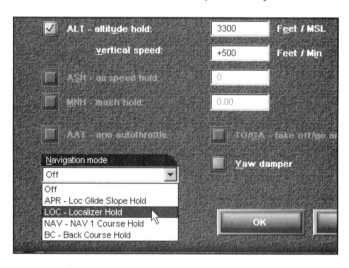

The Autopilot can be used with one of four navigation modes.

ALT—Altitude Hold: This option controls the altitude of the aircraft. You can select a specific altitude using feet above Mean Sea Level and a specific rate-of-climb or descent to get to that altitude. Altitude is set in feet above Mean Sea Level and vertical speed in feet-per-minute. For example, if you want to descend at 800 feet-per-minute all the way down to the ground, you would set vertical speed to -800 feet and leave the altitude field blank. If you

wanted to maintain an altitude of 9000 feet, you would set altitude to 9000 and then set vertical speed to + 0.

ASH—Airspeed: This option is only available when flying the Lear 45 or Boeing 737-400. You can force the autopilot to maintain a specific airspeed using this option.

MNH—Mach: This option is used to maintain a specific speed at high altitudes in the turbine aircraft.

AAT—Arm Autothrottle: The AAT, available only on the Boeing 737-400, will

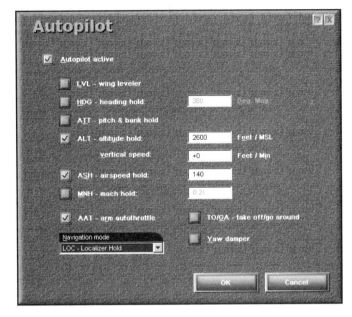

Autopilot options let you control how you want Autopilot to control the plane.

vary the power setting to maintain a specific airspeed. For example, if you're flying at 220 KIAS and begin a descent, the throttles would be pulled back automatically to maintain an airspeed of 220. On problem with AAT is that it is slow to respond to changes in airspeed. This is because it simulates the lag associated with turbine engines when power is changed. Therefore, if you descend using AAT, airspeed will first increase before the change in power is realized. Likewise, in a climb, airspeed will first decrease before dropping off to its original value. The autothrottle can also be armed in flight by hitting Shift + R or by clicking on the autothrottle button on the far left of the autopilot. A red light will appear in this button when it is active.

The autopilot window also has an option called TO/GA (Take Off/Go Around). If you activate this option, Flight Simulator will automatically change the power setting to 90 percent of N1. This comes in handy when you are preparing to take off and don't want to have to manually adjust the throttles to take-off power. If a landing approach goes bad and you want to "go around" and try again, you can activate this option to get the proper power setting while you concentrate on other items in the cockpit. The TO/GA can be temporarily changed by pressing F2 or F3. However, the power will then go back to a setting of 90 percent of N1. The autopilot airspeed modes require Autothrottle to be armed. This includes TO/GA.

The TO/GA option can also be set by hitting Control + Shift + R or by hitting the round button located below the throttles. This button will alight when active and "Tg" will appear in white lights above the engine instruments.

Not located in the autopilot window is the auto spoilers function. This function will automatically extend the spoilers when the aircraft wheels hit the ground to aid in braking. This gives you one less thing to think about when you are concentrating on landing. To toggle the auto spoilers function on and off, hit Shirt + /. If the spoilers are not armed, the spoiler switch, located to the left of the throttles, will be in the highest position next to the "RET" indicator. If they are armed, the spoiler switch will be located below this point next to the "ARM" indicator.

Yaw Damper: This option controls movements around the vertical axis. The autopilot is essentially controlling the rudder inputs.

Navigation Modes: The Autopilot can also track the various navigation radio signals received in the cockpit. The APR-LOC Glide Slope hold will track the glide-slope signal and localizer. The LOC hold will only track the localizer signal. The NAV-NAV2 Course hold will track whatever signal is tuned in to the first NAV radio. The BC hold will track a localizer back-course signal.

Landing Blind with the Autopilot

The autopilot can be used to land when there is zero runway visibility at the airport you are landing at. To give this a try, go to Flights on the main menu and select Challenges. Choose the Landing Blind at Heathrow option.

When the challenge finishes setting up, press P to pause the simulation. Go into the Autopilot and set altitude hold to 2600 feet and airspeed hold to 140 KIAS. Set navigation mode to LOC hold since the glide slope is not yet being received. Click on the AAT option so that power is automatically set by Flight Simulator 98. Press P to restart the simulation. At 11.3 DME, the glide slope will start to be received. Press P again to pause the simulation and change the navigation mode to APR-LOC and Glide Slope Hold.

You should descend at 140 knots. Lower the gear by pressing G and press F7 to lower the remaining flaps. At 80 feet MSL, you will hear the wheels touch down on the ground. As soon as this happens, cut the power using F1,

deploy the spoilers using 'I', and apply the brakes using "Ctrl + .".

When you are on the ground, the visibility will be too low to see much out front. Go into World on the main menu and select Weather. Click on the Cloud Type option and set the User Defined layer to Haze. You will have just enough visibility to see the runway lights.

Try to land with zero visibility at Heathrow Airport, in foggy old London.

Pilot Complacency

A major risk in using the Autopilot is that you can sit back and relax too much while the Autopilot does all the work. If you suddenly want to change your flight plan, you will first need to figure out your current position. In addition, you might miss important check points along your flight route.

If your Autopilot fails, you suddenly have to start flying the airplane again. Those of you who attempted the Checkerboard approach in the last chapter have first-

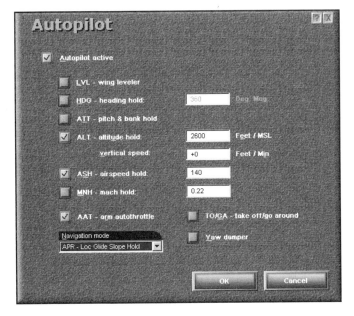

Setting the autopilot to track the glide slope and localizer.

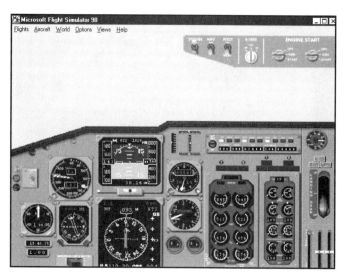

The view out the window isn't much as you descend past 500 feet.

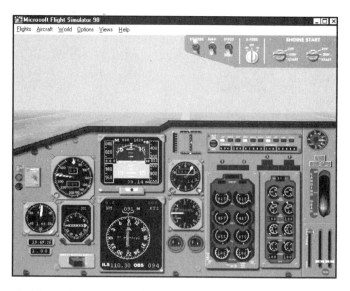

Safely on the ground at Heathrow. That wasn't so hard, now was it?

hand experience of what it's like to suddenly lose this flying aid when you're busy performing other tasks. The aircraft quickly moves away from your desired performance, while you are just beginning to scan the instruments.

SIDs/STARs

When an aircraft is departing or arriving at a busy airport, the Air Traffic Controllers may want it to follow a common route. Instead of taking time to describe this route to the pilot, Air Traffic Control may create SIDs (Standard Instrument Departure procedures) and STARs (Standard Terminal ARrival procedures). These procedures are published in conjunction with approach charts. They describe the route and altitudes a pilot should follow in or out of the airport area.

Let's say you're departing Melbourne International Airport. You would receive the SID that ATC routinely issues outbound flights. Both a

visual and textual description is given. When Runway 9R is used, pilots should fly runway heading until the CAPEN intersection. This is the point where the back-course localizer intersects the 358-degree radial off of the Vero Beach VOR. Then the aircraft should make a left turn to a heading of 360 degrees. The aircraft should maintain 5000 feet MSL or an ATC-assigned altitude.

Now let's say you're making the Brunswick Two Arrival, as shown at right. An aircraft approaching Craig Municipal from Savannah should fly the R-196 off of the Savannah VOR at an altitude of 2200 feet MSL until passing over the Brunswick VOR. The aircraft will then track R-188 off of Brunswick until passing over the Craig VOR. Air Traffic Control will provide radar vectors from that point on to the airport. Specific altitudes which will be assigned to turbojet aircraft are provided on this chart.

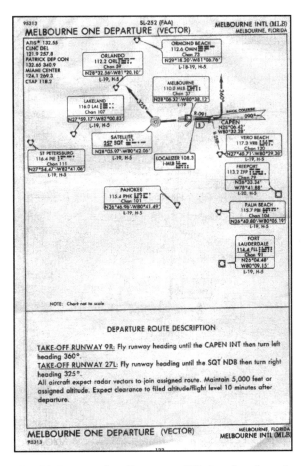

The Melbourne One Departure SID that the airport's ATC issues.

Intercontinental Navigation

In Flight Simulator 98, the primary radio navigation aid is the VOR. The problem is that VORs have limited reception range. Therefore, they are not used for intercontinental navigation. NavAids used for intercontinental navigation are described below. Unfortunately, Flight Simulator 98 does not model these methods.

To navigate in IFR conditions over the oceans in Flight Simulator 98, you can press Y to determine your current longitude and latitude. You can then go to

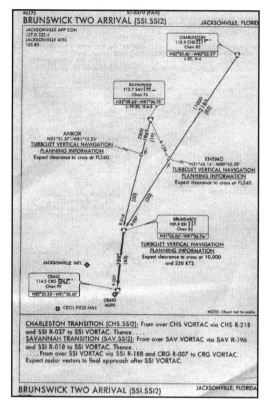

The Brunswick Two Arrival, used during flights around scenic Savannah, Georgia.

World on the main menu and select the Airport Facility Directory to determine the latitude and longitude of the location where you're travelling. Keep your current coordinates displayed so that you can constantly reaffirm that you're flying toward them.

RNAV

VORs often do not provide a direct route to where you want to go. You may find yourself saying things like "If only there was a VOR at Page field—I'd cut 20 minutes off this leg of my flight." RNAV (area navigation) turns this desire into a reality.

Instead of flying to a ground-based VOR, you create a waypoint. If you are using standard VOR/DME RNAV equipment, you simply plug in the distance the waypoint is from a certain VOR and what radial it lays on. On LORAN RNAV-type equipment, you would plug in the latitude and longitude of the location where you want to fly. Behind the scenes, your RNAV is earning its keep by performing a lot of trigonometry you really don't want to deal with. The RNAV is determining your position in relation to both the physical VOR and the waypoint. The result is, instead of having to fly to a physically installed ground-based transmitter, you can fly to any waypoint with known coordinates.

The RNAV receiver will determine what course you need to fly to get to that user-defined waypoint. It also will supply you with some "nice-to-know" information, such as your ground speed and your distance to the waypoint. Some RNAVs can even be integrated into the NAV display. You would be able to track the course just like you would during VOR navigation.

To use RNAV en-route, you need to enter the coordinates of the waypoint into the RNAV. In general VOR/DME RNAV navigation, this is the radial and

DME information of a ground-based VOR. For a LORAN system, the global coordinates would be used. Therefore, you first need to know what these coordinates are. To help you out, both Jeppeson and NOS now include LAT/LON information on low-level en-route charts. Luckily, many LORAN type NavAids come standard with a database of waypoint coordinates. You would simply dial in the waypoint you were after. You can also use your airport and facility directory in Flight Simulator 98 to look up the coordinates of airports and NavAids.

When you start buying approach plates, you will notice an RNAV approach mixed in here and there. However, they are few and far between. One problem with RNAV approaches is that they use at least two waypoints on the approach. If your RNAV does not have the capability to store multiple waypoint data, you will need to re-tune the RNAV during the approach, and therefore, you run a considerable risk of typing in the wrong information. In Flight Simulator, you would need to reference the new set of coordinates and start flying toward them.

VOR/DME RNAV navigation is subject to all the limitations of traditional VOR navigation, such as line-of-sight restrictions. *Scalloping* is caused by the VOR receiver picking up reflected signals off another VOR. This causes CDI to begin to stray from the correct course indication. Not all VOR/DME RNAVs are certified for IFR navigation. If this is the case, the RNAV should only be used to provide back-up navigation data. RNAV navigation is not commonly seen as the filed method of navigation on general aviation flight plans.

LORAN

LORAN (Long Range Navigation) is a type of RNAV navigation that was first developed during World II. This LORAN-A was used primarily by ships. It wasn't utilized much in aviation since it required a lot of manual calculations, which proved unpopular with the flying aces. However, LORAN-C came about in the 1950s. LORAN-C was able to capitalize on advances in the computer industry. With the computer handling the math, LORAN-C soon spread to aviation.

LORAN-C utilizes several chains of ground-based transmitters. These transmitters produce low-frequency pulses at 100 KHz. Therefore, these signals are not subject to the same line-of-sight problems associated with VOR/DME RNAV navigation. Some LORAN-C signals can even be picked up for 2000 miles. Each chain is made up of one master station and several secondary stations. Each pulse the secondary transmitters send out is synchronized with the master transmitter. The LORAN-C receiver compares the time difference between the signals of two secondary stations to the signal of the master station to determine the aircraft's position.

LORAN-C has advantages over traditional VOR/DME RNAV navigation. Aside from being picked up over a further distance, a LORAN-C receiver usually has more computer-processing capability. For instance, a LORAN-C receiver usually stores a database of waypoints which can be easily referenced. In addition, the database may contain data such as MEAs and MOCAs on specific victor airways. The only drawback to these features is that they are a bit more complicated to use. However, if you can handle a computer, you should have no problem figuring out how to program an RNAV receiver. Another problem with LORAN navigation is that the transmitters may need to be taken out of service for maintenance. Like DME/VOR RNAV navigation, LORAN-C requires special IFR certification to be used as the primary method of navigation, with LORAN-C used mainly as a backup system.

GPS

GPS (Global Positioning Systems) are the latest in RNAV technology. The GPS NavStar system is a network of satellites orbiting the globe. The satellites send signals to receivers and measure how much time it takes for the signals to be sent back. This time is then used to calculate the aircraft's position and altitude. Because there are backup satellites ready to come on line, there is little chance of the system coming down for maintenance. The GPS signal is also not subject to the same type of radio-wave limitations, such as line-of-sight factors.

Currently, there's a lot a talk in the industry about "free flight," which will allow pilots to create their own IFR routes. It is estimated that "free flight" will save the airlines millions of dollars. GPS units that are certified for IFR navigation are still a bit expensive, but their costs are gradually coming down. Many of these systems are integrated with moving maps. Basically, the aircraft's position is constantly superimposed on a map. You can see how precisely on course you are and where restricted airspace is around you. You can even superimpose your position on an approach chart, so you can see how you are doing. More advances with GPS technology are right around the corner.

Chapter Nine

FLYING THE NET

Although it's doubtful that you'll tire of playing Microsoft Flight Simulator 98 by yourself any time soon, there's a whole other facet of the program that you can explore whenever you're ready. One of the new features of Flight Simulator 98 is the ability to fly with other desktop pilots on the Internet. Flying in real time with up to seven other pilots over the Net really adds a whole new dimension to Flight Simulator 98, and can also strengthen your instrument flying skills.

Understanding the Internet

Unless you've been hiding under a rock for several years, you've no doubt heard of the Internet. Often referred to as the *Information Super Highway*, the Internet is the vast interconnected electronic system used for the exchange of information and ideas. It's not an online service, although it interconnects computer systems and networks all over the world. The following descriptions will define Internet terms and how they are interrelated.

- The language or protocol (electronic rules that govern how computers communicate with each other) that machines on the Internet use to communicate with each other is called TCP/IP (Transmission Control Protocol/Internet Protocol).
- One popular pastime of Internet frequenters is browsing (known as "surfing the Web"). The Web (World Wide Web or WWW) is comprised of untold scores of hypertext documents.
- Hypertext documents on the World Wide Web are known as Web pages. Web pages are WWW documents presented in a browser window, such as Microsoft Internet Explorer.
- Web pages are linked together by a special protocol named HTTP (HyperText Transfer Protocol).

- A *Web site* is a specific place on the Internet, usually consisting of a set of interconnected pages on the World Wide Web.
- Web sites are arranged on the WWW according to electronic addresses known as URLs (Uniform Resource Locator).
- URLs are always prefaced with "http://". (Note that the two slashes used after the colon are forward slashes.)

Getting Started

The Microsoft Internet Gaming Zone (IGZ or "Zone") is one of the most convenient ways to find other people who share your interest in playing popular games on the Web. The Zone is a place for anyone who enjoys games and competition—from the time-honored strategies of chess and hearts to the hottest recent games from leading developers such as LucasArts, Hasbro Interactive, and (of course) Microsoft.

Flight Simulator 98 is just one of many popular games you can enjoy on the Zone. Besides being free, the Zone's main appeal is as an electronic gathering place where (at any time of day or night) you can find other Flight Simulator pilots. Furthermore, the Zone simplifies connecting with others who use Flight Simulator 98.

Before you can play any Zone game for the first time, you'll need to already have installed the software listed below. Otherwise, you might encounter a message telling you that the Zone software is not detected or that it requires updating.

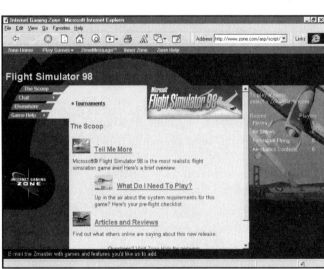

Microsoft's Internet Gaming Zone gives you a convenient way to share the skies with other virtual pilots.

- ActiveX-enabled Web browser like Internet Explorer 3.02 or greater (available at http://www.microsoft.com/ie/default.asp)

- Zone software (To play Flight Simulator 98, you'll need at least the Retail Install version of the Zone software.)
- The game software for the specific game you're interested in playing
- A multiplayer software patch, if the game requires it (As of this writing, none is required for Flight Simulator 98.)

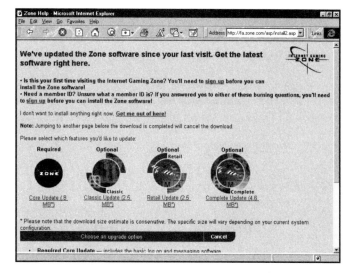

If the current Zone software is not detected, you may see a message like this one when you try and access the Zone.

Before we go over this process, let's make sure your system meets the absolute minimum requirements you need to be able to get on the Zone. Note that if you already meet the system requirements for Flight Simulator 98, you already have most of the hardware and software you'll need.

Zone Requirements

Two lists follow: the first shows the recommended absolute minimum system requirements for the Zone, and the second is the suggested list of what you need to optimize your play performance. As you already know, when it comes to games (and the Web, for that matter), the bigger your hard disk and faster your computer, the better!

Minimum System Requirements

Either

- Microsoft Windows 95 operating system running on a Pentium 75 MHz processor, or higher

or

- Microsoft Windows NT operating system, version 4.0 or higher and the Service Pack 3 running on a Pentium 75 MHz processor, or higher

And the following components:

- 8 MB memory (RAM)
- 15 MB hard disk space (20 MB of additional space may be required for the setup program to complete successfully)
- VGA 256-color, 640 x 480 display
- 14.4 Kbps Internet access
- Microsoft Internet Explorer version 3.01 or higher
- Mouse or compatible pointing device

Recommended System Requirements

Either

- Microsoft Windows 95 operating system, running on a Pentium 75 MHz processor, or higher

or

- Microsoft Windows NT operating system, version 4.0 or higher and Service Pack 3 running on a Pentium 75 MHz processor or higher

And the following components:

- 16 MB memory (RAM)
- 15 MB hard disk space (20 MB of additional space may be required for setup program to complete successfully)
- Super VGA 256-color, 800 x 600 display
- Sound card plus speakers or headphones (for games that require audio)
- 28.8 Kbps Internet access
- Microsoft Internet Explorer version 3.01 or higher
- Mouse or compatible pointing device
- Joystick (for games requiring a joystick)

Tip: *A joystick is handy and fun for action games, but it's not usually required for many of the strategy, card, and board games found on the Zone.*

Making the Connection

Although there are four types of connections that can be used to connect with other players in Flight Simulator 98, you will most likely connect to the Zone using your computer's modem (over the Internet), typically using a dial-in connection or a LAN (Local Area Network) connection. Maybe we should back up a bit.

In order to play any game on the Zone, you must have PPP (Point-to-Point Protocol) access to the World Wide Web. PPP Web access is available through many popular online services such as Microsoft Network (MSN), America Online (AOL) with AOL version 3.0 for Windows 95 or greater, CompuServe (CIS) with CIS for Windows version 3.0 or greater, and through Internet Service Providers (ISPs). The following instructions assume that you already have access to the Web. If you don't have Internet access, you'll need to sign-up for a service like MSN, AOL or contact a local Internet Service Provider.

All connections can be handled through Flight Simulator 98's Multiplayer Connect setup wizard found in the Multiplayer selection under the Flights menu. This wizard will take you step-by-step through the connection process. But if you connect to other players through the Zone, the Zone will handle the initial multiplayer connection automatically for you.

Tip: *You cannot connect to the Internet Gaming Zone if you are using a 16-bit TCP/IP network protocol Dynamic-Link Library (.dll) device driver such as winsock.dll (Windows Network Socket) from SpryNet, GNN, or Trumpet. The only way to fix this problem is to ask your ISP for a full 32-bit networking .dll like wsock32.dll. Be sure to use Microsoft Dialup Networking or some other fully compatible 32-bit layer. Many ISPs ship only 16-bit network support so they don't have to ship two products (one for Windows 3.1 and one for Windows 95).*

Flight Simulator 98's Multiplayer Connect setup wizard will take you through the connection process step-by-step.

Tip: *You'll always be notified of charges, (if there are any) before you start playing any game on the Zone. Also, all software available for download on the Zone is free. Only connect charges (if any) from your online service or Internet Service Provider (ISP) apply.*

Costs

Naturally, before signing up or joining anything, one of the first questions anyone wants to ask is *"How much is this gonna cost me?"* Currently, there are four services offered on the Zone— Classic Zone, Retail CD-ROM ZoneMatch, ZoneLAN, and Zone Exclusive games. Microsoft assures everyone that all of the classic Zone games will remain free to all members *forever*. Now, you're probably wondering what the catch is, right? Well, Microsoft is able to provide this service for free because the funds received from their advertisers help offset development and operational costs.

As new Zone Exclusive games (also referred to as Premium Games) are added to the Zone, they will charge a modest fee to play them. These fees take the form of Daily and Monthly play tickets. Current pricing is $1.95 per day, or $19.95 per month, but keep checking the Zone for current pricing on all Zone Exclusive games. In any case, the existing classic games will always be available free of charge. Flight Simulator 98 currently is also free of charge to play on the Zone, but like all other Retail CD-ROM Zone games, it requires a retail version of the game installed on your hard disk.

Signing Up

Before you can log on to the Zone, you'll need to have the Zone software installed. However, in order to download the Zone software, you need to first sign up. To connect to the Zone, enter the URL below in your Web browser: http://www.zone.com.

From the Zone welcome screen, click on the New Player Signup button. This will take you to the "Sign up here for the new Internet Gaming Zone!" screen.

Address | http://www.zone.com

To reach the Zone, enter http://www.zone.com in your Web browser.

"Wanna Cookie?"

When you access or use the Zone, you may receive a Security Alert dialog box that states that you have received a "cookie" from the Zone and asks if you want to accept it. (A *cookie* is a small Java applet, or "program" a Web server downloads onto the computer of any newcomer to the site.) The Internet Gaming Zone will attempt to download a cookie after you do any of the following:

- Go to http://www.zone.com
- Click Play Games Now
- Select a game from the Games List
- Enter a game room

Although a cookie is really nothing more than a few lines of text that are part of an HTTP (HyperText Transfer Protocol—the communications protocol of the Web) transaction, over the past year or so, there has been a heated debate over cookies.

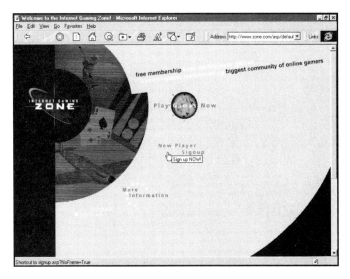

Your journey into the Zone begins when you click the New Player Signup button.

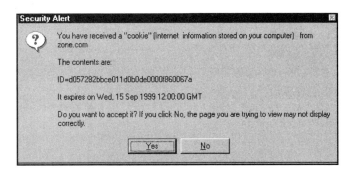

When you access the Zone you may see this Security Alert dialog box, telling you it's "cookie" time.

Among other things, a cookie can help the server determine if you've visited there before, your preferences, your name/handle, and even passwords. What has some Web surfers worried is this action implies that someone is keeping track of you and your actions. While that in itself may not be worrisome to most of us, what's important is how such information is used.

Because the cookie is associated with the browser and is then stored in the database, it *could* be considered an invasion of privacy. However, it's important to note that only an ID is associated with the browser. Cookies can't be used to extract your E-mail address or other personal data, nor can they scan your hard drive for data. There is no way of determining personal information, unless of course, you voluntarily fill out a form and submit it.

The information a cookie passes along to the server (i.e., which pages were accessed and when, and any other information you provide the server) is stored in the Web site's log file or the host company's database—so they have that kind of information, anyway. In any case, the information stored by a cookie is not available to other sources, unless there is a hacker on the channel—a security concern with or without cookies. So, to sum it up, cookies are not evil, secretive things, snooping around to reveal everything about you. Cookies are just a means for Web developers to gather information about users' Web activities without bothering them.

Turning Off Cookie Security Alerts

Cookies are meant to be invisible. You're supposed to be able to traipse all over the Web collecting these things without ever knowing about them. Because of the concerns some have about cookies, the default setting of Internet Explorer is set to notify you with a Security Alert dialog box before accepting any cookies. The problem is that this can be quite annoying and you may wish to turn off this feature.

To turn this feature off, do the following:

1. *Right click the Internet Explorer icon if it's located on your Windows Desktop.(If it isn't, open Internet Explorer by clicking on Start. Then select Programs, followed by Accessories. In Accessories, open Internet Tools and then select Internet Explorer.)*

2. *Click Properties*
   or
   If you've opened Internet Explorer, click Options, which is found under the View drop-down menu selection.

3. *In the Warnings section of the Advanced tab, clear the check box beside Warn Before Accepting "Cookies."*

4. *Click Apply, and then click OK.*

Consequences for Not Accepting Cookies

If, after all of our reassurances, you're still dead-set against accepting cookies, leave Warn selected and just don't accept them. While you'll still be able to participate on the Zone as a

full member, remember that you'll be constantly warned about incoming cookies. Keep in mind that this isn't because the Zone is trying to send you thousands of cookies, but because every time the Zone asks for a cookie and you don't have one, it'll try to send one to you.

> **Tip:** If you're already a Zone member and want to play on the Zone from a different computer than the one you signed up on, all you need to do is download the Zone software onto that machine.

> **Tip:** The Zone membership application form supports uppercase letters in the name field.

Member IDs

When you first sign up as a member, you'll have to enter a Member ID. The Member ID you enter will become your Zone handle. From this point on (unless you re-register under another name again later on and enter the Zone using that ID), you'll appear to everyone on the Zone as your handle, so choose carefully.

Downloading the Zone Software

As we mentioned earlier, before you play any Zone game for the first time, you'll need to install the Zone Software. This is downloaded directly from the Zone.

To download the Zone Software, just click on the Upgrade Software button and you'll be transported to the Install Zone Software page. You'll be given the choice of downloading three different types of software.

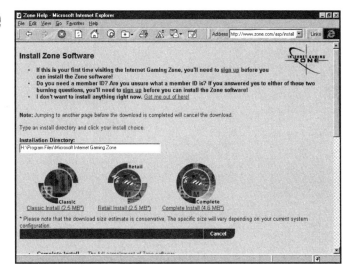

The Install Zone Software page offers three types of Zone software for downloading, depending on the extent of your interests.

- Complete Install—Includes the Zone log-on and messaging plus the Retail Install and Classic Install software.
- Retail Install—The basic Zone log-on and messaging software, plus all the software you need for "matchmaking" retail games on the Zone (purchased separately, such as Flight Simulator 98).
- Classic Install—The basic Zone log-on and messaging software, plus software for all the Zone Classic card and board games.

At the very least, you'll need to have the Retail Install version of the Zone software in order to play Flight Simulator 98 on the Zone. To get this, click on the Retail Install button and follow the Setup instructions.

Authentication and Security Certificates

Every time you download authenticated software, an Authentication Certificate will appear. There are two different types of security certificates on the Web—personal and Web site. A personal certificate is a certificate that you would send to a client authentication server that requires a certificate. A typical situation might be one in which you send personal information, such as your user name and password. Basically, this certificate is a form of guarantee that indicates to the server that you are indeed who you say you are.

A Web site certificate, the kind you'll see on the Zone, is used when a secure Web site (the Zone in this case) sends your copy of Internet Explorer a certificate that provides certain information about security for that Web site. Certificates are issued to a particular organization for a specific period of time. When you open that organization's Web site, Internet Explorer verifies that the Internet address stored in the certificate matches the site you're

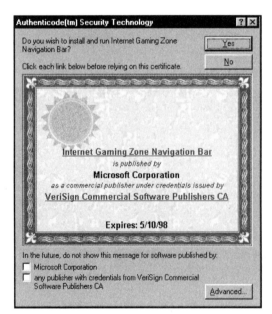

The Zone issues Web site certificates as a means of securing communications between a user (you) and a Web site (the Zone).

currently connected to and that the current date precedes the expiration date. If not, Internet Explorer displays a warning. Essentially, a Web site certificate contains information used for verifying that the site is secure and genuine. This ensures that no other Web site can assume the identity of those associated with the original site.

A certificate can't guarantee absolute security for downloads. Authenticode doesn't check to see if code is free of bugs or malicious intent (viruses). The concept is that you can choose whether to download software based on your knowledge of and trust in a particular software publisher. Just as you know who published the software you purchased from a retail store, you absolutely know who is responsible for the code that you downloaded and ran. To verify a certificate, click each link highlighted on the certificate before relying on it.

> **Tip:** *You'll be sent several Authentication Certificates during the installation of the Zone software. Clicking on the Yes button will continue the download and installation.*

> **Tip:** *Although each ZoneMatch room is named according to the activity played within, most pilots tend not to pay much attention to their exact designation. In other words, just choose a room with pilots gaming if your desired room isn't occupied.*

Where Do We Go from Here?

After downloading and installing the Zone software, first click on the Play Games Now button. Then select Flight Simulator 98 from the Simulator menu option on the Main Zone menu. When you enter the Flight Simulator 98 game room lobby, click on one of the ZoneMatch rooms on the right side of the screen. Once inside a room, chat up other players, arrange some mutual flying time, and join in on the fun. Happy landings!

Multiplayer Basics for Flight Simulator 98

Because Flight Simulator 98 doesn't lock you into certain online flying activities (like aerial combat, for example), you're free to do anything you like. In addition to attempting "stupid aircraft tricks," other popular flight pastimes include formation flying, aerobatics challenges, and playing follow the leader. However, for serious desktop pilots, it's other features that make the multiplayer aspect of Flight Simulator 98 especially interesting: air races around cities or specially created scenery; cross-country flights; flying as an observer/flight instructor; or trying your hand at airport traffic control.

Problems with the Zone?

The Zone uses ActiveX controls and Java applications. If you're unable to view portions of the Zone, your browser's settings may be set improperly. These are symptoms you may experience if the appropriate settings are not enabled in your browser:

- Blank screens
- Some areas of the Zone are not viewable.
- A red "X" appears in place of game room names.
- You see the following message when you log on to the Zone: "We're sorry: We are unable to detect the Internet Gaming Zone software on your system. To troubleshoot this problem, please consult the Log on and Connection Problems section of the Zone FAQ, which you can access by clicking Zone Help."

To configure the proper settings in your browser to attempt to eliminate these problems, do the following:

1. Start Internet Explorer.

2. On the View menu, click Options.

3. On the Security tab, verify that the following options are enabled:
   — Enable ActiveX controls and plug-ins
   — Run ActiveX Scripts

4. Click the Safety Level button.

5. Change the setting from High to Medium.

6. Click OK, click Apply, and then click OK.

Session Settings

You'll be given the opportunity to change your Session Settings after you connect with the Zone, and you can access these settings at anytime during the session by clicking Settings from the Multiplayer selection under the Flights menu. Although the title *Settings* may give you the impression that this is where you set your modem commands and make other technical designations, the actual name of the window is *Session Settings* and this is where your multiplayer game options are configured.

Multiplayer Settings are broken down into two categories—Tracking and Visual Details. Tracking options help you keep track of other players. It's a big world out there (in real life and in Flight Simulator 98, because it models the *whole* world), so it's very easy to lose the (relatively) tiny airplanes of other players.

ADF lock to aircraft:
Sets your ADF to point   at
the selected aircraft
of another pilot.

DME lock to aircraft:
Presents the distance between
you and the selected aircraft
on the DME.

Autopilot to aircraft:
If you're totally lost, setting
this option can mean the
difference between
experiencing hours of fun or
frustration. Don't be afraid to
turn this on. Just be careful
that if you're flying a faster
aircraft, you don't fly into the
other player.

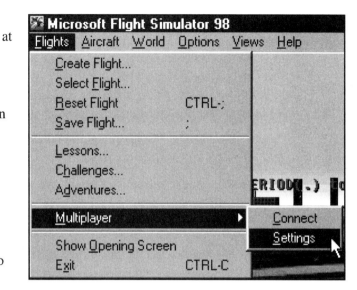

Session Settings, where you configure your multiplayer game options, is found under the Multiplayer menu option.

Display Player Names: Superimposes
the name of each player above their
aircraft. This makes identification a snap.

The Visual Details options are used
to send more detailed aircraft
information to other players. The
drawback to enabling this option is you
may experience some slowdown in
game speed.

At the bottom of the Session
Settings window are the Flight
Conditions buttons. Depending on
whether you are hosting or joining the
session will dictate whether you can Set
or Get Flight Conditions from the host.
This feature allows you to coordinate the various World settings (relating to
weather and time of day) between all of the players.

Tip: *If you have one or more of the Tracking options enabled, you can cycle your target lock/selection through each available aircraft by pressing Ctrl + T on the keyboard.*

Tip: *If you want to catch up to another player, use the time compression function. Press R followed by + to increase and - to decrease the time compression rate. Pressing Ctrl + Shift + F will instantly bring you directly to the selected player.*

Tip: *The Visual Details setting won't affect individual Scenery Settings. Therefore, if one player has scenery set on Dense and another player has their's set to Sparse, the Sparse player won't have as many buildings to worry about as the other player. This can sometimes lead to the "Dense scenery" player seeing the other player fly though buildings, when the Sparse scenery player sees nothing in front of him at all.*

The Multiplayer Connect session setup screen is where you'll set your callsign and determine whether you'll host or join a game.

Tip: *When you begin the setup wizard, you'll be asked to provide a callsign. Rather than just entering your name, sometimes adding the aircraft you'll be flying is a good idea. This way other players will instantly know what you're flying. Of course, this only works if you stay with the same aircraft throughout the session.*

To Host or Not to Host?

When you enter the Flight Simulator 98 ZoneMatch room, you'll have the option to host a multiplayer session or join someone else's session, or join as a player or observer. Basically, the only difference between hosting and joining a session is who actually configures and starts the session. There is no game advantage or disadvantage to hosting or joining a game, although the host of a session does have the ability to limit the number of players and observers in that session.

Player or Observer

Just as you'd expect, a player can fly and an observer can only watch. There are, however, other differences between these two modes of which you should be aware. Some of the differences between being a player and being a observer are:

- As an observer you can switch (ride along) with any of the other players' aircraft. Press Ctrl + Shift + T to cycle through the available aircraft.
- If you begin the session as an observer, you can't switch during the session and become a player.

- To switch to observer mode when you started the session as a pilot, press Ctrl + Shift + O.
- When riding as an observer, Ctrl + Shift + D will lock your cockpit view in the aircraft you are observing.

Tip: *Observers must be "invited" by the host.*

Tip: *Observing flights is a great tool for learning and teaching. For the rookie, both watching and having an observer onboard can really help. Watching how things are done can really drive home some lessons. But let's not forget that having a more experienced pilot in your aircraft talking/typing you through a tricky maneuver or flight can also be extremely valuable.*

Final Notes and Tips

Here are some final notes about flying on the Zone:

- Chat with other players before hosting or joining a game so you can coordinate starting locations and what you'll be doing during the game.
- If you close the Chat window during a multiplayer session, you can call it up again from the Flights menu under the Multiplayer selection, or by pressing Ctrl + Enter. Note that Chat will only be accessible when you are connected to a multiplayer game.

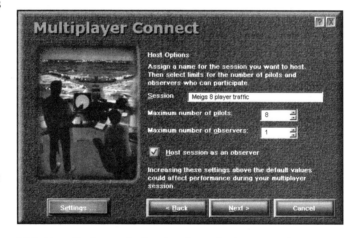

This Host Options window is where the host sets the number of players and observers for the session.

- The Chat window will not be available if you're running a 3Dfx Voodoo-based video card in full screen mode. You need to switch back to windowed mode by pressing Alt + Enter first to see the Chat window— but not to send messages. You can send messages without seeing the Chat

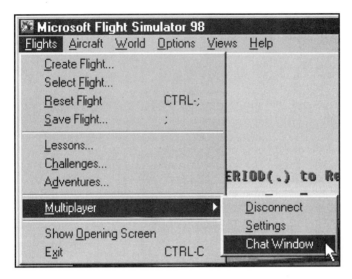

Access the Chat Window from the Flights menu under the Multiplayer selection, or by pressing Ctrl + Enter.

window by pressing Enter first, typing your message, and then pressing Enter again to send the message. Note that you must follow up the whole procedure with Ctrl + Enter to close down the (unseen Chat window or your subsequent key command presses will register as Chat messages.

- Consider joining only those games whose players have good (green-colored) network latency indictors next to their names. These latency indicators are visible on the player list on the right side of the game room screen. You can use the scroll bar to view the rest of the list if there are many players in the room.

- When hosting a game it's often helpful (to attract other players, too) to name your game something descriptive. Name the area where you'll be flying, how many players you'll host, and what type of activity will be taking place.

- If you'd like to connect with other players over the Internet without going through the Zone, all you need is the host's IP (Internet Provider) address, which should be entered in the appropriate box of the Multiplayer Connect setup wizard. The session host can find your IP (Internet Protocol) address by clicking on Start, selecting Run, and then typing WINIPCFG.EXE while connected to your ISP. Note that depending on your ISP service connection, your IP address may change (automatically re-assigned) each time you connect to your ISP.

If you have problems connecting with other players, maintaining connections, re-connecting, or with frame rates during multiplayer games, here are some tips that have been known to help:

- Always start with a clean connection. When your session is over, close all programs, and start over again by making a clean connection to the Zone.
- Do not have Flight Simulator 98 running before hosting or joining a multiplayer game. Let the Host launch the game for you. All players should follow this procedure.
- It takes as long as a couple of minutes for all players to connect together. Be patient. Don't start clicking around and pressing keys until Flight Simulator 98 has finished loading and connecting.
- Accessing the Zone through a proxy server or firewall, you may receive an error message stating that the new Zone does not support your version of Windows. To resolve this problem, do the following:

1. Right click on the Internet Explorer icon.

2. Click Properties.

3. From the Connection tab, click the Settings... button.

4. In the Exceptions box, add the following entry below the line reading "Do not use proxy server for addresses beginning with": *.Zone.com

5. Click OK.

6. Click Apply, and then click OK.

7. Restart Internet Explorer and try accessing the Zone site again.

- Just as when playing in single-player mode, adjusting your visual detail will also help your frame rate during multiplayer sessions.
- Disabling your Web browser connection to the Zone as a proxy connection has been known to solve some connection problems. To do this, select Options from the View menu selection in Internet Explorer. On the Connection tab, un-check the Connect through a proxy server box.

FLIGHT SIMULATOR FEATURES: WHAT'S NEW FOR '98?

It's been said that one can't teach an old dog new tricks, but no one ever considers that it may be that old canines don't *want* to learn anything new. Although Microsoft Flight Simulator 98 has made some changes to what some value as tradition, these changes make Flight Simulator 98 easier to use than previous versions. If you're a Flight Simulator veteran, there are three areas in the new version that you should be especially aware of: key control changes, interface changes, and compatibility issues.

Custom Key Assignments

One of the new features in Flight Simulator 98 is the ability to assign alternate keyboard and joystick inputs for various commands. To give you an example, you can change the landing gear command from G to the another key or even assign the landing gear to operate at the press of a joystick button (provided the new key or joystick button isn't already assigned to another command).

The Assignments feature can be especially handy:

- If you're used to the key commands from another game, you can program them into Flight Simulator 98. This will make you feel more comfortable with the Flight Simulator 98 interface.
- If you don't have a programmable joystick, you can map joystick buttons and stick movement to commands as well.
- If you do have a programmable stick and some odd key combinations won't program properly.

Instrument Flight Techniques
For Microsoft Flight Simulator 98

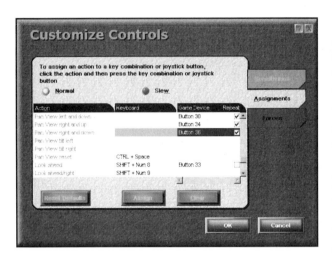

If you want to change the mapping of game commands, Flight Simulator 98's Custom Controls Assignments tab will help you have it your way.

Tip: If you accidentally click Clear and need to know the former command, click the Cancel button. You'll lose all of your changes, but at least you'll be able to start over.

Keyboard and joystick controls are changed through Custom Control Assignments on the Assignments tab. First, select the category of commands you wish to alter by clicking the appropriate radio button. Your choices are Normal and Slew. Slew commands control aircraft positioning, direction, altitude, and location without flying.

Next, find the function you wish to change and double-click on the corresponding Keyboard column (or Joystick column, if that's what you want to change). When prompted, press the key on your keyboard or button on your joystick that you wish to assign to that function. Click on the Repeat box if you want the command to be repeated when the controller button is pressed. You'll be notified if the new key or button conflicts with another command. If that happens, click on the OK button to reassign the control, or click the Cancel button to leave the current assignment as it is. When you've made all your changes, click OK and your changes will be saved. If you click on Cancel, all changes will be lost.

Here are some final notes:

- Keyboard flight control commands will only function if the corresponding flight control is turned off. For example, the arrow keys will not control your airplane if joystick control is enabled.
- The Reset Defaults button only restores the currently selected command.
- Clicking the Assign button has the same effect as double-clicking a selection in the Keyboard or Joystick columns.
- The Clear button will clear the selected command. This will also disable the ability of the Reset Defaults button from restoring the last command.

Interface Changes

Most everything in Flight Simulator 98 is point and click—you literally point to the desired activity or function with your mouse cursor and click on it. In addition to all of the general Windows 95 conventions, such as resizing a window by dragging (clicking and holding) a window border, or closing a window by clicking on the close control box, many of the dials and switches on the cockpit instrument panels also work by mouse click.

For example, you can bring up the radio stack by clicking on the avionics master switch on the instrument panel, and adjusting instrument settings by clicking on a control knob.

The way to work control knobs with a mouse is to notice that the hand pointer/cursor has a plus sign or a minus sign super-imposed on it when you point to a knob. A plus sign means that instrument will increase its current setting with each mouse click. A minus sign will decrease the current setting with each mouse click. Pointing to the right side of each knob will change the pointer to a plus sign, and pointing to the left side of the knob will change the pointer to a minus sign.

Flight Simulator 98 supports all of the general Windows 95 conventions, such as clicking on a close control box to close a window.

Adjust instrument settings by clicking on the control knob.

Clicking on the avionics master switch (shown in the lower left corner of the screen) will bring up the radio stack.

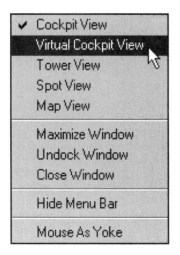

Right click on a window to access a pop-up menu.

Need a fast reminder about an instrument? Quicktips might be just what you're looking for.

Other features associated with Flight Simulator 98's mouse are pop-up menus and Quicktips. Pop-up menus are triggered by a right mouse click and provide quick access to often-used features and settings. Pop-up menus are window sensitive. In other words, right clicking on another window may bring up additional menu choices.

Quicktips are little text reminders that appear when you point your cursor at a hotspot. Flight Simulator 98's hotspots are all located on instrument panels, so if you forget what an instrument is, just point your cursor at it. A second later, a little window with the name of the instrument will appear.

Compatibility Issues

There is no doubt that one of the many features of Flight Simulator that has contributed to its world-wide popularity is its ability to work with third party and user-created add-ons. Flight Simulator 98 continues this tradition. The rest of this section is comprised of notes on compatibility, as well as tips about scenery, adventures, aircraft, panels, and add-on managers.

Tip: *Quicktips may not work at all fullscreen resolutions or on all cockpits.*

Scenery

Flight Simulator 98 is 100 percent compatible with Flight Simulator 5.1 and Flight Simulator 95 scenery. Furthermore, most Flight Simulator 95 scenery installers work fine with Flight Simulator 98. You may need to copy the FLTSIM98.CFG file into a file called FLTSIM95.CFG because a few scenery installation routines look for that file in order to make some changes in it.

If your scenery installer needs a file named FLTSIM95.EXE to work, the Flight Simulator 98 installation CD-ROM includes a file on it. You can find it in the Flight Simulator 98 folder.

Finally, when you use the World: Go to: Airport menu selection, you'll need to click on the Scenery from 6.0 and before button.

Adventures

Any Adventures created with the Flight Shop add-on introduced for Flight Simulator 95 will work with Flight Simulator 98 once they've been converted using the FSCONV.EXE converter or other compiler that's compatible with Flight Simulator 95 (such as APLC32). Both are available on many Web sites listed in Appendix B.

Aircraft

Created aircraft other than those that come with Flight Simulator 98 need to be converted with an updated aircraft and adventure converter designed specifically for Flight Simulator 98. You'll find this converter on the Microsoft Flight Simulator Home page, http://www.microsoft.com/games/fsim/news.htm.

Panels

Because Flight Simulator 98 uses a new high-resolution instrument panel format, older panels are not compatible. Although nothing short of redesigning existing panels will do, it's only a matter of time before newer Flight Simulator 98-compatible panels are available.

Panel and Aircraft Managers

No panel or aircraft managers are compatible with Flight Simulator 98 because its format has changed to what can best be described as a "container" system. Prior versions of Flight Simulator only allowed you to assign panels to a specific class of airplane (e.g. two-engine prop, or four-engine jet, etc.).

Flight Simulator 98 now groups panels and aircraft as individual objects so you can assign panels, sounds, and other art to individual aircraft rather than a class of aircraft. This means a twin engine Beech can have a different panel than a C-47 without requiring the use of an external panel manager. Over and above working with an additional piece of software, this new format saves you from having to exit and restart Flight Simulator 98 just to change panels.

Key Control Changes

Change the key commands on any game and even a casual player will instantly recognize the difference when a pressed key no longer does what it's expected to. Although Flight Simulator 98 has kept most of its traditional key commands, there have been many new features added to this edition. Consequently, there have been many added key commands that Flight Simulator veterans won't know. The following table lists the default key commands of Flight Simulator 98 with major changes from older versions presented in bold lettering).

Note that only the default keys are listed for Flight Simulator 98. This is because of Flight Simulator 98's re-mappable key command feature—Custom Assignments—discussed earlier in this Appendix.

Flight Simulator Key Control Changes

Command	Flight Simulator 98	Command	Flight Simulator 98
Exit Flight Simulator	Ctrl + C	Time Compression select	R
Exit Flight Simulator immediately	Ctrl + Break	Save Flight	;
Pause	P	Reset Current Flight	**Ctrl + ;**
Joystick on/off	K	Decrease selection	-
Sound on/off	Q	Increase selection	=
Slew Mode on/off	Y	Decrease selection slightly	**Shift + -**
Mouse-As-Yoke mode	Ctrl + Num Del		

Flight Simulator Key Control Changes, continued

Command	Flight Simulator 98	Command	Flight Simulator 98
Decrease selection slightly	Shift + =	Mixture full lean	Ctrl + Shift + F1
Select item 1	1	Landing Gear	G
Select item 2	2	Pump Landing Gear	Ctrl + G
Select item 3	3	Brakes	.
Select item 4	4	Brakes (left)	F11
Left Ailerons	Num 4	Brakes (right)	F12
Right Ailerons	Num 6	Parking Brake	Ctrl + .
Left Rudder	Num 0	Spoilers	/
Right Rudder	Num Enter	Arm Auto-Spoilers	Shift + /
Center ailerons and rudder	Num 5	Carb Heat	H
Up Elevator	Num 2	Pitot Heat	Shift + H
Down Elevator	Num 8	Engine select	E
Decrease throttle	Num 3	Jet start	J
Increase throttle	Num 9	Magneto select	M
Trim up	Num 1	Smoke	I
Trim down	Num 7	Lights (all)	L
Cut throttle	F1	Lights (strobe)	O
Decrease throttle slightly	F2	Lights (landing)	Shift + L
Increase throttle slightly	F3	Landing Light Up	Ctrl + Num 8
Full throttle	F4	Landing Light Down	Ctrl + Num 2
Fully retract flaps	F5	Landing Light Left	Ctrl + Num 4
Raise flaps	F6	Landing Light Right	Ctrl + Num 6
Lower flaps	F7	Landing Light Center	Ctrl + Num 5
Fully extend flaps	F8	Directional Gyro Reset	D
Prop pitch low	Ctrl + F4	Altimeter Reset	B
Increase prop pitch slightly	Ctrl + F3	Land Me	X
Decrease prop pitch	Ctrl + F2	Autopilot Master Switch	Z
Prop pitch high	Ctrl + F1	Autopilot attitude hold	Ctrl + T
Mixture full rich	Ctrl + Shift + F4	Autopilot localizer hold	Ctrl + O
Mixture enrich slightly	Ctrl + Shift + F3	Autopilot approach hold	Ctrl + A
Mixture lean slightly	Ctrl + Shift + F2	Autopilot heading hold	Ctrl + H
		Autopilot altitude hold	Ctrl + Z
		Autopilot wing leveler	Ctrl + V

Instrument Flight Techniques
For Microsoft *Flight Simulator 98*

Flight Simulator Key Control Changes, continued

Command	Flight Simulator 98	Command	Flight Simulator 98
Autopilot back course mode	Ctrl + B	Instrument panels toggle	**Shift + [**
Autopilot NAV1 hold	Ctrl + N	Coordinates/ frame rate toggle	Shift + Z
Autopilot Mach Hold	Ctrl + M	Zoom, set to 1X	Backspace
Autopilot Airspeed Hold	Ctrl + R	View Direction Select	Num /
Yaw Damper	Ctrl + D	Pan View Left	Ctrl + Shift + Backspace
Auto-Throttle	Shift + R	Pan View Right	Ctrl + Shift + Enter
Auto-Throttle Takeoff/Go-Around	Ctrl + Shift +R	Pan View Up	Shift + Backspace
		Pan View Down	Shift + Enter
Transponder Select	T	Pan View Reset	**Ctrl + Space**
Com radio Select	C	Look ahead	Shift + Num 8
Nav radio Select	N	Look ahead/right	Shift + Num 9
OBS Select	V	Look right	Shift + Num 6
DME Select	F	Look back/right	Shift + Num 3
ADF Select	A	Look back	Shift + Num 2
VOR1 Identify	Ctrl + 1	Look back/left	Shift + Num 1
VOR2 Identify	Ctrl + 2	Look left	Shift + Num 4
DME1 Identify	Ctrl + 3	Look ahead/left	Shift + Num 7
DME2 Identify	Ctrl + 4	Look down	Shift + Num 5
ADF Identify	Ctrl + 5	Video Stop) (replay or recording	Esc
Send ATC text message	Num +	Text, add to video	,
EGT Select	U	Analysis, stop	\
Checklist View	Shift + C	Panel Window 1, on/off	Shift + 1
View window create	[	Panel Window 2, on/off	Shift + 2
View window close	]	Panel Window 3, on/off	Shift + 3
Map window create	**Shift +]**	Panel Window 4, on/off	Shift + 4
Window switch, next	Ctrl + Tab	Panel Window 5, on/off	Shift + 5
Window switch, previous	Ctrl + Shift + Tab	Panel Window 6, on/off	Shift + 6
View modes, cycle	S	Panel Window 7, on/off	Shift + 7
View modes, backwards	Shift + S	Panel Window 8, on/off	Shift + 8
View types, cycle	Ctrl + S	Panel Window 9, on/off	Shift + 9
View types, cycle backwards	Ctrl + Shift +S	Players, cycle (multiplayer only)	Ctrl + Shift + T
Window view, full	W	Track mode Toggle	Ctrl + Shift + D
Window, bring to front	'		

Flight Simulator Key Control Changes, continued

Command	Flight Simulator 98	Command	Flight Simulator 98
Follow other players	Ctrl + Shift + F	Chat window, switch focus	Enter
Observer mode, switch	Ctrl + Shift + O		
Chat window on/off	Ctrl + Enter	Menu bar	**Alt**

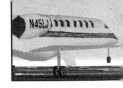

Appendix B

THE FLIGHT SIMULATOR COMMUNITY

If part of the success of Microsoft Flight Simulator can be attributed to its ability to accomodate third-party and end-user created add-ons, one cannot overlook the real strength behind the Flight Simulator universe—Flight Simulator users. The Flight Simulator *community* isn't just a fancy name, it's a real community in every sense of the word. But unlike many other communities, the Flight Simulator community is a global community comprised of people from a wide range of ages and nationalities.

But rather than continuing to tell you why people believe Flight Simulator is worthy of such admiration and loyalty (something only you can decide), let's just talk about what the Flight Simulator community is about and what it has to offer. This section covers how to get support and information, and where to meet others who share your interests in Flight Simulator, computers, and aviation.

Support and Information

If you need help with Flight Simulator 98, obviously the most logical place to seek that help is directly from Microsoft. This is usually a good place to start, but—believe it or not—many times Flight Simulator users themselves have the most up-to-date tips. That's because users within the Flight Simulator community are often the best source for *non-standard* (end-user or third-party developed as opposed to created by Microsoft) modifications, workarounds, and for integration of third-party products. Let's talk about what each source has to offer.

Microsoft on the Web

For many people (and the numbers are increasing every day) the Internet is a convenient way to access information. In addition to the fact that the most current sources are generally found there, another feature the Web offers is the ability to search for information at your leisure 24 hours a day, seven days a week. So, if Microsoft is the first logical place to seek help and information on Flight Simulator 98, Microsoft's Web site is the best reference source for many users with Internet access.

Flight Simulator 98 provides links to Microsoft Web pages in the help menu of the main Flight Simulator 98 window. What you'll find at the following sites is basic product information for setup and configuration help. Although some may believe otherwise, you can't expect assistance for third-party add-ons from Microsoft. Just as this book delivers information "straight from the source" (Microsoft), you should seek help directly from third-party developers of non-Microsoft add-ons.

Here are some of the support pages you'll find most useful for Flight Simulator 98:

Tip: *Internet access is required to connect to Microsoft on the Web help resources.*

Links to relevant Web pages can be accessed in the help menu of the main Flight Simulator 98 window.

Frequently Asked Questions (FAQ): This link originally was to bring you to a list of Frequently Asked Questions (FAQ) about Flight Simulator 98. A FAQ answers common questions in a question and answer format, and is generally the best place to start if you're experiencing problems. If you're experiencing a common problem, the chances are very good that someone else has had the same problem before you, and if this is the case, the answer will be found here.

The FAQ Web page has merged together with the Online Support page listed in the next item. Nevertheless, clicking on the FAQ link will redirect most web browsers to the current page

where you can search the database for your answers.

The Flight Simulator 98 FAQ link points to: http://www.microsoft.com/games/fsim/rp-FAQ.htm

Online Support: As just mentioned, the Online Support page has merged with the FAQ search page: http://www.microsoft.com/games/fsim/rp-support.htm

Flight Simulator Home Page: This is the official Flight Simulator Home Page. Here you learn about the latest news and points of interest about Flight Simulator 98. There are also many links of other popular Flight Simulator 98 web sites as well. http://www.microsoft.com/games/fsim/default.htm

Finally, an often-overlooked source for Flight Simulator 98 information (especially multiplayer help and tips), the Microsoft Internet Gaming Zone. The address is: http://www.zone.com.

Connection Solutions

If you receive an error box similar to the one shown below (saying that Internet Explorer can't connect to the Internet site X when you click on any of the Microsoft on the Web links from Flight Simulator 98's Help menu selection), it may mean that Internet Explorer is not automatically dialing up your ISP.

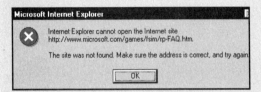

If you receive an error box similar to this it might mean that Internet Explorer is not automatically dialing up your ISP.

One cause for this happening (or rather, not happening) could result from not having the Connect to the Internet as needed option enabled. This option is found by double-clicking on the Internet icon in Control Panel on the Connection tab, as shown on the left.

Not having the Connect to the Internet as needed option enabled is one cause for IE connection error.

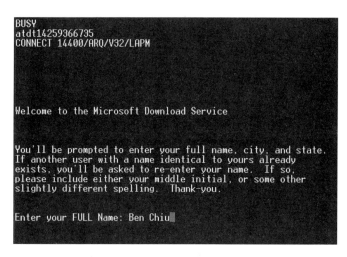

```
BUSY
atdt14259366735
CONNECT 14400/ARQ/V32/LAPM




Welcome to the Microsoft Download Service


You'll be prompted to enter your full name, city, and state.
If another user with a name identical to yours already
exists, you'll be asked to re-enter your name.  If so,
please include either your middle initial, or some other
slightly different spelling.  Thank-you.


Enter your FULL Name: Ben Chiu
```

Use the Microsoft Download Service if you're unable to connect to the Web to download program and driver updates.

Microsoft Download Service

Microsoft Download Service is a fancy name for what most of the computer-oriented public would normally term a BBS (Bulletin Board System) which is a system offering information accessible via computer, modem, and phone line. While technically that definition includes services such as MDS, BBSes are generally much smaller in size and scope.

But the main difference is the Microsoft Download Service is really just that, a source for downloading files.

Although it seems like everyone is connected to the Internet these days, if you haven't felt the need, or are unable to access the Web for some other reason, the Microsoft Download Service may be your best solution under those circumstances.

While you'll likely encounter busy signals, and your connection to the Microsoft Download Service in the U.S. is limited to 14,400 baud, it's one feasible way to download drivers and Flight Simulator updates without hooking up to the Internet or major online service access.

The Microsoft Download Service in the U.S. can be reached at (425) 936-6735 (8 data bits, no parity, 1 stop bit). The Canadian number is (905) 507-3022 (also 8 data bits, no parity, 1 stop bit, but unlike the U.S. number it supports 28,800 baud connections).

Microsoft FastTips

The Microsoft FastTips service (800-936-4100) allows you to access recordings, or order technical information via return fax or mail. If all you're looking for is access to FAQs and you don't have an Internet connection, this

service is an economical option due to it's toll free access and around the clock operation.

> **Tip:** *Microsoft Technical Support Service numbers from around the world can be found in Flight Simulator 98's Help Index under Technical Support, worldwide.*

Talking to Humans

As convenient as all of the automated Microsoft Support options are, there are times when you just need to speak to a human. Unfortunately, the simple fact is some of the automated support services are generally more efficient and often quicker as well. Still, there's nothing quite as reassuring as talking to someone that knows what they're doing.

Microsoft Technical Support comes in two flavors: no charge and charge. The only things that really separate the two (besides the costs) are the hours during which you can reach a Technical Support Engineer.

Microsoft Unlimited No Charge Support

Microsoft's No Charge Technical Support is open from six A.M. to six P.M. Pacific time, Monday through Friday, excluding holidays. While there is no charge for the service, telephone toll charges (if any) do apply. That number is (425) 637-9308.

After Hours Support

Just as the name suggests, Microsoft's Technical Support Engineers are available 24 hours a day, seven days a week including holidays. The only catch is it'll cost you. Most Flight Simulator users would rather wait than pay, but if you absolutely have to talk to a support Engineer right now, this really is a handy service. A listing of After Hours Support numbers and charges can be found in Flight Simulator 98's Help Index under Technical Support, from a Microsoft Technical Support Engineer.

Information and Camaraderie

As we discussed earlier, although Microsoft is the logical place to start seeking information, the Flight Simulator community is where you'll often find the most up-to-date information and tips. The world of Flight Simulator enthusiasts is mostly located on both the Internet and on public online service forums. These are the places where you'll be able to meet, communicate and interact with other Flight Simulator enthusiasts. So, in essence, the following sections

Newsgroup software for IE can be found on the Microsoft Internet Explorer Internet Mail & News site located at http://www.microsoft.com/ie/imn.

The microsoft.public.simulators newsgroup—the friendliest Flight Simulator newsgroup on the Web.

contain the very heart of the Flight Simulator community.

USENET Newsgroups

Just as ISPs have replaced BBSes, Newsgroups have (for the most part) replaced BBSes as the preferred electronic gathering places. Therefore, it really shouldn't come as a surprise that many cyber-savvy Flight Simulator pilots gather on USENET (the actual designation that encompasses all newsgroups).

microsoft.public.simulators

Microsoft's public simulators newsgroup is the most popular newsgroup for Flight Simulator aficionados because just as there are newsgroups dedicated to other sims, microsoft.public.simulators is devoted to only Microsoft simulators (read: Flight Simulator) so virtually everything discussed here is related to Flight Simulator.

Sound like the perfect place to gather? There's more. The microsoft.public.simulators newsgroup is hosted by two volunteer MVPs (Most Valuable Players). Although their presence is to help everyone with problems (and they really do exemplary jobs) and not to *police* the group, this newsgroup is by far the most tame and new-user friendly. If you want to get your feet wet, this would be a good place to start.

rec.aviation.simulators

Although the rec.aviation. simulators newsgroup is technically a newsgroup that discusses aviation simulators of all types (general aviation, combat, helicopter, stand-alone, etc.) from *all* manufacturers, GA sims like Flight Simulator 98 are the topics of most of the discussions. While you'll see postings regarding Flight Simulator in this newsgroup, many of these postings are *cross-posted* (posted to multiple newsgroups) from microsoft.public.simulators but not always. Anyway, it's definitely worth checking out what goes on in this newsgroup.

This newsgroup's demeanor could be rated about average for volatility, and the language tends to get a bit lewd on occasion. Still all in all, the trade-off for information seems to be worth it if you are selective about what you read.

Newsgroup Blues

Although Microsoft hosts its own newsgroup dedicated to Microsoft Simulators, the Internet and subsequently USENET are, for the most part, un-moderated. This means most users are responsible for maintaining their civility. Most of the time this isn't a problem as the majority of users self-regulate the group by peer pressure, but sometimes things do get out of hand with name-calling and foul language.

While this may sound intimidating, the newsgroup experience really isn't as traumatic as that may sound. That's because you can lurk (watch and read, but contribute very little or nothing at all) in a newsgroup and no one will ever know you're there. From that "invisible" perspective, you can explore the newsgroups and search out the information you seek from the numerous postings without any fear of being hassled or otherwise. If you can put up with the occasional upheaval between other users or the pushy know-it-all users that appear every now and then, newsgroups can be a fun, informative, and social gathering spot.

If you've never accessed a newsgroup before, you might have to download newsgroup software update if you don't already have the full version of Microsoft Internet Explorer. You can download this software from the Microsoft Internet Explorer Internet Mail & News site at http://www.microsoft.com/ie/imn.

comp.sys.ibm.pc.games.flight-sim

The comp.sys.ibm.pc.games.flight-sim newsgroup probably contains—all at once—the best and the worst the Internet has to offer for flight simulators. This is probably the best gathering place for knowledgeable pilots. Unfortunately, it also is frequented by visitors with some of the worst attitudes imaginable. The overall atmosphere of this newsgroup has been described as the *Wild West*. In other words, this newsgroup isn't for the faint of heart.

Discussions of aviation simulators from all manufacturers and of all types (but mostly GA-related) can be found in the rec.aviation.simulators newsgroup.

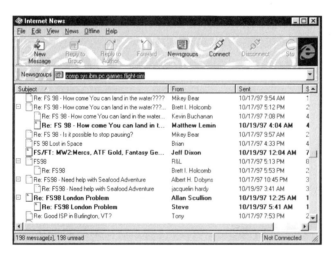

The main topics of conversation in comp.sys.ibm.pc. games.flight-sim are usually combat sims.

Furthermore, combat sims are overwhelmingly the main topics of conversation and Flight Simulator 98 posts (especially those that don't include conspiracy theories, or attacks from fans of competing GA simulators) never add up to more than a few posts. So, if you skip this group, you probably won't miss much about Flight Simulator 98. Lurk at your own discretion.

Other Flight Simulator Sites

The World Wide Web is chock full of hundreds of commercial and private sites that feature Flight Simulator, Flight Simulator 98 products, files, utilities, and related interests. As you might imagine, it'd be a major undertaking to document all of them. So instead, we'll just cover a small sample of offerings from the Flight Simulator community on the Web. From there you'll be able to surf from site to site by clicking on hot links located at each Web site.

AVSIM Magazine— The Online Resource for Aviation Simulation

Short for Aviation Simulaton, *AVSIM* is one of the largest depositories of Flight Simulator knowledge on the Web. AVSIM.COM has links to databases for Scenery Textures, IUP (Indiana University Of Pennsylvania) Flight-Simulator E-mail list messages, and the extremely useful Tech Database for installation, hardware and setup as well as real flight procedure information. And that's just scratching the surface!

Computer Simulation Games

Although the Mining Company's site is more along the lines of a typical *E-zine* (a Web-based magazine), filled with product reviews and articles dedicated to computer-based entertainment of all types, the Computer Simulation Games section offers many Flight Simulator-related links. Overall, it's a well-thought-out and pleasant site to visit that as of this writing offered a new online chat room.

AVSIM Magazine: (http://www.avsim.com) is absolutely packed with Flight Simulator information.

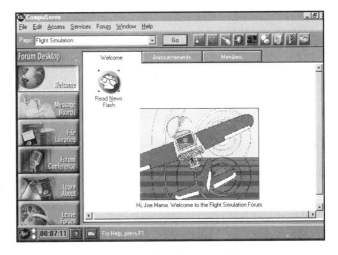

Although more like an E-zine than anything else, Computer Simulation Games (@The Mining Company: http://compsimgames.miningco.com) does contain plenty of useful Flight Simulator-related links.

Whether you're interested in desktop flight or the real thing, FlightSim.Com is a treasure trove of information. (http://flightsim.com).

Flight Simulator Ferdy's Page:
http://www.milenium.com/~ferdy/.

FlightSim.Com

FlightSim.Com is one of the most popular sites on the Web, for many reasons. One reason is because it's devoted to both flight simulators *and* real world aviation. Searchable file areas, public and private message forums, product reviews, photo galleries, news, and how-to tips are just a few of the valuable offerings you'll find here. Although you need to register to access the wealth on FlightSim.Com, there is no charge to use this site.

Flight Simulator Ferdy's Page

Ferdy's Flight Simulator Web site is just one example of the many privately maintained sites available on the Internet. Here you'll find many types of freeware, aircraft art, scenery, and utilities for Flight Simulator. Be sure to check out the Aircraft of the Week section when you visit.

MicroWINGS

MicroWINGS is the official site for The International Association for Aerospace Simulations. The lines are a bit

blurred about whether MicroWINGS is a publishing business that puts out an excellent magazine covering flight simulations requiring membership for a subscription, or an organization that just happens to provide an excellent magazine for its members. In either case, the MicroWINGS site is filled with news, links, and information of interest to Flight Simulator fans. Membership not required for access.

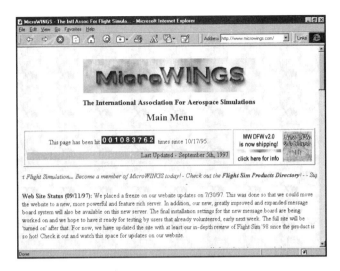

MicroWINGS: http://www.microwings.com.

Roberts Dutch Flight

This site is an excellent example of not only how far around the world the Flight Simulator community extends, but it's also a tribute to the dedication and creativity of its citizens. On this page you'll find the Web author's Flights around the Netherlands. These user-written adventures are comprised of flight plans and charts for excursions around the land of tulips as well as other Flight Simulator-related links and files.

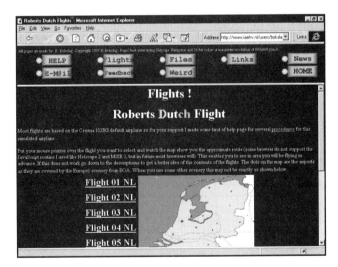

Roberts Dutch Flight: http://www.iaehv.nl/users/bokslag/.

simFlight

simFlight is an interesting combination of user-maintained Web sites in the form of commercial style E-zine. Here you'll find articles and information about Flight Simulator 98 from some of the most dedicated Flight Simulator enthusiasts from around the world.

simFlight: http://simflight.com.

*The World Wide Guide to Flight Simulation:
http://www.wwguide.com.au.*

The World Wide Guide to Flight Simulation

Based in Australia, the World Wide Guide site is generally considered to be (as the site itself claims) "the World's best guide to the world's best resources for MS Flight Simulator." Here you'll discover lot's of interesting links to information, scenery, artwork, and tutorials. Although the site may no longer have what some would consider state-of-the-art graphics, it's one site you really shouldn't miss.

Aviation Sites

Because Flight Simulator 98 is a simulation of GA flight, many of the resources primarily designed to assist real world aviators can directly apply to and enhance your Flight Simulator experience. When you consider that the Flight Simulator community is also comprised of many actual pilots, it should come as no surprise that many real-world aviation sites also have sections dedicated to Flight Simulator.

AirNav

Free of charge and detailed, AirNav is a searchable data base of airports and navigational aids in the U.S.. Because the information on this site is designed for real world pilots, the information you'll find here is more detailed than that found in Flight Simulator 98's Airport/ Facility Directory.

Landings

Links to real world and simulation aviation links are the least of what the Landings site has to offer. You'll find news, weather, classifieds, a cyber Marketplace, and a whole host of interesting things to see that aviation enthusiasts (real and PC-based) are sure to find interesting.

US Government Office of Aeronautical Charting and Cartography

Although you won't be able to access navigation charts online, this is a useful source to find information on updates, catalogues and current purchasing information for NOAA publications.

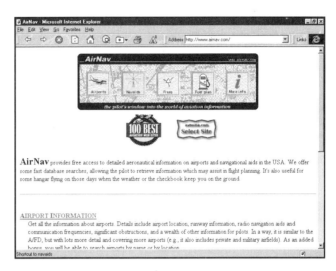

AirNav: www.airnav.com.

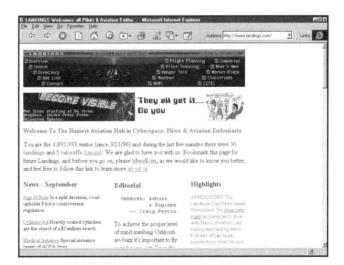

Landings.com: www.landings.com.

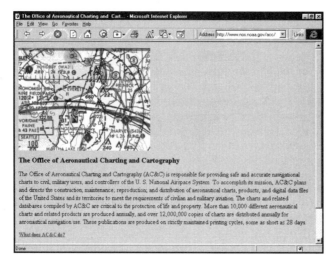

The Office of Aeronautical Charting and Cartography

The Office of Aeronautical Charting and Cartography (AC&C) is responsible for providing safe and accurate navigational charts to civil, military users, and controllers of the U. S. National Airspace System. To accomplish its mission, AC&C plans and directs the construction, maintenance, reproduction, and distribution of aeronautical charts, products, and digital data files of the United States and its territories to meet the requirements of civilian and military aviation. The charts and related databases compiled by AC&C are critical to the protection of life and property. More than 10,000 different aeronautical charts and related products are produced annually, and over 12,000,000 copies of charts are distributed annually for aeronautical navigation use. These publications are produced on strictly maintained printing cycles, some as short as 28 days.

What does AC&C do?

Tip: *Just as with everything on the Web (or in print, for that matter), the old adage you can't always believe everything you read definitely applies. The information you read on any Web site, even the most professional-looking ones, should be viewed with a discerning eye. It's usually not that people intentionally pass along unreliable information, but sometimes it happens.*

US Government Office of Aeronautical Charting and Cartography: http://www.nos.noaa.gov/acc/.

Online Service Forums

Back before the Internet explosion, online services reigned supreme. And even though there were those who predicted that USENET newsgroups would bring an end to the big online forums, those forums are still alive and well today. An online forum works essentially the same way that a newsgroup where people post and exchange messages. However, the online forums are a bit more complete because they offer file areas as well.

Perhaps the biggest appeal for forums is that they are moderated by members themselves. People are appointed to moderate and regulate what happens on the forums unlike the wide-open and often untamed USENET newsgroups. Unruly and troublesome members are usually quickly and quietly dealt with so the atmosphere found on these forums is generally considered to be the most hospitable.

The tradeoff for this stability is cost of entry, because access to most major online services is predicated on having a paid membership to that service. Fortunately, most services have some sort of a "try before you buy" trial period where you can explore the service before actually joining. On the other hand, many members of online services don't object to paying a monthly or hourly

fee for access due to the fact that service charges tend to keep out some of the "undesirables." Whether this is true or not seems to depend upon whom you ask.

America Online (AOL)

The Flight Simulations Resource Center (keyword: FSRC) on America Online has a healthy number of discussion groups and file sections. Here you find people interested in Flight Simulator and third-party Flight Simulator add-ons, as well as nearly every other flight simulator ever produced. To receive the free trial AOL software, you can contact AOL at (800) 827-6364 or contact them via the Web at http://www.aol.com.

CompuServe

CompuServe's world famous Flight Simulation Forum (FSFORUM) has always been a popular gathering place for Flight Simulator enthusiasts.

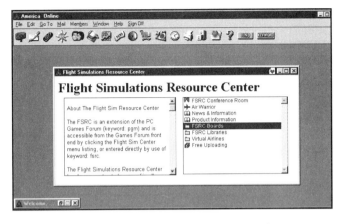

America Online's Flight Simulations Resource Center.

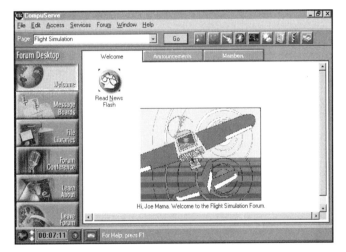

CompuServe's world famous FSFORUM.

As of this writing, AOL has taken over CompuServe. However, FSFORUM (although not certain) is reportedly going to continue, at least for the foreseeable future. Fortunately, like AOL, CompuServe offers a free trial period. You can contact CompuServe at (800) 848-8199 or on the Web at http://www.compuserve.com.

THE ART OF THE INSTRUMENT SCAN

Flying instruments is one of the most challenging and rewarding of aviation experiences. Besides that, it's fun. Instrument flying satisfies and gratifies a pilot's inherent need to be master of the universe, the airplane and the environment (not necessarily in that order).

Instrument flying is comparable to playing a video game in three dimensions. It costs more and there are no Klingons to shoot down, but you can earn a chance to make another flight if you're good. So let's see what it takes to be good.

The Scan Plan

The *instrument scan* is the clue and the glue, the foundation of all instrument flight, yet it's the one thing at which many instrument pilots are deficient.

Perhaps that shouldn't come as a surprise, given the way we teach instrument flying. Instead of an agreed-upon and systematic method for scanning, pilots are often left to their own devices when it comes to mastering the airplane's devices. If you've been an instrument flight instructor for any period of time longer than, say, a week or two, you will see a wide and amusing array of scan techniques. You'll see pilots who appear to follow a fly around the cockpit, all the way to the radical head twister who keeps half of North America's chiropractors in business by grinding down his cervical vertebrae.

My initial instrument instructor (there were several) insisted on tapping the instruments with his metal pointer, his baton leading my eyes in scan. Most conductors confine themselves to Bach, Beethoven, and Brahms. Not this one. He would say, "OK, [tap, tap] look here [tap] (airspeed indicator); look there [tap] (attitude indicator); don't look at that [tap] (heading indicator), look at this one [tap] (turn coordinator)." For a long while, I thought that's what the instruments were called: *here*, *there*, *that*, and *this one*.

Many pilots end up surviving, rather than mastering, every IFR flight. They deserve better. Properly done, instrument flying is a pleasure and you get to bask in the post-flight glow of a complex job well done. Along the way, you also get the comfort of realizing that you know what to do. The individual tasks required of an instrument pilot are not inherently difficult; assembling them into a smoothly functioning, seamless whole, however, does take a plan. So, let's make one.

The Three Steps

Most aviation manuals present the instrument scan as a disjointed process. You're instructed to look at certain instruments, at certain times, under certain conditions. You're never provided a series of steps to follow that work under all conditions. It's like attending dance school where you're shown individual steps but not shown how they're connected. You attend your first real dance only to look completely goofy as you stomp the floor like a guy who really hates bugs.

The following three-step instrument scan connects the steps into a continuous process. These three steps are executed every time a major attitude change is made. (A *major attitude change* occurs whenever the airplane transitions from one attitude to another, such as when going from a turn to straight and level or a climb or a descent, or any combinations of these.) All three steps should take approximately 15 seconds to complete. Here are the three steps of the scan, in the order they should be done:

STEP 1: Select attitude, power, trim & confirm.

STEP 2: Radial scan the primary instruments.

STEP 3: Trim using the VSI and monitor-scan the Big-6 instruments.

In step one, the airplane is put in the desired attitude, power is adjusted and an initial twist of trim is applied to hold the airplane in this attitude. The correct operation of the most critical instruments is then checked by a confirmation process. In step two the primary instruments are then scanned in an organized fashion, and small corrections are made to fine-tune the airplane to the proper attitude. The final trim adjustments are made in step three and the airplane's new attitude is monitored on the six main panel instruments otherwise known as the "Big-6." This is the big picture of how the instruments are scanned in

this three step process. The specific details and reasons for each of the three steps follow.

Step One of the Scan

The first step in the three-step scan is to select the attitude, power, and trim conditions for the new flight attitude. Execute this first step by focusing on the attitude indicator and selecting (from previous experience) the attitude that educated approximation says will provide the flight conditions desired. The implication here is that you have or are acquiring knowledge of the predetermined attitudes necessary to make the airplane climb, turn, and descend as commanded.

After the first few hours of instrument flying, you should immediately decide on an array of specific power settings and flight attitudes which allow the airplane to do exactly what you wish. These power settings and flight attitudes are values or reference points on the tachometer and attitude indicator. In a light, general aviation trainer, climbs are typically done with full power and a five to ten degree nose up pitch attitude. This usually results in a consistently good cruise-climb speed. Most turns are accomplished with a 15 to 20 degree bank. This is close to the bank necessary for a standard rate turn at normal cruising conditions.

Remember, a standard rate turn simply means that the nose of the airplane changes direction at three degrees per second in the horizontal plane. The easiest way to determine the bank required for a standard rate turn is to drop the last number off the airspeed and add the number five. If the airspeed is 125 Knots then the bank required for standard rate is 12 + 5 or 17 degrees. If the airspeed is 90 then the standard rate bank is 9 + 5 or 14 degrees. If the airspeed is 600 knots then the bank required is 65 degrees. This could be real interesting for the passengers of jet airplanes! There is a good chance some of the older passengers will experience a dislodging of their uppers. The general rule is never to exceed 30 degrees of bank under IFR conditions, even if a steeper bank is required for a standard rate turn.

Besides, someone once suggested that most airline pilots avoid steep turns because of the debilitating effects of G-forces on posture. Many years spent in a pilot seat makes you look like a graduate of the Quasimodo posture school.

No pilot worth his or her weight in slow Hobbs meters (the device that measures how much pilots pay for airplane rental) denies that looking outside at the earth's horizon is a good thing. The earth's horizon allows you to keep your airplane in the correct attitude for flight. In fact, most pilots flying VFR (visually, under Visual Flight Rules) spend upwards of 90 percent of their time referencing the visible horizon. Why should this be any different during instrument flight? When the earth's horizon is no longer visible, the airplane's attitude indicator (artificial horizon) is a most welcome substitute.

Step one of the instrument scan suggests that the attitude indicator be exclusively observed during major attitude changes. This is certainly contradictory to what you may have been told about instrument flying. It's often considered a punishable offense to stare at any one instrument. For the most part, this is a good rule (except when it comes to step one of the scan).

The Air Force Instrument Flying Manual AFM 51-37 states: "The attitude indicator is the only instrument which you should observe continuously for any appreciable length of time. Several seconds may be needed to accomplish an attitude change required for a normal turn. During this period you may need to devote your attention almost exclusively to the attitude indicator to ensure good attitude control."

Since the USAF is in the business of flying aircraft, it's a sure bet that they gave this statement a great deal of thought. Problems with instrument scan often occur when pilots spend too little rather than too much time observing the attitude indicator.

Many years ago, a study of military and professional pilots discovered something interesting. When cameras were targeted on the eyes of these pilots during their instrument scan, it was discovered they spent 85 percent of their time looking at the attitude indicator. It's reasonable to conclude that this behavior evolved because it is imminently useful and efficient. If this behavior is good enough for professionals, then it's wise to emulate it.

The attitude indicator is a complete instrument. Unlike any other instrument it contains both pitch and bank information. Therefore, it's reasonable to focus on this instrument when changing attitudes. Of course, if attitude indicators never failed, there would be no concern with them being the center of a pilot's attention. As an entry instrument, it is the core of the scan. But you cannot be obsessed with its presence nor crippled by its absence. Instruments do fail, often with disastrous consequences for the pilot addicted to the attitude indicator and rejecting all other sources of information. Knowing how to detect instrument failure and correct for it is the defensive countermeasure which balances the emphasis on the attitude indicator.

In the final part of step one of this scan, you compare and validate the results of control input to the response of the attitude indicator. This is the confirmation process which ensures the attitude indicator is working properly. In other words, the attitude indicator should respond according to how you move the flight controls. If control pressure is applied to make a right turn, the attitude indicator should show a right turn deflection in proportion to the amount of control input. A slight amount of back pressure on the controls should show a gradual increase in pitch on the attitude indicator. Any discrepancy between control input and attitude response sthat consult the turn or pitch triangle of agreement. (Keep in mind that it's only necessary to check this triangle of agreement if you suspect the attitude indicator or any other flight instrument is in error. In other words, it's not necessary to check the turn or pitch triangle of agreement every time a major attitude change is made.)

The Turn Triangle of Agreement

A triangle of agreement occurs when three instruments (those providing either all pitch or all bank information) respond at a similar rate and in a noncontradictory manner. For example, the turn triangle of agreement consists of the attitude indicator, turn coordinator and magnetic compass. All three of these instruments respond to a turn. When turning, these instruments should reflect similar rates and similar directions of turn.

In the event you suspect a discrepancy in the operation of the attitude indicator, the other two instruments of the triangle should be consulted, starting with the turn coordinator. If the turn coordinator does not reflect the attitude indicator's expected direction and rate of turn, the magnetic compass should be checked for movement. The instrument in disagreement with the other two is the one to eliminate as failed. For instance, if the attitude indicator reflects a turn and the compass shows a heading change, but the turn coordinator indicates a constant heading, the turn coordinator has probably failed. The majority wins. It's just like professional wrestling, which, by the way, isn't real. Whether it's Wally, the Flying Cadaver Creator or Herbert, the Organ Donor Provider, the wrestler who has the most fans usually wins.

On most modern day general aviation airplanes, the turn coordinator is electrically operated, the attitude indicator is vacuum- powered and the magnetic compass is blessed and powered by Mother Nature. This means that each of these three turn indicators is operated by an independent power source. Generally, they won't all fail at once (and if they do, you're just having a bad

Magnetic Compass

160 KNOTS 60
140 80
120 100

A.T.

9 1
8 2
7 3
6 5 4

30.15

DC. ELEC.
PITCH INFORMATION

TURN COORDINATOR
L R
2 MIN

33 N 3
30 W E 6
24 S 15
12

10 15
5 VSI
0 20
5
10 15

The turn triangle of agreement consists of the attitude indicator, turn coordinator and magnetic compass.

"air" day). This is why these three instruments make up the turn triangle of agreement. Why isn't the heading indicator part of this triangle? The heading indicator on many airplanes is vacuum-powered. Since it operates on the same power system as the attitude indicator, a failure of the vacuum system renders both these instruments inoperative.

Several years ago, a high performance, single-engine, general aviation airplane entered a repair shop to have work done on the instrument vacuum system (the vacuum system isn't something used to keep the airplane clean. It's a pump that provides spin for the gyros of certain instruments). Apparently the mechanic forgot to put the air filter on the intake line, which allows air to be drawn from inside the engine cowling and over the gyro instruments by the vacuum pump. The aircraft departed IFR and entered a solid wall of precipitation. Water was drawn through the air intake of the vacuum line and into the vacuum system. The pilot stated that he looked up at his instruments and saw water filling up the attitude indicator and the heading indicator. Wow! Now that's something his instructor probably never told him about. What would most pilots think if this happened to them? They might think the mechanic installed an auto-timed, self-lubricating, gyro system. The moral here: Be prepared. Instruments can and do fail.

There is a little-used instrument that is actually easier to use than the magnetic compass for detecting turns—the ADF (Automatic Direction Finder). It's my opinion that pilots should never fly instruments without having the ADF tuned to a station with a strong signal. In the event the turn triangle of agreement needs to be consulted, ADF needle movement is a strong indication that the aircraft is turning, and in what direction the turn is made. In the

unfortunate event that all your gyro instruments fail, the ADF could provide enough information to keep your wings level and the airplane under control.

The Pitch Triangle of Agreement

The pitch triangle of agreement consists of the attitude indicator, vertical speed indicator and alternate static system. The attitude indicator and the VSI (Vertical Speed Indicator) operate on separate power sources (vacuum and static pressure). Neither the airspeed indicator nor the altimeter should be used as the third instrument in the triangle, because both these instruments operate on the same static source as the VSI. If a pitch discrepancy exists between the attitude indicator and the VSI, it is possible the static source is blocked. Therefore, the altimeter and airspeed indicator may also be in error.

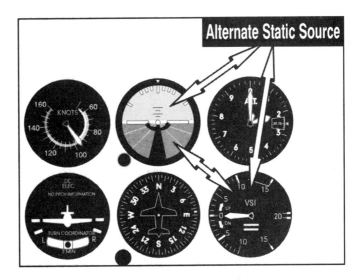

The pitch triangle of agreement consists of the attitude indicator, vertical speed indicator and alternate static system.

The appropriate action is to eliminate the VSI as a source of error. Simply activate the alternate static source and note any change in VSI indication. If the VSI's indication doesn't change with the selection of the alternate static source, then the attitude indicator is probably in error. If the VSI's indicator does change, then leave the alternate static source open. If the source for alternate static air is inside the cockpit, there will be a slight jump of the needle due to the cabin's lower pressure.

Setting Power in Step One of the Scan

After the initial attitude is selected, the power is adjusted for the desired flight condition. If selecting a climb, the power is added as the nose is raised. This reflects the old adage, "Pitch, plus power, equals performance." There is no need to look at the tachometer when entering a climb in fixed-pitch propeller airplanes, since the climb is usually accomplished with full power (throttle full forward). In high performance airplanes, usually the propeller control is moved forward first, followed by the throttle as the aircraft enters climb attitude. The appropriate tachometer or manifold pressure settings are made by taking a quick glance at the engine instruments. Initially, this setting need only be approximate. A more precise setting can be made when the new attitude is finally established. When you gain experience you'll establish power settings by sound alone!

To enter a descent, the power is reduced first, then the attitude is adjusted. The more smoothly these two actions become integrated, the less indicated airspeed variance there will be. It's often not necessary to even look at the power gauges when the initial power reduction is made. These settings can be approximated, with experience, by sensing the throttle's position and by sound. Make sure you keep a keen eye on the attitude indicator during the attitude change, thereby maintaining complete control of the aircraft in the transition.

Once an attitude is selected and power adjusted, trim is added to keep the selected attitude constant. This initial "gross" application of trim should be just enough to keep the airplane's attitude from wandering. When twisting the trim wheel, all "Wheel of Fortune" fans should avoid the temptation of yelling, "Come on, one thousand!" In other words, give the trim wheel a couple of good turns as experience indicates, then go on to step two. The final and more accurate application of trim is completed in step three.

Step Two of the Scan

Step two of the three-step scan procedure is to radial scan of the primary instruments. This is done for two very important reasons. First, the primary instruments are those that allow you to fine-tune the attitude selected on the attitude indicator. Second, the primary instruments allow you additional confirmation that the attitude indicator is reading correctly. (*See footnote at end page, Appendix C.)

Readily identifying, in flight, which instruments are primary for a given flight condition is difficult for many new instrument pilots. After all, you have six main instruments to choose from. You don't, however, need to look at all of them to fine-tune the airplane's attitude. Experienced professionals know exactly what instrument they need to look at to make the airplane fly precisely. In fact, skill at instrument flying lies not so much in scanning all the instruments, but learning in what instruments to invest time. When time is spent

efficiently, the airplane is easily controlled. This is where instant recognition of the primary instruments becomes very important for successful instrument flying.

There are always three primary instruments for any condition of flight: one for pitch, one for bank, and one for power. Primary instruments are those that dispense the needed information to precisely accomplish the intended maneuver (i.e., climb, turn, descent, etc.). These instruments are primary in the sense that they reaffirm that the previously selected attitude is correct. If you know which instruments are primary, you'll avoid ocular waste while

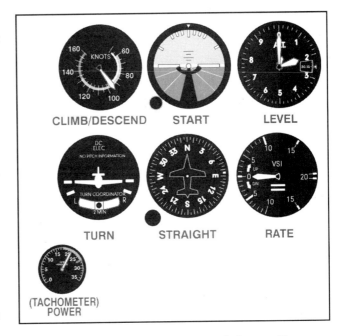

These instruments are primary controls for specific conditions of flight.

scanning instruments. The best way to understand these primary instruments is to tape the words shown in the diagram at the top of this page, under each instrument on the panel (write them on a thin, sticky strip of a Post-It note and place this directly under each instrument on your computer's screen). The FAA considers the word bank to be associated with either holding headings or heading change. This makes sense, considering controlling the angle of bank is directly related to the control of the heading.

For example, in straight and level flight, pilots should look at the panel and find those instruments labeled as straight and level. The heading indicator is primary for bank (going straight), the altimeter is primary for pitch (remaining level) and the tachometer is primary for power. In constant airspeed climbs or descents, airspeed is always the primary pitch instrument. In a turn, the turn coordinator is always primary for bank. The primary instruments for a climbing turn are: airspeed for pitch, turn coordinator for bank, and tachometer for power. The primary instruments for a level turn are: altimeter for pitch, turn

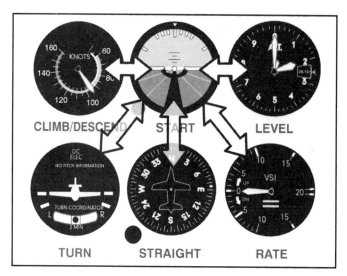

The radial scan begins with the attitude indicator and takes in all of the primary instruments.

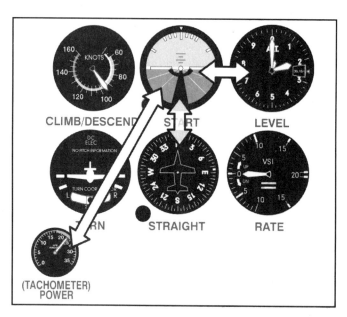

The proper scan for straight and level flight.

coordinator for bank, and tachometer for power.

In a straight climb or descent, at a specific rate, the VSI is primary for pitch and the heading indicator is primary for bank. Additionally, if a specific airspeed is necessary for the constant rate descent (and it most often is on ILS approaches), then the airspeed indicator becomes primary for power. This is one of the rare situations where the tachometer is not primary for power as listed. Think of it this way: What is the job to be accomplished and what is primary to do the job? The job, on a constant rate descent, is to maintain a specific airspeed, heading and rate. The only instrument that can do the job of telling the pilot if the airspeed is correct is the airspeed indicator. Power is modified to maintain this specific airspeed.

To determine which flight instruments are primary, look at the words under each instrument making up the intended flight condition. This visual prompt precludes the

awkward mechanics of having to rigidly memorize which instruments are primary (a difficult task for the neophyte when instrument relationships may not be understood). This is the same visual method used by the order-takers at McDonalds. You say, "Hamburger" and they push the button with the hamburger picture on it. (If you said, "Beautiful weather," they might answer, "I'm sorry, I don't have that button.") After flying IFR with the primary instruments labeled as shown, they'll be easier to recognize and your instructor will eventually remove them from the panel.

Step two directs you to radial scan these primary instruments. To radial scan means to begin the scan at the attitude indicator which is marked Start. Then you move to the primary instrument, extract information from it, return to the attitude indicator and make any necessary correction in attitude. This is called the radial scan because the visual scanning track is from the attitude indicator out to the primary instrument, then back to the attitude indicator, making what appear to be spokes radiating from the attitude indicator to all the primary instruments, as shown in the figure at the left.

The attitude indicator is marked Start because this is where all attitude changes begin. It's very important that you understand how the radial scan is accomplished. Your eyes move from the attitude indicator to a primary instrument, where you observe its reading or detect its movement, then return to the attitude indicator and make an attitude adjustment to stabilize the primary instrument. Thus, radial scanning a particular instrument means going back and forth between that instrument and the attitude indicator as necessary.

If straight and level flight is the goal, you should radial scan the heading indicator, the altimeter, and the tachometer. The secret to radial scanning is to start at the attitude indicator, proceed to a primary instrument, snatch information, then return to the attitude indicator and make a small attitude adjustment to effect the correct performance. Each of the three primary instruments should be quickly radial scanned at least once, before spending additional time radial scanning any one instrument in particular. This scan immediately identifies how close the airplane is to the planned attitude.

For straight and level flight, radial scan the heading indicator by observing it, then returning to the attitude indicator. If you notice a heading deviation, make a small change in bank on the attitude indicator to stop, then correct this change. Use five degrees of bank correction on the attitude indicator to return to a heading that's not off by more than 20 degrees. The altimeter is radial scanned next by observing it, then returning to the attitude indicator. If the

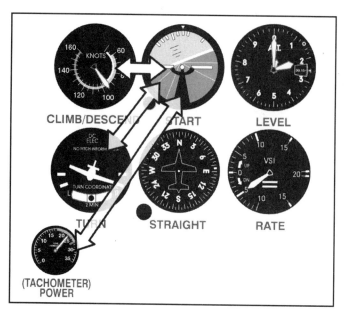

The proper instrument scan for a descending turn.

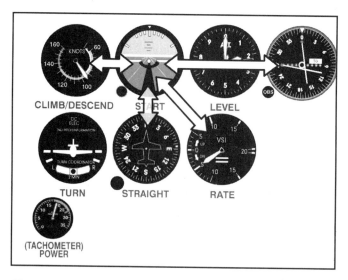

The proper instrument scan for an ILS approach.

altimeter needle is moving or didn't indicate the proper altitude, a small correction in pitch (as appropriate, depending on the amount of deviation) is applied to the attitude indicator.

The tachometer is radial scanned last. Look at the tachometer and make any necessary final adjustment in the setting, then immediately return to the attitude indicator. Usually there is no need to radial scan the tachometer more than once during a major attitude change. If carburetor ice is suspected or detected, then radial scan the tachometer more often. After radial scanning all three primary instruments, you should alternately radial scan the altimeter and heading indicator, making small corrections on the attitude indicator to stabilize these instruments.

The diagram at the top of page 14 shows the proper instrument scan for a descending turn. The primary instruments for this condition are: airspeed for pitch, the turn coordinator for bank, and the tachometer for power.

The power is reduced as a left, 15 degree banking turn, of approximately three degrees nose down pitch is selected. An initial application of trim is applied to stabilize the airplane, thereby completing step one of the scan. The airspeed indicator, turn coordinator, and tachometer are initially radial scanned and small adjustments to the attitude indicator are made to make the primary instruments indicate correctly.

The diagram at the bottom of this page shows the proper instrument scan for an ILS approach. The ILS approach requires that a constant rate descent be maintained, as well as a specific airspeed. The VSI becomes primary for pitch control; the heading indicator, primary for bank control; the airspeed indicator, primary for power. Remember, despite not being labeled as a primary power instrument in the diagram on page ten, the airspeed indicator is the one exception to primary instrument identity. The throttle position is predicated on maintaining a specific airspeed; therefore the airspeed indicator becomes primary for power.

Step Three of the Scan

The last step requires you make the final trim adjustments using the VSI, then monitor scan the new aircraft attitude on the BIG-6 instruments. Step three is accomplished once all the primary instruments are radial scanned and are indicating the proper values. If rudder trim is available it should be used first, followed by aileron trim, then elevator trim. For most small general aviation airplanes, the elevator trim will usually be the only one available on the aircraft. To properly trim the airplane for pitch, the VSI should be used. This instrument is very sensitive to small pitch changes and will indicate almost immediately the direction of movement. The VSI also has a large, noticeable needle swing that is visually easy to identify. When leveling off, or when established in a climb or descent, trim for a constant VSI indication.

A gradual easing of control pressure usually identifies if the airplane is or isn't properly trimmed. There is never any reason to let go of the controls when trimming to see what the airplane does. This causes pilots more heartaches than it's worth. By letting go of the controls, an untrimmed airplane could rapidly deviate from the planned flight attitude, depending on just how out of trim it was. You must now return the airplane to its previous flight condition before you re-trim. It's so much easier to ease up on control pressure, observe VSI needle movement and make a corresponding change in the trim. Very small adjustments in trim can now be made without having to recapture a runaway airplane. Another valid reason to hold onto the controls while trimming is turbulence. In turbulent air, you can still apply aileron control to keep the wings level while trimming for pitch.

Once the airplane is properly trimmed, you have the advantage of using your rudder to control the direction of the aircraft. Simply apply a slight amount of rudder pressure to keep the airplane on its desired heading. This frees your hands up to sort charts, tune radios, and complete cockpit chores that often require the use of two (or more) hands. The airplane may wander up and down a trickle, but generally won't stray a great deal from the desired fight condition.

After the final trim adjustments are made, the six main panel instruments are monitor scanned. This is often done in a sideways fashion going from the top row to the bottom row of instruments or in a clockwise, circular fashion. Select any particular scanning pattern you feel comfortable with. The objective is to monitor deviations from the established attitude. When deviations are noted, small adjustments are made on the attitude indicator to maintain the desired flight conditions. Monitor scanning is the condition in which you'll spend most of your time while on instruments. Step three, therefore, is performed continuously until a new flight attitude is desired (thus requiring a major change in attitude). All three steps of the scan procedure are repeated when making this major attitude change.

The first two steps of the three-step scan process typically take about ten seconds, with each step taking about five seconds. There are instances where you've completed step two of the scan and might not be able to move on to step three. In turbulence, or when you're on an instrument approach, you may find yourself obliged to rapidly radial scan the primary instruments to maintain precise control of the airplane. Remember, radial scanning is a lot of work. It is possible to radial scan all the instruments on the panel, but this is usually unnecessary and can become very tiresome. Radial scan only those (primary) instruments necessary to control the airplane.

Tips from the Professionals

Over the years, some professionals have reported a rather unusual method of detecting instrument deviation once the airplane's attitude has been established and the aircraft trimmed. These pilots focus their vision in the center of the

panel, just underneath the attitude indicator. Relying upon only their peripheral vision, they watch for any instrument movement. In much the same way a speed reader is taught to take in three or four words at a glance, instrument pilots can absorb information from clusters of instruments at a single glance. Developing peripheral vision takes practice but it does seem to represent the higher art of instrument flying. Until then, when step three of the scan is completed, keep your eyes moving around the panel while looking for attitude deviations.

The radial scan becomes extremely useful for scanning non-control items in the aircraft. Everyone remembers the perilous experience of driving an automobile with an attack bumble-bee flying about inside. From the outside, the hand movements make the driver look like a hyperexcited person who overdosed on caffeine, yet is still trying to land a B-29. People don't usualy crash their car in such instances, because of the way they allocate their time and attention to the problem. They look at the road, then look away while hunting for the little critter, then look back at the road again. While the little varmint is yelling, "Tora, Tora, Tora," the insect is being radial scanned with the road serving as the starting point. The road, in this instance, is similar to how the attitude indicator is used in the radial scanning process.

Radial scanning is useful when scanning approach plates, radios, engine instruments, or copying clearances. When you're forced to look away from the panel, the secret to controlling the airplane is to return to the attitude indicator every few seconds and keep the attitude where it was before you looked away.

With a little experience you'll see that as long as a specific attitude is maintained on the attitude indicator, the primary instruments hardly move. As a demonstration, I usually cover up all the instruments except the attitude indicator and have my student maintain a straight and level attitude for several minutes. When I uncover the instruments, there is often no deviation whatsoever in altimeter and heading indications.

Subtle Secrets

After a certain amount of exposure to instrument flying, many pilots start to notice subtle secrets that make instrument flying easier. Professionals understand that these little bits of information are what add polish to the art of instrument flying. In many cases, these subtle clues directly contradict what these pilots were taught about instrument procedures early in their flying career.

For instance, does the airspeed indicator have a lag in its response? Many instrument pilots say it does. Experienced professionals know this just isn't accurate. If a pilot walked out to an airplane and blew into the pitot (pee-toe) tube, two things would happen. One, all the valves on the airplane mechanic's heart would seize with shock at such a sight. (Never blow into a pitot tube, under any circumstance!) The delicate pressure sensing mechanism inside the instrument would be immediately damaged. Second, the instant a pilot blew into the pitot tube, the airspeed needle would immediately indicate Mach 3. There would be no appreciable lag whatsoever in this instrument.

The apparent lag in the airspeed indicator is caused by the airplane's inertia (its resistance to changing speed). When the nose is raised, the airplane begins losing speed. It may take a few seconds for the airplane to settle down to a new velocity. This implies that you should select a specific attitude, then wait for the airspeed to settle down to its final value. If the airspeed is still off its assignment, then change the attitude and wait for the new indication. Chasing the airspeed needle is a common error among new instrument pilots. It is, however, an error an experienced professional avoids making. That's why professional pilots stop an airspeed deviation first, then apply a correction to return the needle to its desired position.

When you get a few instrument flying hours under your belt, you'll learn that time is often saved by memorizing a few specific power settings for desired conditions of flight. Setting 1,900 RPM on the tachometer yields a constant rate descent of approximately 500 feet per minute at 100 knots in most small airplanes. The difficulty arises when the RPM is set while the airplane is above the intended approach speed. Professionals are aware that when power is reduced from the cruise setting to 1,900 RPM, the higher airspeed will have a pinwheel effect on the propeller and result in a temporarily higher RPM. When the airplane slows to the new approach speed, the decrease in wind blowing on the propeller causes the RPM to settle to a lower value (of course this assumes that you're not flying an airplane with a constant speed propeller). An experienced professional handles this problem by setting the tachometer about 50 to 75 RPM higher than the desired setting when slowing the airplane.

Experienced professionals know the attitude indicator offers its own brand of instrument error. At the completion of a 180 degree turn, the attitude indicator will experience its greatest error due to precession, indicating a slight climb and a slight turn in the opposite direction. This precessional error tends to cancel itself out if an additional 180 degrees of turn is made in the same

direction. When making a turn of approximately 180 degrees, be prepared for the attitude indicator to precess and anticipate a slight error. This precessional error varies between instruments and will generally take from five to 15 seconds to completely disappear. This emphasizes the value of the primary instruments during this short period.

The vertical speed indicator is an instrument that has not received the credit it deserves. While the VSI does have a slight lag, you can learn to anticipate this and become fairly proficient at flying specific descent rates.

Practice using the VSI for constant rate descents in smooth air until you can keep the needle within 50 feet per minute of a specific value. If you can do this you'll easily pass the ILS portion of the toughest ATP (Airline Transport Pilot) checkride, even if it's with the notorious inspector Pinkslip. I've seen pilots who can keep the needle paralyzed at a specific rate. They made the needle look like it was broken and frozen! These pilots realize that precision control of the VSI is the key to shooting enviable ILS approaches.

The VSI, once mastered, provides additional useful information for the precise control of an aircraft. Most pilots also find the VSI useful for helping maintain level flight within the ten to 20 foot mark. Sometimes it's easier to use the VSI to identify trends away from level flight because of the large swing arc and greater sensitivity of its needle. Taking time to learn to fly the VSI with precision pays off handsomely.

There are many boring things to do in life, but instrument flying isn't one of them. The art of flying instruments is a challenging test of your mettle. Instrument flying offers you the opportunity to master your airplane and yourself. A rather sophisticated form of satisfaction results from this combination. Perhaps this is why most instrument pilots are so happy. They realize the scope of their accomplishment. I should warn you, however, that looking really happy at the airport is often inconvenient. The FAA might become suspicious and make you take a drug test. Be cautious!

(Appendix C was originally published as "The Art of the Instrument Scan," in *Rod Machado's Instrument Pilot's Survival Manual,* Copyright 1997 and 1991, by Rod Machado. Published by The Aviation Speakers Bureau, P.O. Box 6030, San Clemente, CA 92674-6030. This appendix was updated by the author and is reprinted through the courtesy of the author and publisher.)

*Footnote:

The primary instruments, with the exception of the heading indicator, operate on power systems that are separate and independent from the attitude indicator. This implies that a failure of one power system will be noticed as a discrepancy between the primary instrument and the attitude indicator. In many aircraft, the heading indicator operates on the same vacuum system as the attitude indicator. Since the heading indicator is primary for bank when performing any "straight" maneuver (i.e. straight and level, straight climb or descent), there may be concern about how the attitude indicator's accuracy can additionally be determined in this condition. In addition to checking control application against attitude indicator response, there are a couple of ways erroneous bank information on the attitude indicator would be noticed. First, the turn coordinator is in the pilot's peripheral vision when the heading indicator is being scanned. Any failure of the attitude indicator would probably be observed on the turn coordinator, when the heading indicator is radial scanned. In other words, if the heading indicator isn't moving, and the turn coordinator is, the vacuum system may have failed; therefore, the turn triangle of agreement should be consulted. Second, the heading indicator and the attitude indicator, in a failing mode, may indicate conflicting attitude information. This may occur as the gyros spin down and behave in a peculiar manner. Despite the attitude indicator and the heading indicator operating on the same power system, these additional means of detecting vacuum failure should be comforting to the pilot.

Appendix D

INSTRUMENT FLIGHT RESOURCES

En-route charts, approach procedures, and SIDs/STARs can be used with Microsoft Flight Simulator 98. To order the kind of maps used by actual aviators, try contacting the following sources.

National Ocean Service
Phone: 1-800 638-8972
Internet: www.nos.noaa.gov/aaa/welcome.html.

Jeppesen
1-800-621-5377.

Sporty's Pilot shop
1-800-Lift Off.

The following books can enhance your knowledge of Flight Simulator and instrument flight skills:

Microsoft Flight Simulator 98: Inside Moves
Microsoft Press/PC Press
Ben Chiu
1997
ISBN 1-57231-635-7

Instrument Flying Handbook
U.S. Department of Transportation
Federal Aviation Administration
1980
Reprinted by ASA publications
ISBN 1-56027-086-1

Rod Machado's Instrument Pilot's Survival Manual
The Aviation Speakers Bureau
Rod Machado
1997
ISBN 0-9631229-0-8

Rod Machado's Private Pilot's Handbook
The Aviation Speakers Bureau
Rod Machado
1996
ISBN 0-9631229-9-1

The Pilot's Manual: Instrument Flying
Aviation Supplies and Academics, Inc.
Trevor Thom
1993
ISBN 1-56027-186-8

Instrument Flight Training Manual
Professional Instrument Courses
Peter Dogan
1991
ISBN 0-916413-12-8

Glossary

Abeam: Fix located off the aircraft's wing tip in a no-wind situation.

ADF (Automatic Direction Finder): Radio receiver which can pick up frequencies between 200 and 1,600 kHz and display the direction the wave is coming from. A special type of ADF is the RBI (Relative Bearing Indicator).

Aircraft control: The techniques used to make control inputs based solely on the information the instruments provide.

Aircraft performance: Obtained aircraft heading, altitude, airspeed, and rate of climb.

ALS (Approach Lighting System): Lighting systems used to direct the pilot to the runway during low visibility.

ASR (Airport Surveillance Radar) approach: Non-precision approach which relies fully on ATC guidance.

Attitude: The combination of pitch and bank.

Attitude instrument flying: Procedures to control the aircraft solely by reference to the instruments.

Bank: Angle formed between the lateral axis of the plane and the natural horizon.

Bearing: A magnetic course to or from an NDB.

CDI (Course Deviation Indicator): Pointer on the VOR display used to determine the position of aircraft in relation to a set course.

Charts: Description of approach procedures. Also known as *plates*.

Circle-to-land approach: Landing on a runway different than the runway the approach procedure leads to.

Clearance: Permission to enter controlled airspace.

Cone of confusion: VOR error when the aircraft is above a VOR.

Contact approach: Pilot request to perform a visual approach rather than an IFR approach if there is at least one mile visibility and the aircraft can remain clear of clouds.

Control instruments: Instruments used to set aircraft performance.

COP (Change Over Point): Specifies when to switch from one VOR to another on an airway.

Crab: Technique used to compensate for wind drift.

Currency Requirements: Flight requirements that the pilot must complete after receiving a rating to keep the rating active.

DH (Decision Height): Lowest point on a precision approach; acts as the MAP.

FAF (Final Approach Fix): Point on a non-precision approach where the aircraft can begin the final approach segment.

FAP (Final Approach Point): Point on a precision approach where the aircraft intercepts the glide path and can then begin the final approach segment.

Final approach segment: Approach segment where the aircraft begins its final descent for landing.

Fix: A location identified by a distance and course from at least one navigational aid. Also known as a *station*.

Frequency: Number of wave cycles completed in a unit of time.

Full approach: Approach performed using the initial and intermediate segments.

Glide path: The combination of glide slope and horizontal guidance during an approach.

Glide slope: Vertical path provided by the ILS ground-based transmitter.

Gyro drift: The tendency of the directional gyro to lose its calibration over time.

Gyros: Instruments that use the principles of gyroscopic precession to operate.

HAA (Height Above Airport): Aircraft height above the highest point of the airport at the end of the approach.

HAT (Height Above Runway Threshold): Aircraft height above the runway threshold at the end of the approach.

High-frequency waves (H/F): Radio waves transmitted between 3,000 kHz-30 Mhz.

IAF (Initial Approach Fix): Starting point of an approach.

IFR (Instruments Flight Rules): Flight procedures used when flying solely by reference to the aircraft instruments.

IFR approach procedure: A method for allowing an IFR-equipped aircraft to descend from cruising altitude to a minimum altitude in IFR conditions.

IFR Configurations: Predetermined pitch and power settings used to achieve desired aircraft performance.

IFR Minimums: Visibility and cloud clearance below VFR minimums.

ILS (Instrument Landing System): Precision approach providing a glide slope and horizontal guidance.

Initial approach segment: Provides a method to turn the aircraft to the correct heading for the inbound approach path.

Instrument cross check: The system used to observe the instruments during IFR flight. Also known as *scanning*.

Instrument interpretation: Understanding how instrument displays relate to aircraft performance.

Intermediate approach segment: Transitions the initial and final approach segments.

LDA (Localizer-type Direction Aid): Non-precision approach using a localizer which does not produce an approach path along the extended centerline.

Leading radial: Reference radial used on an instrument approach to prevent overshooting the inbound course.

Low-frequency waves (L/F): Radio waves transmitted between 30-300 kHz.

MAP (Missed Approach Point): Point where the missed-approach procedure must be executed.

Marginal VFR: Visibility between three and five statute miles.

MEA (Minimum En-route Altitude): Lowest published attitude on a route that guarantees obstacle clearance and ensures adequate signal reception on the route.

Medium-frequency waves (M/F): Radio waves transmitted between 300-3,000 kHz.

Middle Marker: Navigational aid used to determine the aircraft's position on the approach path.

Minimums: Designates the lowest altitude the aircraft can descend to during an approach and the visibility requirements necessary to perform the approach.

Missed approach segment: Approach procedure flown if the pilot has not maintained enough visual contact to land the aircraft by the end of the final approach segment.

MLS (Microwave Landing system): Little-used precision approach which uses radio waves located between 5,031-5,091 Mhz.

MOCA (Minimum Obstruction Clearance Altitude): Lowest obstacle clearance attitude on the route with adequate signal reception only within 22 miles of the VOR.

MRA (Minimum Reception Altitude): Minimum altitude a receiver can pick up an intersection point on a route.

MSA (Minimum Safe Altitude): Provides obstacle clearance within a 25-mile ring of a pecified NavAid.

NavAid: Ground-based radio navigation aid.

NDB (Non-directional radio beacon): Ground-based navigation aid which emits a radio wave with frequencies located between 190-535 kHz.

Non-precision approach: IFR approach that provides horizontal guidance to the runway or airport environment.

NOS (National Ocean Service): Branch of the government that produces U.S. Terminal Procedures.

PAR (Precision Approach Radar) approach: Precision approach which relies fully on ATC guidance.

Partial Panel: Flying IFR with one or more of the primary instruments malfunctioning.

Performance instruments: Instruments used to determine aircraft performance.

Pitch: Angle formed between the longitudinal axis of the airplane and the actual horizon.

Precision approach: IFR approach that provides horizontal and vertical guidance to the runway.

Procedural instrument flying: Procedures to navigate the aircraft solely by reference to the instruments.

Radar-vectored approach: Approach where ATC issues radar vectors so that the aircraft flies directly to the final approach segment.

Radial: A magnetic course from a VOR.

Radio navigation: Any method based on radio waves used to determine the aircraft's track over the ground.

Reverse Sensing: Aircraft's position in relation to a course is displayed on the VOR in a manner opposite the normal display.

RVR (Runway Visual Range): Visibility on the runway as measured by the transmissometer.

Scud running: VFR flight in IFR conditions and/or flying dangerously low to stay below IFR conditions.

SDF (Simplified Directional Facility): Non-precision approach.

SID (Standard Instrument Departure): Published route used to quickly identify a routing to exit the airport area and get established on an airway.

Special VFR: A clearance to operate under VFR in IFR weather conditions if the flight visibility is at least one SM and the aircraft remains clear of clouds.

Standard rate turn: Turn made at three degrees-per-second.

Station passage: The point when an aircraft passes over a fix.

Straight and level flight: Flight that remains on a constant heading and altitude.

Straight in approach: Landing on the same runway the approach procedure leads to.

STAR (Standard Terminal Arrival Route): Published route used to quickly identify a routing to transition from an airway to the airport area.

Transmissometer: Instrument used to measure runway visibility.

Ultra high frequency waves (UHF): Radio waves transmitted between 300-3,000 MHz.

Very high frequency waves (VHF): Radio waves transmitted between 30-300 MHz.

VFR (Visual Flight Rules): Flight procedures used when flying using visual references.

VFR Minimums: Visibility and cloud clearance requirements necessary for VFR flight. Generally referred to as when flight visibility is greater than three statute miles and the cloud ceiling is greater than 1,000 feet.

VFR On Top: Flying VFR on an IFR flight plan to rise above a layer of clouds.

Victor airways: Airway system consisting of VOR routes published on IFR en-route charts.

Visual approach: ATC-issued or pilot-requested visual approach while on an IFR flight plan.

VOR (Very high frequency Omni-directional Radio range): Ground-based navigational aid which emits radio signals between 108.0 and 118.0 Mhz.

Zone of ambiguity: VOR error when the aircraft is located near the area separating the TO and FROM flag readings.

Index

Stop Struggling & Start Learning!

ROD MACHADO'S INSTRUMENT PILOT'S SURVIVAL MANUAL

A serious book written in a refreshing and humorous style!

← **IFR and Complete General Aviation Text** →

A Learning Experience You Won't Forget!

Rod Machado's Private Pilot Handbook

The Ultimate Private Pilot Book

Learn everything you need for:
● The FAA private pilot exam
● Biennial flight reviews
● Updating & refreshing your knowledge

A complete information manual by one of aviation's best-known and most humorous teachers. More than 1,100 original illustrations & photos

"As if your instructor is explaining everything in PLANE English."

Rod Machado's Instrument Pilot's Survival Manual

This unique book contains a wealth of interesting and exciting information on instrument flying. Rod's 26 year of flying experience makes this an important resource. Chapters include: Scanning, Ice & Thunderstorm Avoidance, Jep & NOS Chart Usage, Pro Thinking, IFR Departure Skills, Cockpit Management and much more.

This book is unlike any other book on instrument flying you have encountered. Illustrated with humorous drawings and containing some of the most spectacular reports of pilots gripped by the problems of instrument flight, it's sure to educate and entertain you. Written in a humorous manner, this 232 page book will prepare you to be a more educated and proficient pilot. Excellent for any IFR student, experienced professional pilot or as an IFR refresher. **$29.95**

Rod Machado's Private Pilot Handbook

This book is a serious text written in a fun and witty style. With more than 1,100 illustrations and photos and 64 pages of full color, this 572 page manual make preparation for the FAA private pilot oral and knowledge exams (flight reviews too) a pleasant and enjoyable experience. Here's some of what's inside:

- Easy to understand analogies and examples for technical subjects such as engines, aerodynamics, flight instruments and the airplane's electrical system
- METAR & TAF weather codes
- Airspace made E-Z with 3-D color illustrations
- Step-by-step planning for a cross country flight
- Clear, down-to-earth explanations of pertinent FARs
- Easy navigation methods of VOR, GPS and ADF
- Practical tips and techniques for ensuring a safe and enjoyable flight **$34.95**

"ROD HAS CREATED THE (Private) BOOK THAT HAS ALWAYS BEEN NEEDED AND WILL SET THE STANDARD FOR EVERYTHING THAT FOLLOWS...All the material you could ever want to need to know in a clear and precise manner... has a comprehensive index (what a concept)... you'll be asking your self why someone didn't do something like this along time ago."
Vicki Cruse-Campbell, US Aviator Magazine

"...it's a ball to read. AFter seeing most of the IFR tests available, I'd strongly recommend this book to anyone considering initial or brush-up on instrument training."
Bill Cox, Senior Editor, Plane & Pilot

IF YOU LIKED THE VIRTUAL, YOU'LL LOVE THE REALITY.

As a virtual pilot with Microsoft's amazingly realistic Flight Simulator, you've developed a "hands-on" feel for the challenge and fun of flying your own plane. Now, we challenge you to experience the next level – with a $35 discovery flight in a real Cessna aircraft. Imagine: for less than the cost of this software, you can take the controls and discover how easy it is to turn your virtual skills into real ones. Visit our website to find your nearest Cessna Pilot Center.

$35 DISCOVERY FLIGHT

COUPON NOT VALID UNTIL ACTIVATED.
Visit our website www.cessna.textron.com to activate your coupon today!

PLEASE ENTER YOUR ACTIVATION NUMBER HERE: _____

Once activated, this coupon entitles the bearer to one $35 discovery flight at a participating Cessna Pilot Center.

Valid only at locations in the U.S. and Canada. Must be 16 or older to redeem discovery flight coupon. Coupon expires 12/31/1998.

Cessna
A Textron Company